ONE NATION UNDER BASEBALL

One Nation

Under Baseball

How the 1960s Collided with the National Pastime

JOHN FLORIO AND
OUISIE SHAPIRO

Foreword by Bob Costas

University of Nebraska Press
Lincoln and London

Manufactured in the United States of America

Library of Congress Cataloging-in-Publication Data
Names: Florio, John, 1960– author. | Shapiro, Ouisie, author.
Title: One Nation Under Baseball: How the 1960s Collided with the National Pastime / John Florio and Ouisie Shapiro; Foreword by Bob Costas.
Description: Lincoln: University of Nebraska Press, 2017. | Includes bibliographical references.
Identifiers: LCCN 2016029038
ISBN 9780803286900 (hardback: alk. paper)
ISBN 9781496200808 (epub)
ISBN 9781496200815 (mobi)
ISBN 9781496200822 (pdf)
Subjects: LCSH: Baseball—United States—History—20th century. | Baseball—Social aspects—United States. | Baseball players—United States—Biography. | African American baseball players—United States—Biography. | Discrimination in sports—United States—History—20th century. | BISAC: SPORTS & RECREATION / Baseball / History.
Classification: LCC GV863.A1 F65 2017 | DDC 796.3570973/0904—dc23
LC record available at https://lccn.loc.gov/2016029038

Set in Whitman by John Klopping.

For the 26 guys who introduced
me to the joy of baseball:
my dad and the 1968 Yankees

JF

For my first coaches:
Alan and Chuck Shapiro

OS

Foreword Bob Costas

Politics and social issues have no place in sports. *Sports*. Sports is a respite from all that. It's where I go to escape. Sports are sacrosanct, and even to acknowledge, let alone delve into, the countless times that larger issues intersect with sports is out of bounds.

Believe me, I am familiar with these arguments—if you can call them that. Curiously, they seem to be raised only by those who disagree with, or are made uncomfortable by, the athletes and commentators who dare to address pertinent subjects beyond a late-inning pitching change or an early-round draft choice. Just as curious, political views that align with their own are, of course, seldom a problem.

I shudder to think what additional ad hominem attacks, misrepresentations and sheer falsehoods would have been directed at Jackie Robinson, Hank Aaron, Curt Flood, Marvin Miller, and the rest had the internet, cable television, and talk radio existed during that time.

In *One Nation Under Baseball: How the 1960s Collided with the National Pastime*, John Florio and Ouisie Shapiro focus on the 1960s, the most turbulent American decade of the second half of the twentieth century. Despite the protests of the "Shaddup and tell me the score" crowd, the forces affecting and profoundly changing America were also having a dramatic effect on sports and, for our purposes here, on baseball in particular.

Labor relations, players' rights, shifting population centers, the opening of new baseball markets, the emergence of television as a major factor, the evolving role of the sports press, the increasing willingness of young people to assert their individuality and challenge the status quo. And, of course, the persistent issues of race. They all affected baseball as surely as they did America as a whole. In fact, in some cases, sports—baseball included—weren't just touched by these issues, they personified them.

In the pages that follow, careful research, telling details, and rich and revealing personal stories combine to give us a better sense of how those dynamics affected and, in some ways, transformed baseball.

It is often said (with appreciation and a fair measure of truth) that baseball is a constant in an ever-changing world. That its rituals, traditions, and familiarity are a huge part of its appeal. A source of comfort as much as of interest. Agreed.

But that does not mean that baseball exists in a bubble and somehow can (or should) be immune to the social forces raging around it. That has never been the case. And perhaps no period of time proved that point as well as the 1960s did.

The '60s were a time of conflict, progress, tragedy, triumph, and unforgettable events in the nation and its pastime. *One Nation Under Baseball* connects the two in revealing and insightful fashion. Hope you enjoy it as much as I did.

A Note to the Reader

One Nation Under Baseball relies on first-person interviews and archival materials. When quoting from our interviews, we have omitted attribution. When quoting from secondary sources, such as books, newspapers, and magazines, we've provided attribution within the narrative.

1

I'm calling on behalf of Senator Kennedy.

That's what the guy had said, and if Mudcat Grant were white, he may have trusted him. But for black ballplayers like Grant, prank calls were commonplace—and in some cases dangerous. They came at all hours, in all forms, and were often accompanied by death threats. This one had come by way of a ringing telephone in Grant's room at the Sheraton Cadillac in Detroit, the majestic hotel in which the twenty-five-year-old pitcher was staying with the rest of the Cleveland Indians.

The caller was still talking. "Mr. Kennedy would like to have breakfast with you."

"I'm sorry," Grant said and quickly hung up.

The phone rang again. And again. And again.

Grant ignored it each time, and went back to reading the morning paper. It was Labor Day 1960 and barely eight o'clock. He was scheduled to pitch the first game of a doubleheader against Detroit in a few hours. The game was meaningless—the Tigers and the Indians were both out of contention—but it mattered to Grant. One more win and he'd match his career high of ten, which he'd posted each of the previous two seasons.

Suddenly, there was a knock on the door. Grant got up off the bed and looked through the peephole. Standing in the hallway were two white men wearing identical suits and deadpan expressions—and flashing ID cards. They looked official enough, so Grant let them in.

"Mr. Kennedy is a big fan of yours," they said, explaining that they worked for the Massachusetts senator. "He'd like you to join him for breakfast in the hotel."

Hard as it was to believe, the phone calls had been legit. Grant got dressed and, within minutes, was sitting in the hotel dining room sharing eggs and coffee with the man who'd won the Democratic nomination for president six weeks earlier. John F. Kennedy told Grant how much he admired the black ballplayers that had been pioneering integration in the Majors; he went on to say that he'd followed the career of Grant's former roommate, Larry Doby, who'd broken the color line in the American League three months after Jackie Robinson had done the same with the Dodgers in the National League.

Sitting across from each other, Kennedy and Grant made for an odd couple: one an Irish-Catholic politician, born into money and prestige, his skin tanned, his collar starched, his thick, nasal Boston accent unmistakable; the other a brown-skinned southerner, the grandson of a slave raised in the blinding hatred of Jim Crow. (Racism had followed Mudcat into the minors, which is where he got his nickname. Some white teammates, upon seeing James Timothy Grant for the first time, said he had the face of a Mississippi mudcat—and the derisive moniker had stuck.)

"You're from Locawoochee, Florida?" Kennedy asked.

"Lacoochee," Grant said, correcting the senator's pronunciation of his birthplace, surprised the man knew so much about him.

Grant explained that it was in Lacoochee's black quarters, fifty miles northeast of Tampa, that his mother, Viola, had raised him and his six siblings. He could barely remember his father and namesake James, who'd been a log cutter at the local mill; the elder James had fallen ill on the job and died of pneumonia when Grant was a young boy.

The town Grant described to Kennedy was the Lacoochee of the late '40s and '50s, the one whose mill shut down once the area had run out of cypress trees, the one that had gone into an economic tailspin shortly thereafter.

Grant told Kennedy, too, how his elementary school teacher had introduced him to a wide range of music, and how his mother, who'd worked as a maid and directed the choir at Mount Moriah Baptist Church, had taught him to sing. But he didn't sugarcoat his story: He was raised in the Deep South, where, for blacks, opportunities had been practically nonexistent. He told the senator about the tumbledown row house that had served as his elementary school, about the school's secondhand books, about the books' torn and missing pages.

Still today, Grant has vivid memories of the indignities he'd suffered as a kid in Lacoochee. These are Mudcat's words, from Bill Staples and Rich Herschlag's *Before the Glory*:

The very minute you walked out of your house, there were incidents that were out of line. As a black person, you had water fountains you couldn't drink from. There were restaurants you couldn't go into. You had to always watch where you were and know what you were going to do, because there was something that was going to happen to you every day. You knew of lynchings. You would hear it in the night, and if you didn't, word came through the next town that somebody was hanged or somebody was castrated. There used to be a law called "reckless eyeballing." If they saw you looking at a white lady, you could be charged with "reckless eyeballing." Sometimes, whites would get drunk, go riding through town, and fire guns into your house. That was done to my family. I remember my mother putting me down by the fireplace to keep the bullets from hitting me. That was called "nigger-shooting time."

Kennedy listened intently for nearly an hour, and when the two finished eating, he thanked Grant for his time and reassured him that he was working with Congress to end segregation.

Soon after their meeting, Kennedy stood on a makeshift podium in Detroit's Cadillac Square and addressed sixty thousand enthusiastic supporters. His pro-labor speech praised collective bargaining, called for an increase in the minimum wage, and, echoing his conversation with his new friend Mudcat Grant, called upon America to put an end to bigotry: "I take my case to you because I know you agree with me that racial discrimination must be eliminated everywhere in our society; in jobs, in housing, in voting, in lunch counters, and in schools."

That same day, Mudcat Grant toed the rubber on the mound at Briggs Stadium. He pitched seven innings, striking out ten, but lost the game, 4–3.

Still, the day put a checkmark in a win column that no baseball fan could see. Grant had just met the man who might become president, and he seemed to care genuinely about the plight of blacks in Lacoochee and the rest of the country.

By 1960, the world was changing. Blacks were speaking out, mobilizing; they were demanding equality, forcing America to confront its bigotry, to wake up from the slumber it had been in.

One such voice belonged to Jackie Robinson.

Known in various circles as a pariah, a sacrificial lamb, and a national icon since breaking baseball's color line, Robinson had retired from the Brooklyn Dodgers after the 1956 season and had become a familiar face at civil rights protests.

Unlike Mudcat Grant, Robinson had little regard for John Kennedy. Rather, he was a loyal supporter of the Republican nominee, Vice President Richard Nixon. He wasn't alone. Black voters had long backed the GOP; it was the party of Lincoln, the party of emancipation. Conversely, it was Democrats who during Reconstruction had formed the Ku Klux Klan, the organization bent on restoring white supremacy. And while the advent of the '60s saw an evolving ideology in both parties, blacks were still an important voting bloc. As late as 1956, black Americans helped get Dwight D. Eisenhower reelected, with 39 percent of their vote.

"I wanted to be fair about things, so I went to see both Kennedy and Nixon," Robinson told Roger Kahn in *The Boys of Summer*. "Now, Nixon seemed to understand a little bit of what had to be done. John Kennedy said, 'Mr. Robinson, I don't know much about the problems of colored people since I come from New England.' I figured, the hell with that. Any man in Congress for fifteen years ought to make it his business to know colored people."

Robinson also took issue with Kennedy on another matter. The senator, an avowed liberal, had courted a handful of ultraconservative southern governors during his campaign. Most insiders and journalists recognized that Kennedy was in the political fight of his life and had little choice but to solicit every vote he could get. Still, the ballplayer-cum-activist insisted the senator had sold his soul to a devil known as the segregated South.

Robinson preached from his pulpit, a nationally syndicated column in the *New York Post* (written with playwright William Branch).

"As long as he continues to play politics at the expense of 18,000,000 Negro Americans," he wrote in June 1960, "Senator Kennedy is not fit to be president of the United States."

In September, Robinson took a leave from the paper to campaign for Nixon.

In October, his words came back to haunt him.

The precipitating incident was a sit-in at Rich's Department Store in downtown Atlanta—a protest that included civil rights leader Martin Luther King.

King had deep roots in Atlanta. It was the city in which he'd been born and where he'd spent most of his thirty-one years fighting racial injustice. (He spent four years at Boston University in the 1950s earning a doctorate in theology.) It was also where he and fifty-nine other black ministers and civil rights leaders had founded the Southern Christian Leadership Conference (SCLC), with the mission of abolishing segregation and putting an end to racial injustice.

At Rich's, King and a group of college students challenged the store's segregation policy by requesting service in its "white-only" restaurant, the Magnolia Room. When they were denied, the protesters remained seated—waiting to be served or arrested, whichever came first.

Similar sit-in protests had been spreading throughout the South for months, starting in February when four black freshmen at North Carolina's Agricultural and Technical College took seats at the Woolworth's lunch counter in Greensboro, North Carolina.

The Greensboro five-and-dime, with its marble stairs, rose-tinted mirrors, and twenty-five thousand square feet of retail space, allowed black shoppers to spend their money throughout the store—but not at the luncheonette. The students, Joseph McNeil, Franklin McCain, David Richmond, and Ezell Blair Jr., took seats at the counter, and when no one would serve them, they asked why they weren't welcome.

"We don't serve colored here," the clerk told them.

Following their well-rehearsed strategy, all four stayed put on their chrome stools, opened their textbooks, and studied quietly, staging a sit-in so un-Greensboro-like that even a black dishwasher called them stupid, ignorant troublemakers.

But twenty-four more students joined the protest the next morning, and still more the day after that. Soon hundreds of students, including coeds from nearby Bennett College, had packed the store, pressuring Woolworth's into serving black shoppers a fresh-brewed cup of equality.

It wasn't long before groups of white segregationists rolled onto South Elm Street by the truckload, hurling racial epithets, pelting eggs at the passive protesters, even burning them with scalding coffee and setting their clothes on fire. The F. W. Woolworth Company kept silent on the matter. The only word coming from its headquarters in New York City was that the company had a policy of adhering to local custom—which in Greensboro, included the segregation of public dining facilities.

After a week of raging tension and hostility, a phoned-in bomb threat put an end to the sit-in—but the Greensboro lunch counter was still off limits to black customers. Five months later, after suffering nearly two hundred thousand dollars in losses as a result of further demonstrations, picketing, and boycotts, store manager Clarence Harris had arranged for three black employees to order a meal at the counter, thus officially desegregating the Greensboro Woolworth's. By the middle of October, another 150 lunch counters in variety stores throughout the South had followed suit. Although many of its stores in the Deep South remained segregated, F. W. Woolworth insisted that progress was being made.

That wasn't the case at Rich's Department Store in Atlanta.

Upon refusing to leave the Magnolia Room, Martin Luther King and his fellow activists were promptly arrested. Charges were dropped against many of the demonstrators, but King and thirty-five others remained in custody, refusing bail on the grounds that they had not violated the law.

While awaiting arraignment, King drafted a statement to the judge, defending his right to assemble peacefully to "seek service just as any other citizen." He explained his actions by saying, "If by chance, your honor, we are guilty of violating the law please be assured that we did it to bring the whole issue of racial injustice under the scrutiny of the conscience of Atlanta. I must honestly say that we firmly believe that segregation is evil, and that our southland will never reach its full economic, political, and moral maturity until this cancerous disease is removed."

Dekalb County judge J. Oscar Mitchell was unmoved by King's statement. Instead, he found King guilty on a series of trumped-up charges unrelated to the sit-in and sentenced him to four months' hard labor in a public works camp.

Jackie Robinson turned to his chosen leader, Richard Nixon, for help in freeing King—but the vice president refused.

As Robinson continued trying to bend the inflexible Nixon, Senator Kennedy stepped in. He called Coretta Scott King to reassure her that she had his support.

"I want to express to you my concern about your husband," Kennedy is quoted as saying in Coretta Scott King's *My Life with Martin Luther King*. "I understand you are expecting a baby, and I just wanted you to know that I was thinking about you and Dr. King. If there is anything I can do to help, please feel free to call on me."

Robert Kennedy, the senator's brother and campaign manager, feared that news of the conversation would jeopardize the southern vote and, therefore, Kennedy's chances of election. Still, he was furious enough to call Judge Mitchell at the courthouse and appeal to his sense of justice. The next morning, King was released on a two-thousand-dollar bond.

When Robinson asked Nixon why he hadn't intervened to help King, the vice president accused his opponent of grandstanding. Robinson was dismayed and went so far as to tell Nixon's speechwriter, William Safire, "Nixon doesn't deserve to win."

Despite increased pressure from other civil rights activists to switch his allegiance to Kennedy, Robinson couldn't bring himself to divorce the Republican candidate. Against the advice of his wife, Rachel, he stuck by Nixon, insisting that the GOP would once again be the party of emancipation.

But the damage had been done.

Once Kennedy had gone to bat for King, black voters shifted so strongly to the Democratic ticket that they tipped as many as five states in the senator's favor.

The lead held, and the following month, Kennedy defeated Nixon by a wide margin in the electoral vote, 303 to 219, but by a mere one-tenth of one percent in the popular vote. It was one of the closest elections in American history.

After the election, the *New York Post* dropped Jackie Robinson's column.

Still, the ex-ballplayer remained committed to the losing side.

2

Baseball. Hot dogs. Ice cream. For sports fans, nothing beat Florida in the spring of 1961. This was where fourteen of the eighteen big league clubs got in shape for the season. The atmosphere was casual. Fans strolling around could stop and chat with stars like Mickey Mantle, Hank Aaron, Stan Musial, Bill White, and Harmon Killebrew.

This was the Sunshine State.

It just didn't shine on everybody.

Even though the Supreme Court had mandated the integration of public schools in 1954, southern states were still clinging to their own Jim Crow laws and keeping blacks from gaining equal footing. The laws, holdovers from the 1800s, had created two societies, one "colored" and one "white," and covered virtually every sphere of human contact—not only schools but also restaurants, swimming pools, libraries, restrooms, phone booths, railway cars, and drinking fountains. The accommodations were nominally "separate but equal," but there was no doubt as to which ones were preferable.

Just as protesters across the South were organizing sit-ins to integrate lunch counters and retail establishments, black ballplayers training in Florida were launching their own struggle to desegregate public facilities, particularly housing.

The New York Yankees and the St. Louis Cardinals shared Al Lang Field, a seven-thousand-seat facility along the St. Petersburg waterfront. White fans could sit anywhere they liked, including the premium, shady seats behind home plate. Black fans were confined to the "colored" section down the right field line, unprotected from the scorching subtropical rays.

Jim Bouton, a white, twenty-two-year-old pitcher from Ridgewood, New Jersey, joined the Yankees in Florida after an impressive 14-8 season with the club's Class-B team in Greensboro.

"When I drove down to spring training," Bouton recalls, "we passed a couple of small towns that had giant billboards: Knights of the KKK, with [images of] horses and hoods. And I thought, 'Whoa.' That was part of going through red dirt, clay country. One time, we stayed overnight somewhere and I saw a sign that read, 'Nigger, don't let the sun go down on you in this town.'"

The issue, of course, was especially galling to black players making the same trip.

Bill White, the thickly built, six-foot first baseman on the Cardinals, had been raised in racially mixed Warren, Ohio. As White describes it, his hometown was progressive enough to have integrated schools, but it wasn't advanced enough to elect a black official or to discontinue its practice of disinfecting public swimming pools after blacks had swum in them. White had attended Hiram College as a premed student, lettered in basketball, football, and baseball, and would have looked as natural working in a medical lab as running the bases at Al Lang Field. White had spent four years in the minors, two of them in the South, and done a year of military service in Kentucky. He had been bounced from "white-only" establishments, called "nigger" to his face, and at one point chased onto the team bus, protected only by his bat-wielding teammates.

"If you were a black man and [a bathroom] didn't say "colored" on it, you'd best not go in," White says when speaking about Florida. "For black ballplayers, especially those from the North, it was like suddenly being transported to apartheid South Africa."

In 1959, when arriving to his first spring training camp in St. Pete, White had taken a "colored" taxi from the airport to the team hotel. Once in the lobby, he gave his name to the desk clerk and asked for his room key.

As White recalled in his memoir, *Uppity*, the clerk looked at him as if he "had dropped in from another planet."

The hotel employee then directed White to another "colored" cab and told him he'd be staying across town. He gave White the address of a widow, Mrs. Williams, who rented rooms to "colored" players.

The cab delivered White to the Williams home. As he was settling in he was greeted by Cardinals teammate Bob Gibson.

White was tired, hungry, and pissed-off.

"So this is the way it is here?" he said to Gibson. "Black players can't stay in the team hotels?"

Gibson, who was in his second spring with the Cardinals, shrugged. "Welcome to St. Petersburg."

White could hardly forget those injustices. "I was called words I had never even heard before," he told *Ebony* magazine. "Having to sit on that bus while the other guys went in and ate. . . . Not being able to go into a gas station to use the bathroom, not being able to stay in a decent hotel. . . . It was a bitter experience for me. You don't forgive those things when people treat you like dirt—*worse* than dirt."

Like many black players in St. Pete, White often found himself at the home of Ralph Wimbish, a physician who was also president of the local NAACP. Wimbish and his wife, Bette, had organized a number of sit-ins at lunch counters and public facilities in the area; they also opened their home to ballplayers, inviting them to unwind with a barbecue and a dip in the pool. When those players were stuck without housing, Dr. Wimbish would drive them around town knocking on friends' doors—or, in some cases, he'd simply put them up in eight-year-old Ralph Jr.'s bedroom. White wasn't the only regular; other familiar faces included those of Gibson, Cardinals center fielder Curt Flood, and Yankees catcher Elston Howard.

"It was a professional black community," recalls Arlene Howard, Elston's widow. "They embraced the black ballplayers because the white population didn't. The whole area was very restricted. You couldn't go to restaurants; you couldn't do anything. I remember Al Lang Field. That was the first time I'd seen signs on restrooms: 'colored' and 'white.' And the water fountains. I'd deliberately drink out of the 'white' one. The South had its own rules and regulations; it was still fighting the Civil War. The South was bad, and the Wimbishes were a shining beacon."

Ralph Wimbish Jr. saw it all through a youngster's eyes: a world of successful blacks—athletes, entertainers, professionals—marginalized in a segregated society.

"We had people come through our house that normal people wouldn't have, like Jesse Owens [and] Cab Calloway," he remembers. "And there was Elston Howard. He was my favorite. He was such a nice guy. He stayed in my room just like Cab Calloway did. It was just great being able to hang out with them. I remember Elston would come down when pitchers and catchers came early, and he'd be in my bedroom and I'd be down the hall."

Howard had joined the Yankees in 1955. He was six-two, built like a lumberjack, and soft-spoken, which some people took for subservient. His demeanor was similar to that of many first-generation black Major Leaguers: he couldn't find trouble if it were waiting inside his baseball mitt. For that reason, along with his outstanding baseball skills, Yankees general manager George Weiss had chosen him to break the team's color barrier.

Weiss's other option had been first baseman Vic Power, a highly talented Puerto Rican prospect who'd played with Howard on the Yankees' Triple-A team in Kansas City. But Power approached baseball as he did life: with a smiling face and an open mouth. One story places him in the Deep South, facing a white judge as he defended himself on a jaywalking charge. When asked why he'd broken the law, Power said, "I thought the 'Don't Walk' sign was for whites only."

In Power, Weiss saw the devil: a young black man who didn't know his place. He began spreading word that the flashy fielder lacked hustle. Power, figuring the team was looking for an excuse to dump him, responded by saying, "What do they want me to do? Mow the lawn in the outfield, too?"

For Weiss, the final word on Power came in the form of hearsay: Power was seen driving with a white woman in his Cadillac convertible. Before the Caddy's engine had cooled, Weiss had traded him to the Philadelphia Athletics—never bothering to ask about his companion, who, it turned out, was a light-skinned black woman who answered to the name of Mrs. Power.

It wouldn't have mattered to Weiss. Power was a loose cannon; Howard wasn't. Weiss knew he could count on Howard to abide by the implicit list of dos and don'ts that baseball had designed for players of color. *Do* keep your mouth shut at all times. *Don't* express your opinion. And for god's sake, *don't* be seen alone with a white woman.

For Weiss and the Yankees, Howard's stoic demeanor was carte blanche to serve him a steady diet of indignities. In the minors, they'd taken him from the outfield and put him behind home plate when the team's big-league catcher, Yogi Berra, was in the prime of his career—thus slowing Howard's ascent. In Florida, they separated him from his white teammates, who were staying at the Yankee Clipper hotel.

"It just wasn't Elston's personality to raise hell," says Wimbish Jr., who went on to write *Elston and Me* with Arlene Howard. "It just wasn't his nature, as opposed to someone like Bob Gibson, or particularly Bill White. . . . [Elston] was just happy to be playing baseball for the New York Yankees. That was quite an achievement. He was getting a World Series check every year, which back then was a lot of money. He didn't want to rock the boat."

Which is how Howard found himself at Ralph and Bette Wimbish's house, cooling off at the pool alongside Bill White and a collection of other black players, a quiet yin to their outspoken yang. But time was running out. Later that spring, in an attempt to pressure the Yankees and the Cardinals into forcing their hotels to integrate, the Wimbishes stopped offering their home to ballplayers. Howard, White, and their fellow black teammates had to find other accommodations.

That's when the Ku Klux Klan threw a flaming cross onto the Wimbishes' front lawn.

Nobody recognized the ghost of the Confederacy more readily than sportswriter Wendell Smith.

The Detroit-born Smith had gone to West Virginia State College, where he was a pitcher on the baseball team and a sports editor on the school newspaper. Smith showed promise at both, but when his skin color ended his baseball career, he took a job as a sportswriter with the black-owned *Pittsburgh Courier*—and vowed to advocate for black athletes. In the '30s and '40s, he and a handful of other black journalists tried to integrate baseball by writing open letters to club owners and bringing black players to tryouts. Most notably, it was Smith who advised Branch Rickey to sign Jackie Robinson as the game's first black player.

In 1961 he was still waging war against Jim Crow.

Smith's new campaign was to desegregate Florida's spring training facilities, and having moved to the white-owned *Chicago's American*, he now carried more weight and reached a broader readership. The first column of his campaign, "Negro Ball Players Want Rights in South," hit the newsstands on January 23, 1961. In it, he wrote of the modern-day ballplayer, but he could have been describing the four freshmen who had demanded seats at Woolworth's a year earlier.

Here are some of Smith's words: "The Negro player resents the fact that he is not permitted to stay in the same hotels with his teammates during spring training, and is protesting the fact that he cannot eat in the same restaurants, nor enjoy other privileges. At the moment he is not belligerent. He is merely seeking help and sympathy and understanding, and a solution."

For months Smith kept up the pressure. "What a Negro Ballplayer Faces Today in Training." "Negro Stars Find Themselves Caged." "Negro Diamond Stars Tired of Second-Class Citizenship in South." In one article he quoted Birdie Tebbetts, catcher turned executive vice president of the Milwaukee Braves, as saying, "My boys do not mind being subjected to the Jim Crow laws in the spring. They are happy, perfectly satisfied with their lowly status." Smith fired back, noting that Tebbetts displayed the "courage and fortitude of a baby chick," and suggested that such cowardice might be how he ended up with the nickname "Birdie."

Smith often quoted the ballplayers directly, starting with the Braves' Henry Aaron, who'd grown up in Alabama and was no stranger to the appalling caste system of Jim Crow. Aaron, who'd already won an MVP award, was staying in a boarding house in the black section of Bradenton, twenty-five miles south of St. Petersburg. The home, owned by local schoolteacher Lulu Mae Gibson, was crammed with players who couldn't find housing elsewhere.

Aaron told Smith, "There is really one room for four men, and last year, there were eight or ten living there. Beds have to be put in the hall, and if players don't hustle to the bathroom in the morning, the last man doesn't get any hot water."

Smith took his campaign to Sarasota, where he interviewed Ed and Lillian Wachtel, a white, Jewish couple from New York who rented rooms to players of any color on the Chicago White Sox. Their motel, the DeSoto, was a green, one-story building off Sarasota's main thoroughfare with a neon sign advertising heating, air conditioning, and overnight stays. For players of color, it was a roof and a bed. For locals, it was an issue. That strip of highway ran through the white section of town.

Smith wrote that the Wachtels had taken "a daring risk" in their stand against Sarasota's systemic bigotry.

He wasn't exaggerating.

He let Ed Wachtel do the talking.

> When it was first discovered that I was going to accept these players, people called us all hours of the day and night and demanded that I refuse them. They warned that if I didn't, they would bomb us out. We received calls from men who said they were members of the Ku Klux Klan and that they were going to burn a fiery cross on my front lawn. . . . Naturally, my wife and I were frightened. . . . However, I think the community is beginning to accept the fact that this isn't such a bad thing after all. I receive only one or two daily threats by telephone now, and the police no longer consider it necessary to guard the place around the clock.

In exposing bigotry in Sarasota, Smith reignited a simmering feud between White Sox owner Bill Veeck and the team's official hotel. Since purchasing the club in 1959, Veeck, a World War II veteran from Chicago, had been pushing the Sarasota Terrace to integrate.

This was standard fare for the famously out-of-the-box thinker, who was often at odds with his baseball brethren. In 1947, as owner of the Cleveland Indians, Veeck had signed Larry Doby as the American League's first black player. Before that, Veeck had bought the Milwaukee Brewers, a minor league club that trained in Ocala, Florida. One day Veeck made his way to the "colored" section of the stands, sat down and watched the game with the fans. When the sheriff ordered him to leave, Veeck refused—delighting those around him but irking the local official. The situation quickly escalated into the hands of the Ocala mayor, who showed up at the park to repeat the sheriff's order. This time, not only did Veeck stay put, but he also threatened to pull his team from the city, cancel its six-week stay at the Ocala Hotel, and contact the national media. The mayor, no doubt calculating lost revenue, lost jobs, and, perhaps, lost votes, backed down. Veeck sat in the "colored" section for the rest of the spring.

Now armed with Smith's articles, Veeck squared off against the Sarasota Chamber of Commerce and used the same tactic: He threatened to pull his team out of town if the Terrace wouldn't capitulate. But this time he was in a tougher fight than he'd imagined. The Terrace adamantly refused to offer a bed to a black guest.

Stymied and in poor health, Veeck had little choice but to keep his team at the Terrace, although he did provide his non-white players with a chef, maid service, and transportation to and from the park. Later that season, he would sell the team to Arthur Allyn Jr., who, having deeper pockets than Veeck, would purchase the Terrace and integrate it himself.

In Wendell Smith's view, the battle in Florida was still raging, but the troops were advancing.

In 1961 baseball wasn't the only sport dealing with segregation. In Washington DC, where President Kennedy was confronting the difficulties of an increasingly unstable government in South Vietnam and a burgeoning civil rights movement at home, the Washington Redskins were a blight on the new administration. Of the eighty-three black players in the NFL, not one was on the 'Skins.

The team's owner, Laundromat tycoon George Preston Marshall, made no bones about his distaste for black players and insisted that an all-white team was a legitimate draw for southern markets.

"We take most of our players out of Southern colleges and are trying to appeal to Southern people," the native West Virginian told the *New York Times*. "Those colleges don't have any Negro players."

Washington Post sportswriter Shirley Povich routinely mocked Marshall and the bottom-dwelling Redskins, saying their team colors were "burgundy, gold, and Caucasian." When covering Redskins games, the Pulitzer Prize–winning columnist called an opponent's touchdown "integrating the end zone" and a lopsided score "separate but unequal."

Baltimore sportswriter Sam Lacy wrote in the *Afro-American* that his "column has never advocated suicide, but in George Preston Marshall's case, it would be readily forgivable."

In March, Stewart Udall, the newly appointed secretary of the interior, issued an ultimatum to the Redskins: integrate or find a new home.

It was the first such warning ever made to a professional sports club. Since public funds were behind the team's stadium, Udall reasoned, the Department of the Interior was the Redskins' landlord and could deny use of the park if Marshall continued his discriminatory hiring practices.

Marshall scoffed at the ultimatum, telling reporters, "I'm surprised that with the world on the brink of another war, [the government is] worried about whether or not a Negro is going to play for the Redskins."

Marshall's lawyers had a different reaction, assuring the White House that their client intended to comply with Udall's directive.

Jackie Robinson, now a vice president of the Chock Full o'Nuts coffee company, wrote to the secretary, "Your stand on the hiring policy of the Washington football team is both inspirational and encouraging. You have made your position quite clear, and we applaud you for it."

Marshall wrote off Robinson as quickly as he had the government. "Jackie Robinson is in the business of exploiting a race and making a living doing it," he said. "I'm not. He doesn't qualify as a critic."

When Wendell Smith asked Marshall why he resisted so strongly the hiring of black players, Marshall replied, "That's like asking me when I stopped beating my wife. . . . Why do you ask such a question?"

"Because," Smith said, "we want to know."

"Well, I've told you," Marshall said. "I haven't seen any I thought were good enough. Does that answer your question?"

Finally, NFL commissioner Pete Rozelle convinced Marshall to comply. Apparently, Marshall's fellow owners weren't relishing the negative publicity he was generating—especially since the league had a two-year, nine-million-dollar television deal to protect.

Marshall finally backed down, and on December 4, the Redskins made Heisman Trophy–winner Ernie Davis the top overall pick in the NFL draft. Davis, perhaps the first football player to root against hearing his own name, refused to play for an outspoken bigot, and a week later he was traded to Cleveland for two black players, running back Bobby Mitchell and halfback Leroy Jackson.

The newly integrated Redskins would have a turnaround season in '62, finishing 5-7-2—prompting sportswriters to name the secretary of the interior the NFL's most valuable player.

While Udall and Marshall had been slugging it out over racial integration in the NFL, Floyd Patterson was using his platform as heavyweight champion to advance the cause of civil rights. An Olympic gold medalist, the much-admired Patterson had carried the title for five years, lending it for a short time to Sweden's Ingemar Johansson.

When negotiating his highly anticipated rubber match with Johansson for March 1961, Patterson insisted that the Miami Beach Convention Hall suspend its Jim Crow seating policies for the fight. He gave Miami mayor Lee Powell and the fight's promoter, Feature Sports, no choice but to agree—and insisted they put it in writing. Not trusting that they'd fulfill their promise, Patterson doubled down by adding another clause: If Patterson were to hear about any transgressions during the fight, the promoters would be "penalized" ten thousand dollars, all of which would go directly to the NAACP.

It was a small but noteworthy blow to segregation—and it landed squarely on Jim Crow's jaw. After Patterson knocked out Johansson in the sixth round, the *New York Times* observed, "Negroes were spotted freely among the predominantly white crowd in all sections, and so far as could be noted, no incidents arose from the integrated setup."

When it came to integration, baseball wasn't enjoying the same success as boxing. The tension over training accommodations in Florida had reached a tipping point, and in this case, a social event knocked it over—specifically, the 1961 St. Petersburg Chamber of Commerce's annual "Salute to Baseball" breakfast.

The guests of honor were the Yankees and the Cardinals, and when the invitation was posted on a bulletin board in the shared clubhouse, it was immediately clear that only white players had been invited. When asked why blacks were excluded—studies revealed they ate breakfast, too—Cardinals public relations man Jim Toomey said the event was limited to players living in the team hotel.

"I decided to invite only the Cardinal players who were staying at the hotel [Vinoy Park] where the breakfast was held," Toomey told inquiring writers. "Since it was scheduled at 8:15 a.m., I thought it would be inconvenient for those not staying at the hotel."

He went on from there, pointing out that Stan Musial, Lindy McDaniel, and Joe Cunningham, three white players who'd chosen to live off-premises, had also been excluded. What he didn't mention was that black players had never been given the option of living at the hotel in the first place.

It didn't help Toomey that Yankees public relations director Bob Fishel offered a different response. When Elston Howard asked whether he was invited to the breakfast, Fishel simply said yes, all players were welcome.

Some black players were willing to let the incident slide, writing it off as standard discrimination and counting the days until spring training—and their stay in Florida—ended.

Bill White wasn't one of them.

"I wanted to go very badly," he told the press. "I think I'm a gentleman and can conduct myself properly. This thing keeps gnawing away at my heart."

When asked for his reaction, Toomey said that White was certainly welcome. He went on to say that he'd wanted to extend a belated invitation to White but hadn't been able to find him. The excuse rang hollow, given that White and Toomey both worked for the Cardinals and that White was reliable, professional, and could be found playing first base at Al Lang Field.

Wendell Smith jumped on Toomey's response in the *Pittsburgh Courier*.

"That confession illustrates the absurdity of the 'problem,'" Smith wrote. "Apparently, Toomey, an executive of the St. Louis Cardinals, does not know how to contact the Negro players on his club. . . . The point is that many baseball executives lose all contact with the Negro players after the latter leave the ballpark where training is conducted. And, of course, the Negro players lose all contact with the officials, as well as their white teammates."

Smith then turned his crosshairs on the chamber of commerce. "The entire blame for this particular situation cannot, of course, be heaped upon the shoulders of Toomey. The St. Petersburg Chamber of Commerce must bear the brunt, because it is clearly obvious that the breakfast invitation had a 'white only' label."

Bill White recalled the incident years later in his memoir, *Uppity*.

"I saw the list included a couple of rookies who'd never swung a bat in the majors," he wrote. "The idea that the local bigwigs wanted to honor unproven players while ignoring proven players because of the color of their skin rankled me. . . . No, it more than rankled me. Combined with all the other crap that black players had to take, it made me furious."

White vented his fury to Associated Press sportswriter Joe Reichler in an interview about the incident—and Reichler sent his story out over the wire. The black-owned *St. Louis Argus* picked up the story and added an editorial comment of its own, saying, in essence, that if this was how the company that owned the Cardinals, Anheuser-Busch, treated its black players, then the city's black residents should return the favor by boycotting the company's beer.

The mere mention of the word boycott woke up Anheuser-Busch executives, as well as the Cardinals.

Eddie Stanky, White's minor league manager who was now working in the Cardinals' front office, was never a bigot but always a company man. He took White aside and advised him to keep his feelings to himself. Similarly, Roscoe McCrary, a reporter from the *Argus*, suggested that White might want to revise his earlier comments.

White refused to back down. He figured he was in a noble fight and that if he got kicked out of the sport he loved he could go back to college and attend medical school.

Surprisingly, White's most encouraging conversation was with the head of Fleishman-Hillard, Anheuser-Busch's public relations company. Al Fleishman was sympathetic to White's cause.

"The last thing you want to do now is cool down," Fleishman told him. "You need to keep the pressure on their ass."

White did just that, continuing to speak his mind whenever given the opportunity.

It wasn't long before the chamber of commerce, no doubt receiving pressure from Anheuser-Busch, backed down. It insisted that the whole brouhaha surrounding the "Salute to Baseball" breakfast had been one giant misunderstanding—and extended official invitations to both Bill White and Elston Howard.

The Yankees ordered Howard to attend and he complied.

But there was no power great enough to convince White to show up. In his words, he "didn't want to eat with those bigots, anyway."

When Branch Rickey signed Jackie Robinson to the Brooklyn Dodgers in 1947, his partner and legal counsel, Walter O'Malley, ducked Florida's Jim Crow laws by moving the team's spring training facilities to Havana. O'Malley, who had an almost fanatic attachment to the bottom line, realized that integrating spring training would help the club acquire the top players from the Negro Leagues. The following year, he skirted Jim Crow again. He built the Dodgers their own spring training complex, Dodgertown, out of an old army barracks on Vero Beach, a barrier island in the heart of Florida's citrus country. O'Malley figured the place was so hard to reach—drivers had to cross a one-lane wooden bridge—that city officials would agree to ignore how it was run. He was right.

The result was a mini-utopia. Black and white players shared dormitory housing, not to mention a dining facility, fishing hole, orange grove, barbershop, post office, training fields, and a pitch-and-putt, nine-hole golf course. Five years later, as president of the team, O'Malley built the Dodgers their own 6,500-seat ballpark, Holman Stadium.

Don Zimmer played with the team for six seasons in the '50s. "Every morning, they would blow a whistle, just like in the army, and you'd get in the chow line," he told the *New York Daily News*. "You never knew who you'd be standing there with. There'd be kids from Class D ball right next to Walter O'Malley and his wife, Kay. There was no class system. Everybody ate together."

O'Malley's son, Peter, remembers Dodgertown as a cross between a campsite and a small college campus. And its spartan accommodations—no phones, radios, televisions, or air conditioning—fostered a sense of camaraderie.

"I think [being housed together] was almost our secret weapon," O'Malley says. "Everybody hadn't seen each other all winter long and they come together in Florida. The weather's cold and windy in the beginning, and there was no heat in the rooms. And everybody would gather in the lobby by the stove, drink coffee, and talk about the cold, windy night, or the rainy night, or the leaky barracks. They shared the experience, and it absolutely brought the organization together."

Still, this was the South, and the authorities had their limits. They insisted that Holman Stadium remain segregated for public events, including exhibition games—and they stuck to it. The city police showed up at the Dodgers' first exhibition game and, on three different occasions, ordered black fans to move farther away from white fans, squeezing them deeper into the "colored" section in the right-field corner.

Walter O'Malley was in a tough spot. He wanted the publicity and the ticket sales that came with integration, but he didn't want to pay to uproot his team. Yet like Veeck and other owners, he knew his only clout was the threat of taking his team—and the cash flow it generated—out of Florida.

In August 1961, O'Malley responded to a letter from the Major League Baseball Players Association inquiring about race relations in Dodgertown.

"There are local ordinances that are not in keeping with our thinking," O'Malley wrote. "Our relations with the local political administration are not cordial at the moment and we have been giving some thought to transferring our [spring training facilities] to the West Coast unless we see signs of improvement."

The following spring—1962—Peter O'Malley, now the director of Dodgertown, met with a biracial committee of local citizens seeking to improve race relations. Two days later, he lost his patience with Jim Crow and painted over all of the signs at Holman, desegregating its entrances, restrooms, water fountains, and seating sections.

When asked what prompted him to take the matter into his own hands, Peter accepts no credit for defying local policies or for standing up to the local authorities. "It was an easy decision," he says. "It was clear to me that it was a mistake and wrong to distinguish these restrooms. It had to change. And I remember standing up on the back of a pickup truck taking down the sign that said [white only]. I just knew it was the right thing to do, it was a no-brainer."

With the painted-over signs, city officials had little choice but to tacitly waive the segregated-seating ordinance at Holman. But *Los Ange-*

les Herald-Examiner columnist Melvin Durslag noted that Peter's popularity in Vero Beach "hadn't thickened."

Peter didn't care. He invited black committee member Ralph Lundy to watch a game with him at the newly integrated ballpark. The greatest spectacle for Lundy wasn't on the field, it was in the grandstands. Black fans were confused and disoriented, tentatively making their way to the formerly segregated section.

Dodgers left fielder Tommy Davis remembered encouraging the fans to leave the right field corner and sit behind home plate.

"We almost had to push them," he told *Sports Illustrated*. 'Get up! Everything's O.K. now.'"

Segregation may have been defeated within the walls of Holman Stadium, but until President Kennedy's successor, Lyndon Johnson, signed into law the Civil Rights Act of 1964, Jim Crow was still waiting just outside the ballpark—and inside many other parks throughout the South.

3

New York 1962. A bustling city of fedoras, chesterfields, and cigarettes. President Kennedy, on a visit to the city, took in the Broadway musical *How to Succeed in Business Without Really Trying*. Louis Armstrong & His All Stars filmed a concert at Pathé Studios at 134th and Park. Twenty-one-year-old folk singer Bob Dylan performed his newest song, *Blowin' in the Wind*, at Gerde's Folk City in Greenwich Village.

And corner newsstands hawked seven major dailies.

It seemed there was a paper for everybody. The well-heeled read the morning broadsheets, the *New York Times* and the *New York Herald Tribune*. Conservatives grabbed the afternoon broadsheet, the *New York World-Telegram & Sun*. Blue-collar readers had their pick of the mass-market morning tabloids, the *Daily Mirror* and the *Daily News*. Sports fans also picked up the afternoon tabloid, the *New York Journal-American*, or the city's most liberal paper, the *New York Post*.

But on Sunday, December 9, the city's 1,300 newsstands had no papers to sell.

In the wee hours of the morning, the Linotype machines in the *Times*'s composition room had stopped clattering, the presses stopped roaring. Members of Local 6 of the International Typographical Union, better known as Big Six, had grabbed their typewriters, coffee mugs, and lunchboxes and walked off the job. By the time the sun rose over the East River, nine other unions had joined them, shutting down the *Times*, the *News*, the *Journal-American*, and the *World-Telegram & Sun*.

Hours later, the publishers of the *Herald Tribune*, the *Mirror*, and the *Post* announced they, too, were suspending publication.

In all, more than nineteen thousand newspaper employees had gone on strike—and left New York baseball fans without a single paper with which to follow their teams.

At the heart of the walkout was automation. The workers were railing against the inevitable: computerized typesetting machines that would automate the pressroom and make their jobs obsolete.

The president of Big Six, Bertram Powers, a debonair forty-year-old Irishman with a tenth-grade education, had worked as a printer at various papers around New England before settling in New York. Having come up through the ranks, Powers made it his mission to get every possible penny for his members. To some, he was a formidable negotiator. To others, he was a stubborn, counterproductive bully. The latter group often questioned whether he even liked newspapers—or the people that ran them.

It may have been that Powers was so blinded by typesetting machines he didn't see that another technology—television—was making far greater inroads into his turf. TV was gaining a voice in news and politics and had already proven to be a primary influence in the 1960 presidential race. (In the first of the four televised debates between Kennedy and Nixon, viewers polled almost two-to-one in favor of Kennedy, primarily because of the way the candidates came across on screen. Where Nixon looked thin, pale, and tense, Kennedy appeared young, robust, and confident.)

With their newspapers taken away, New Yorkers were leaning even more heavily on television. They also began reading magazines and books more thoroughly—and soon found themselves enjoying a calmer life, one without an incessant barrage of newspaper headlines vying for their attention.

In a February press conference, President Kennedy laid into the unions.

"The situation has long since passed the point of public toleration," Kennedy said. "Collective bargaining has failed. The most intensive mediation has failed. This is a situation which is bad for the union movement all over the country, bad for the newspaper managements, and bad for the New York citizens, more than five million of them, who are newspaper readers."

On March 31, 114 days into the stalemate, Mayor Robert Wagner and mediator Theodore W. Kheel reached a settlement with Powers and the other union presidents. The publishers agreed not to modernize technology without the consent of the unions; they also agreed to increase wages to an average of $152.63 a week from $145, and to reduce the workweek to thirty-five hours from thirty-six and a quarter.

But those figures didn't include the cost of the strike.

Six hundred forty-nine million papers had gone unprinted, costing the publishers more than $108 million in advertising and circulation revenue. The downtime had cost the striking workers $50 million in lost wages. The damage was so steep that four papers would fold by 1967. Only the *Post*, the *News*, and the *Times* would be healthy enough to make it through the '60s.

By all accounts, the strike had been catastrophic for the New York newspaper business. Writers, editors, columnists, copyboys, and photographers had stretched their wallets along with the printers and pressmen, dipping into savings and relying on strike fund benefits to put food on their tables. Many never returned to their jobs.

On the other hand, those who adapted to the new New York flourished.

Clay Felker, an editor at the *New York Herald Tribune*, took over the paper's Sunday supplement and hired popular newspaper writers such as Jimmy Breslin and Gail Sheehy to appeal to a hipper audience. When the *Tribune* shut down, Felker raised one million dollars and created the groundbreaking and hugely successful *New York Magazine*. Another group of editors launched the *New York Review of Books*, a highbrow magazine that filled its pages with in-depth book reviews, literary commentary, and cultural essays. News columnists, now freelancing, stretched their talents to come up with longer-form pieces that would appeal to readers' new sensibilities—and sold them to magazine editors.

When it came to the sports page, few writers emerged from the strike as unscathed as Dick Young. If anything, the *New York Daily News* columnist was more influential, and more popular, than he was before. His syndicated column, "Young Ideas," had flourished during the strike, mainly because it reached far beyond the boundaries of New York, filling the pages of hundreds of major dailies throughout the country, not to mention the national weekly *Sporting News*. While just about every other New York sportswriter had been out of action, Young was churning out as many as four thousand words per week.

A self-taught writer with a thick shock of salt-and-pepper hair, Young grew up during the Depression, when Hollywood glorified newspapermen. Cut in the mold of Clark Gable, Spencer Tracy, and Pat O'Brien, Young was intoxicated by the smell of press ink—and the notion of having a typewriter where he could spit his vitriol. He soon found the ideal platform on which to begin: the *Daily News* was New York's most widely read morning paper, reaching more than two million loyal blue-collar readers.

It was no surprise that Young appealed to the workingman. He'd had his own share of struggles and had developed a strong, no-excuses work ethic along the way. Born in the blue-collar Manhattan neighborhood of Washington Heights, Young was three when his parents divorced and his father, a Russian Jew, took off for California. He was fostered to a family in New York City until he was twelve, and after high school he tried to finagle his way into acceptance at Los Angeles Junior College, claiming California residency to qualify for in-state tuition rates. (He said he was living with his father even though the elder Young had since remarried and moved to another state). The administration soon caught on and forced him to leave when he couldn't scratch together the seventy-five-dollar non-residency fee.

With no college education to put on his resume, Young returned to the East Coast and found work with Franklin Roosevelt's relief program, the Civilian Conservation Corps, helping to build bridges on Cayuga Lake in Upstate New York. When he heard that the *Daily News* was looking for eager young reporters, he threw himself in front of Harvey Duell, the paper's managing editor, begging for whatever he could get. The effort paid off, and in 1937 Duell made him a messenger for eighteen dollars a week. Young took it gladly; he ran errands for the *News* during the day while attending classes at New York University at night. He was soon getting better-paying assignments, one of which was on the sports desk. In five years, he was covering the Dodgers. In twenty, he was the most widely read sportswriter in America.

"I didn't even want to be a sportswriter," Young told Ross Wetzsteon of *Sport* magazine in 1985. "I wanted to be a hotshot newspaperman like Walter Winchell. I wanted to be a stop-the-presses guy, competing with the other paper for the scoop and for the girl. I didn't go for that fancy writing—still don't. Some guys think they can fool a sports fan with, quote, good writing, unquote, but the fan knows when he's being bullshitted by a cute line. If you've got the story, you report it. If you don't, you write it. A newspaper isn't like a book, for Christ's sake. When you're through with it, you throw it out and buy a new one."

Young's was a no-nonsense style, and his column gave readers a generous helping of opinion—most of it acerbic.

The late Phil Pepe started covering the Yankees for the *New York World-Telegram & Sun* in 1961. "[Young] had a way of talking to the people the way people talk to each other," he said in an interview in 2015. "And he also had a way of incorporating in his stories the language of the major league player. He's the first guy, as far as I can tell, who called runs batted in 'ribbies,' because that's what the players called it. Dick Young was very creative. He was like the everyman. He was a blue-collar guy and he wrote for the blue-collar reader."

Young knew his trade. One story puts him and *Daily News* colleague Joe Trimble in Yankee Stadium for game five of the 1956 World Series. Don Larsen had just thrown the first perfect game in Series history. Bill Gallo was in the same press box that day and he recounted the Young-Trimble story years later in the *Daily News*.

> Trimble was covering the Yankees. He had a deadline to get the story in, but after the game, he suddenly started to sweat. He sat at his typewriter, staring at a blank piece of copy paper. Then he turned to me and said, "Get Dick Young over here, please. I'm stuck." In twenty seconds, Dick knocked out the line "Don Larsen, the imperfect man, pitched the perfect game." Period. This was all Trimble needed to get him started on what was to be one of his best efforts. Joe received several awards throughout the years for this piece.

Years later, Trimble himself recounted the incident at a party in midtown Manhattan in honor of Young, who was leaving the *Daily News*. "I never told this story," Trimble said to the roomful of newspapermen, "and what's more, and what makes me feel so good about it, Dick Young never told this story either."

For every writer that looked up to Young, there was an owner or a player who preferred to steer clear of him. They knew that Young's pen was as sharp as a bayonet. In Young's view, he had no agenda, just a responsibility to protect the game from those who threatened its integrity.

Robert Lipsyte arrived at the *Times* in 1957, fresh out of Columbia University. "[Young] saw himself, and spoke of this, actually, as the conscience of baseball," Lipsyte says. "I once saw Richie Ashburn on the Mets' charter fall out of his chair onto the plane floor when Dick said he was the conscience of baseball. 'What the fuck are you talking about?' But he did feel that way."

When the Lords of Baseball, as Young derisively called the owners, were celebrating the defeat of a Senate proposal to exempt baseball from antitrust laws, Young called the sport "a money-grabbing, prestige-purchasing monopoly that has taken on the shameless aspects of a floating crap game." He added, "There is very little civic pride or public devotion in the breasts of the Lords of Baseball. They attempt to peddle their product on the basis that the local team belongs, in truth, to the fans, but that is an unmitigated fraud. . . . Baseball moves along with all the nobility of a medicine show; less, in fact. At least a snake-oil huckster doesn't make threats of what he might do if not given municipal handouts."

George Vecsey's career overlapped with Young's. Vecsey spent the '60s at *Newsday* before moving to the *Times*. "Young was a hardhead and didn't care what people thought," Vecsey says. "The part of him that was nice enjoyed younger people, unless we proved ourselves to be dolts and idiots, in which case he'd scream at you in the press box or over dinner somewhere. He was a tough, miserable, ornery guy but also a shining light for those of us who came along."

Young's popularity was based on his willingness to tear down superstars as quickly as he did young sportswriters.

One of his favorite whipping boys was Jackie Robinson. In his opinion, Robinson saw the world through only one lens—that of race.

As reported in Bill Madden's book, *1954*, Young once told Robinson, "That's the trouble with you, Jackie, and the difference between you and Campy [Robinson's black teammate, Roy Campanella]. I can go to Campy and all he ever wants to talk about is baseball. But with you, it always sooner or later gets back to social issues. I'm telling you as a friend that the newspapermen are saying Campy's the kind of guy they can like, but that your aggressiveness, your wearing your race on your sleeve, makes enemies."

Of Yankees superstar Mickey Mantle, Young wrote, "He is emotionally immature. Actually, he's a pretty nice guy, all things considered. He's not too bright, and he's not too friendly, but he has many fine qualities—aside from his ability to hit a baseball."

Young saved most of his venom for the television crews that began invading the clubhouses during the press strike, taking advantage of the newspaper blackout. Unfortunately for Young, the crews only multiplied after the strike ended.

Former Yankees public relations director Marty Appel remembers Young's antipathy toward television. "Oh, he hated the guys with the TV cameras," he says. "He'd behave rudely to them—standing in front of their lens during a press conference. He didn't like the occasional privileges they might get, as their financial support of baseball was growing, so he never did come to terms with that, come to peace with that. . . . The guys who would show up just for pregame and then leave, wouldn't stay for the game, and you'd see them once a week or something like that, he just didn't have much respect for them."

Steve Jacobson joined *Newsday* in 1960 after four years as a copy boy at the *Daily Mirror*. "What did I learn from Dick Young?" he says. "Not to take shit from television. The television people were very abusive. Young would curse into a television microphone. A television guy would stand on the outside of the crowd and listen to the newspaper's questions and record the answers and Young would deliberately curse into his microphone so [the television network] couldn't put it on the air. He was fearless that way."

Vecsey agrees. "The locker room was our turf, the writers' turf," he says. "Dick protected his turf as viciously as any capo. He was a tough SOB. Twice in postseason baseball I saw live crews come in and some foof with hair says, 'Okay, we're going live.' I learned from Dick, what do you do? You stand into the microphone and you say, 'In a pig's ass you're going live!' . . . Dick saw the enemy, and to put it into cowboy terms, he knew the West was changing and he went down hard."

But television was here to stay, and even Young had to see that his kingdom wasn't only being invaded—it was being conquered. To stay relevant, he and his fellow newspapermen would have to step out of the press box and bring the fans what they couldn't find elsewhere: an up-close, personal look at their uniformed heroes, warts and all.

4

In 1962 Ford Frick occupied the office of baseball commissioner. But the real king of the hill, the man who truly ruled the game, was Walter O'Malley. The fifty-nine-year-old Dodgers owner—an impeccably dressed businessman who wore round wireframe glasses, kept his hair slicked straight back, and usually held a stogie between his lips—had come to power a decade earlier during a drawn-out political battle with the leaders of New York City.

O'Malley's story is one of ambition and perseverance. By nature, he was unlike his fellow Lords of Baseball, nearly all of whom had been born into wealth. (The Yankees' Dan Topping traced his fortune to the tin industry; the Cubs' P. K. Wrigley inherited a chewing gum empire; the Phillies' Bob Carpenter was heir to the chemical giant DuPont; Red Sox owner Tom Yawkey was the grandson of a timber and iron ore tycoon.)

No, O'Malley had seen good times and bad. Growing up in the borough of Queens, he witnessed his father, Edwin, go from dry goods merchant to commissioner of public markets, a city hall job that brought the elder O'Malley a fair degree of affluence. But after leaving public office, he tried and failed at several other businesses. And in 1929, when the American economy collapsed, Edwin's modest fortune went down with it.

The family may have gone broke, but lack of money didn't squelch Walter's ambitions. He graduated from the University of Pennsylvania; then, when he was too strapped to continue studying law at Columbia, earned a law degree by attending night classes at Fordham. As Andy McCue, the author of *Mover and Shaker*, put it, "he was out of the Ivy League and back with the Catholic strivers."

Determined not to repeat his father's financial missteps, the newly minted attorney spotted opportunity in the least likely of places: the Great Depression. He built a law practice by representing bankrupt companies—helping them emerge from ruin, and helping himself to a tidy slice of the pie. He also invested wisely, elbowed with bigwigs in Brooklyn, and in 1942 positioned himself to replace Wendell Wilkie as chief legal counsel for the Brooklyn Dodgers. Two years later, he teamed up with Branch Rickey and John L. Smith, and together they bought a minority interest in the ball club. In 1945 the group took full control of the team.

Technically the Dodgers' vice president, O'Malley had never quite gotten used to the "vice" in his title. He sparred with Rickey, the team's president, on most everything, especially when it came to who should be in charge. O'Malley won that argument in 1950, when he steamrolled over Rickey, buying out his shares and assuming full control.

As president, O'Malley had made it his first order of business to ensure that his club would be profitable. As he saw it, the biggest threat was Brooklyn itself. The borough's population of more than 2.7 million made it the city's largest, but residents had been fleeing by the thousands. O'Malley recognized the migratory pattern: Brooklynites were heading for the wide open spaces of Long Island, where homeowners could buy cars, barbecue in the backyard, and watch the ballgame in roomy dens.

In O'Malley's view, Brooklyn was no longer the borough it had been in the heyday of the Dodgers. According to Dick Young, O'Malley had once said, privately, that the borough had become "full of blacks and spics and Jews."

O'Malley had been right about one thing: attendance was a problem. In 1955, the year the Dodgers won the World Series, barely one million fans had come out to the park—a 43 percent drop from its peak attendance in 1947, the year Jackie Robinson made his debut. A decade later, the last of the Brooklyn trolleys had shut down, and the club's biggest asset, Ebbets Field, was in decay. Worse yet, the park could handle only seven hundred parking spaces for its thirty-two thousand seats.

Again, O'Malley had studied the forces at play and mapped out a path to prosperity. Instead of saving Ebbets Field, he'd build a new stadium, one that would draw fans from the suburbs, luring them with attractions for the whole family. He claimed to have his eye on downtown Brooklyn—specifically, the abandoned Atlantic rail yards at the intersection of Flatbush and Atlantic Avenues. He appealed to the city's mayor, Robert Wagner, and its even more powerful parks commissioner, Robert Moses, offering to build a six-million-dollar stadium on the site.

"He was in love with that site, there's no doubt about that," recalls Peter O'Malley. "It was because of rapid transportation. All the subways in New York went through Atlantic and Flatbush. In addition, the Long Island Rail Road ended at Atlantic and Flatbush. His goal was to design, pay for, maintain, and landscape, where appropriate, a stadium. He didn't want a taxpayer facility. [But] he needed help assembling the land."

Moses had dismissed the idea, insisting that O'Malley wanted the land at too great a discount and the city would end up paying tens of millions of dollars to finance the stadium. Instead, Moses proposed a site he'd coveted since the '30s: Flushing Meadows in Queens.

O'Malley wanted no part of it. For starters, the site was remote. The Long Island Expressway had yet to be completed, so suburbanites would've been confined to a single highway, the Grand Central Parkway. Taking the subway from almost anywhere in Brooklyn required going through Manhattan, and the train from Long Island didn't reach the Meadows. Few fans would come from Manhattan or the Bronx; those boroughs had the Giants and the Yankees. Worse yet, the site itself was little more than a marshy dumping ground for the company that burned all of Brooklyn's garbage. Flushing Meadows was a wasteland of ashes, horseshit, and rats.

Moses felt certain it could be turned into a public park. He urged Peter Campbell Brown of New York's Office of City Construction, "I hope you won't give the time of day to Walter O'Malley's latest 'offer.' What Walter says about foundation problems at Flushing Meadows is rubbish. We know every yard of it. No trouble with parking and the open spaces and the building would be on piles."

O'Malley had called the letter "a further bit of sabotage" that showed there was "no sincere administration desire to work out a solution here in Brooklyn."

So for O'Malley, it was Atlantic Avenue or bust—or, more accurately, Atlantic Avenue or Los Angeles. He'd made little secret of his interest in moving the Dodgers to the West Coast. In LA, he could build his dream stadium surrounded by a nexus of multilane highways and vast parking lots, making it easy for fans to get to and from the park. Plus, LA offered a booming middle-class economy. Spurred by the entertainment and defense industries—not to mention a sizable amount of unionized manufacturing—the city's population had been exploding since the end of World War II; real estate development had replaced oil and agriculture as the area's leading industry. If O'Malley moved his team there, he'd have the third-largest baseball city all to himself. Attendance was a no-brainer, and the prospect of charging TV viewers to watch Dodger games was tantalizing.

Brooklyn borough president John Cashmore pleaded with O'Malley to stay, insisting he was doing everything he could to clear the Atlantic site. "I don't think I would be able to ever again face a youngster in Brooklyn or anywhere, if I didn't do everything I could within reason to keep the Dodgers in Brooklyn," he wrote in a telegram to O'Malley. "Please hold everything—and tell Los Angeles to go find itself another baseball team."

Moses, apparently, felt the cause was already lost. He figured if O'Malley had wanted to stay in New York, he'd have accepted the Flushing Meadows site. In his view, O'Malley was simply looking for a way to leave the city without being flogged in the history books. Why else would he have made a deal with Cubs owner Philip K. Wrigley to swap the Dodgers' farm team in Fort Worth, Texas, for the Cubs' Triple-A team in Los Angeles, along with territorial rights?

Moses's logic made sense.

It did seem as though O'Malley was liquidating his assets to raise funds for a stadium in Los Angeles.

He'd unloaded the Dodgers' minor league park in Montreal for one million dollars.

He'd sold Ebbets Field for three million dollars with a plan to lease it.

He'd also defended his purchase of a forty-four-passenger Convair plane by saying, "If a club should go to the West Coast, it would have to fly and it would have to own an airplane." This, of course, was true—but it was an especially bad sign considering that the fifteen other Major League teams were clustered in the Northeast and Midwest, close enough to each other for train travel.

It's impossible to know when precisely the decision had been made, but it was clear the fight was all but over.

Whatever Moses had seen in the grassy fields of Flushing Meadows, O'Malley had begun to picture in the lucrative Los Angeles sprawl. The two visions were 2,800 miles—and millions of dollars in revenue—apart.

At the end of the 1957 season, O'Malley made it official. After two years of name-calling, backstabbing, and headline-grabbing, he'd pulled the Dodgers out of Brooklyn and brought them to Los Angeles, crushing the hearts of loyal Dodgers fans who'd sat in the stands at Ebbets Field and watched Jackie Robinson make history.

Red Smith, the venerable writer whose syndicated column appeared in the *New York Herald Tribune* and later the *New York Times*, saw the Dodgers' move as nothing more than a play for power and money.

"It had always been recognized that baseball was a business," he wrote, "but if you enjoyed the game you could also tell yourself that it was also a sport. O'Malley was the first to say out loud that it was all business—a business that he owned and could operate as he chose."

Dick Young performed his own postmortem. Spewing forth in the *Daily News*, he told his readers, "Preliminary diagnosis indicates that the cause of death was an acute case of greed, followed by severe political implications. And, now, Walter O'Malley leaves Brooklyn a rich man and a despised man."

By all accounts, O'Malley had wrestled with the decision, but in the end he chose the wide-open frontier of the West.

The city of Los Angeles, in its haste to build a home for the iconic Dodger franchise, condemned the three hundred acres of Chavez Ravine in the name of urban renewal, driving more than a thousand Mexican American families from their homes in the process. Rather than creating modern public housing, which the city had promised the displaced residents, it handed over the land to O'Malley, cheating its taxpayers of $4.7 million.

Few people, other than those residents, seemed to care.

In 1962 O'Malley moved his team into its new home, Dodger Stadium, a fifty-six-thousand-seat Shangri La complete with one pitching rubber, four bases, and sixteen thousand parking spots.

A glimpse of the 1962 sports headlines showed that fortunes were being made on the baseball field. At least that's what the owners were saying.

Look at the golden boys, Willie Mays and Mickey Mantle. The two stars were each earning ninety thousand dollars. You could buy a house for less than half that.

What the owners neglected to mention was that the league's minimum salary was six thousand dollars, and that the typical baseball player's career lasted four years, nine months.

Dick Young, ever the champion of the working class, sympathized with the poorly paid rookies, asking, "How many Lords of Baseball have priced groceries lately?"

Most players took second jobs during the offseason to make ends meet, and to prepare for life after baseball. The Tigers' Norm Cash worked on a ranch and auctioned hogs. The Giants' Willie McCovey sold cars. Dick Radatz, a rookie reliever for the Red Sox, spent the winter as a furniture mover and substitute teacher. One group of players, including Frank Robinson, Al Jackson, Dick McAuliffe, and Jim Bouton, formed a basketball team and played against high school teachers in the New York area for fifty dollars apiece.

The players were caught in a bind. When their contracts arrived in the mail at the beginning of the year, they had three choices: sign, ask for more money, or quit. There was little room for negotiation and no freedom to look for a job with another team. The entire employment system came down to paragraph 10a of the Uniform Player's Contract, the so-called reserve clause, which the owners interpreted to mean they could renew a player's contract year after year as long as the club desired to keep him. If a player didn't like it, his only option was to find another line of work.

If it seemed one-sided, it was.

Ebony magazine summed up the situation as follows:

> Once a player signs with a major league baseball club, he signs for his baseball lifetime. If he is a kid who grew up on the sandlots of a small southern town and nothing much is known about his ability, he usually signs for as little as $90 to $100 a week and a train ticket. If he is an outstanding high school or college player with a national reputation and several clubs vying for his services, he might get as much as $100,000 as a bonus and other concessions just for

signing a contract. No matter what he gets . . . that club owns him for life.

Red Smith was more direct than Young or *Ebony*, indicting the reserve system for giving owners "the right to buy and sell men like hogs."

Smith told the story of Peahead Walker, who'd earned fame as a college football coach in North Carolina. In 1937 Peahead was managing a minor league baseball team, the Snow Hill Billies. The club's owner, local businessman Josiah Exum, sat Peahead down and told him the Yankees were interested in their catcher, Aaron Robinson.

"Now, listen, Peahead," Exum said. "George Weiss is coming after Robinson. . . . You sit in with us but let me do the talking because that's my business. He'll offer $5,000, I'll ask for $15,000 and we'll settle for $10,000, but you keep quiet."

When Weiss arrived, he offered $5,000, just as Exum had predicted.

Exum pulled Peahead from the room.

"I sold lumber and did good," Exum said in the privacy of the hallway. "I sold coal and made money, and now I'm selling hardware. But this is the first time I ever sold a man. [I'm not about to bargain over a human being.] I'm taking the $5,000."

These kinds of transactions weren't limited to obscure players such as Robinson. Even the big stars had no control over their destiny.

Mickey Mantle had had a spectacular season in 1956; he hit 52 homers, batted .353, drove in 130 runs, and won the Triple Crown. The following spring, he walked into George Weiss's office, confident that the Yankees' general manager would gladly double his $32,500 salary. Instead, Weiss gave him a take-it-or-leave-it proposal that outdid all others: accept the team's offer or have his many illicit affairs exposed to his wife.

Mantle recounted the story to Dave Anderson in the *New York Times*. "[Weiss] told me I was too young to make that kind of money," he said. "Then he threatened to show my wife reports from private detectives he had gumshoe me and Billy Martin. He threatened to trade me for Herb Score and Rocky Colavito."

Weiss had stuck to his blackmailing guns, but Yankees co-owner Del Webb caved and agreed to pay Mantle sixty thousand dollars.

"Weiss never forgot it," Mantle told Anderson. "After [I won a second straight MVP award], he tried to cut me $5,000."

What Mantle hadn't known—and what would have certainly shed some light on the negotiations—was that Weiss received a percentage of every dollar he cut from the team's payroll.

In 1962 the Yankees won the pennant—their twenty-seventh in franchise history—and then beat the Giants in the World Series. Playing on a perennial winner meant more than bragging rights. For many Yankees players, the bonuses that came in the postseason amounted to more money than their salaries. The old guard—Mantle, Ford, Berra, and Howard—were so accustomed to winning, they'd come to treat the extra money as part of their pay. But the rookies used it to make ends meet. Roy Hamey, a longtime Yankees employee who'd taken the reins from Weiss, even used the bonuses as a negotiating tactic. His advice for rookies was always the same, "Look, son, you're wearing Yankee pinstripes, you'll get a World Series check."

Tony Kubek, the Yankees' All-Star shortstop, hadn't caught on to Hamey's game until later in his career.

"I used to think that if you were honest with the front office they'd be fair with you," Kubek told David G. Surdam, author of *The Postwar Yankees*. "I found out that isn't so. They simply want to get you as cheaply as they can."

What Kubek took from the experience was a lesson: The better a player was at bargaining, the more money he'd make.

One such bargainer was Jim Bouton, who'd had a respectable rookie season in 1962. He went 7-7, compiled a 3.99 ERA and earned the minimum, seven thousand dollars. Hoping to be rewarded, Bouton asked for a five-thousand-dollar raise the next spring.

Dan Topping Jr., who'd been put in charge of signing lower-level players, handed Bouton a contract and told him to sign on the bottom line. The document guaranteed Bouton nine thousand dollars if he made the team—and seven thousand dollars if he didn't.

Bouton was incredulous. "What do you mean *if* I make the team? I was with the team the whole year; why wouldn't I make it? Why would you even want to plant that kind of doubt in the mind of a rookie pitcher?"

Topping skipped past the comment and reminded Bouton that he'd be earning more money in October.

"Don't forget, you'll get a World Series share," he said. "You can always count on that."

"Fine," Bouton said. "I'll sign a contract that guarantees me $10,000 more at the end of the season."

Topping reminded Bouton that the Yankees didn't modify contracts. After going back and forth, he agreed to nine thousand dollars, regardless of whether Bouton made the club.

Bouton refused to sign.

Later that day he got a call from Hamey.

"Lookit, son," Hamey yelled into the phone. "You better sign that contract, that's all there's gonna be. That's it. You don't sign that contract you're making the biggest mistake of your life."

Bouton, young, cocky, and nobody's fool, hung up.

Two days later Topping approached Bouton again and asked him how much he wanted.

Bouton stuck to his number: twelve thousand.

Topping came back with ten.

Bouton countered with ten-five, and they called it a deal.

While Bouton and the Yankees were duking it out in the spring of 1963, Jim Brosnan, a middling reliever on Cincinnati, was battling with Reds owner, Bill DeWitt. The pitcher, a stateside army man who wore horn-rimmed glasses, smoked a pipe, and was as comfortable quoting Dickens as he was throwing a 2-0 fastball, had had a long-burning love affair with writing; he'd spent his off-seasons as an advertising copywriter and wrote articles for *Life* and *Sports Illustrated*. It was only natural that he'd get around to writing a book about baseball. Still, nobody expected his truth-telling diary, *The Long Season*. In it, Brosnan deviated sharply from the hero-worshipping formulas found in books like *Joe DiMaggio: Lucky to Be a Yankee* and *Willie Mays: The "Say-Hey" Kid*. Instead, Brosnan chronicled the 1959 season from an insider's point of view—he shared his love of martinis, his attitude toward managers, and the financial struggles and inner doubts that came with being a professional pitcher. He released a second memoir, *Pennant Race*, two years later.

Consider this excerpt from Brosnan's second book: "To get to [Cincinnati's] Crosley Field, I usually take a bus through the old crumbling streets of the Bottoms. Negroes stand on the corners watching their homes fall down. The insecurity of being in the second division of the National League leaves me. For 25 cents, the daily bus ride gives me enough humility to get me through any baseball game, or season."

Or this one from *The Long Season*, when Brosnan finds out he's been traded: "I sat back on the couch, half-breathing as I waited for indignation to flush good red blood to my head. Nothing happened. I took a deep breath, then exhaled slowly. It's true. The second time you're sold you don't feel a thing."

DeWitt set out to silence Brosnan, and he did it by using every owner's favorite weapon: the reserve clause. After the season, he gave Brosnan his new contract. Brosnan, seeing that his pay had been cut the maximum 25 percent, refused to sign and handed it back. DeWitt grabbed a pen and circled paragraph 3c, the bit of language that allowed teams to control a player's conduct on and off the field, and slid the paper back to Brosnan.

"Why are you invoking [that clause] against me?" Brosnan asked.

"What are you going to do about it?" DeWitt said.

"But why me?"

"Because you say things that are not good for baseball."

What DeWitt meant, obviously, was that Brosnan said things that weren't good for DeWitt.

Brosnan negotiated, but in the end, took a 10 percent cut and agreed, in writing, to show Reds' management anything else he wrote about baseball before it was published.

In an interview with Milton Gross of the *New York Post*, Brosnan explained the agreement. "I'm not allowed any more to write about baseball, talk on radio about it, or make any remarks on television without first having the gist of the statements cleared by the front office."

"You're being censored," Gross told him. "That's unconstitutional."

"Obviously," Brosnan admitted. "But so is the reserve clause."

The following season, Brosnan was traded to the White Sox who told him he couldn't write a word while wearing a Sox uniform.

Brosnan played out the rest of his contract. Then, at thirty-three, after being offered another pay cut, he quit altogether.

In Los Angeles, Maury Wills wasn't faring all that much better with Dodgers general manager Buzzie Bavasi. In their first year at Chavez Ravine in 1962, the Dodgers had missed out on the pennant by one game—but Wills had stolen a record 104 bases and beaten out Willie Mays for the National League MVP.

It made sense that Wills expected a sizeable raise from the thirty-five thousand dollars he'd been making—but he was dealing with Bavasi, a renowned skinflint and disciple of Walter O'Malley.

How tough was Bavasi? Three years earlier, he'd released Carl Furillo when the thirty-eight-year-old outfielder tore a calf muscle. Furillo had sued the Dodgers, invoking the contractual clause that prohibited teams from releasing players who had become disabled. When Bavasi realized he had no legal leverage, he settled, giving Furillo the twenty-one thousand dollars remaining on his contract. But Furillo paid the price: after fifteen years of service, a National League batting title, and a world championship, the baseball lifer couldn't find a team that would hire him as a player or as a coach.

According to Bavasi, Furillo had "had his day in the sun" and "it was over."

Dick Young saw things differently and accused the Dodgers of blackballing Furillo, presumably to send a message to other players. "[Furillo] had the nerve . . . to threaten a breach-of-contract suit against the Dodgers," Young had written in the *Daily News*. "He had caused trouble. Club owners have a strange way of equating trouble. A ballplayer can get into all sorts of it, presumably, as long as it is not with them. They will tolerate a man who waves a gun in public, or a player picked up on a morals rap, or a paternity suit. Furillo has done none of these things. His was a greater crime. He threatened to sue a ball club."

So when Wills walked into Bavasi's office, he knew what he was up against. He stated his case—as an MVP he deserved to enter the same stratosphere as Mays and Mantle—but there was no trophy great enough to sway Bavasi.

"I thought I was going to get me a raise, maybe get a new car," Wills said years later. "All I wanted was a Ford station wagon. I came out of [Bavasi's] office in ten minutes happy I was still on the team."

Eventually, Bavasi did put Wills on par with Don Drysdale, the Dodgers ace who'd just won the Cy Young award. Both players were now earning forty-five thousand dollars, making them the highest-paid players in the Scrooge-like organization. In agreeing to the raise, Bavasi advised Wills not to tell his teammates he was earning so much money. Wills obliged, too embarrassed to tell them he was earning so *little* money.

Bavasi had much to gain by keeping player salaries private. The same was true for all general managers. If players couldn't compare numbers, they'd never know what they were worth. One such victim was Tommy Davis, who'd just won the 1962 National League batting title and was hoping to make twenty-five thousand dollars.

Bavasi boasted to *Sports Illustrated*.

> I told my secretary Edna Ward to fix me up a phony contract calling for $9,000 for Tommy Davis.
>
> I told Edna, "Now, when that stubborn kid comes into my office today, wait about ten minutes and then call me outside so I can leave him in there alone."
>
> I carefully put the [phony] Davis contract on my desk where it could be seen, and I marked its exact position. The kid came in, and he and I talked for a while, and then Edna came in and said, "Mr. O'Malley wants to see you for a minute."
>
> "Oh, excuse me," I said and stepped out.
>
> I gave it about five minutes, then I coughed loudly and walked back into my office. Sure enough, the fake contract had been moved. And all of a sudden, the kid is saying, "All right, Buzzie, maybe I'm being unreasonable." He said he'd sign for $12,000. I wound up giving him $18,000.
>
> I've pulled that phony-contract stunt a dozen times, and I'll do it every chance I get, because this war of negotiation has no rules.

In light of the climate in which he operated, Bavasi was a master negotiator. But he had to know it was only a matter of time before players started comparing notes.

5

In 1963 Birmingham, Alabama, had the dubious honor of being the country's most racially divided city.

It was there that Martin Luther King had waged a series of nonviolent protests targeting segregation—and where the commissioner of public safety, Bull Connor, responded by unleashing the city's firemen and police officers on the demonstrators. The ad hoc militia turned high-pressure hoses and raging water cannons on the black protesters, and salivating German Shepherds on civilians as young as six years old.

On May 13, Jackie Robinson flew to Birmingham to lend support to King's cause. With him was Floyd Patterson, who'd lost the heavyweight championship to Sonny Liston eight months earlier and was in the midst of training for a rematch.

The two athletes arrived in Birmingham just as the city was spiraling into more violence. Two nights earlier, members of the Ku Klux Klan had bombed the home of the Reverend A. D. King, Martin's younger brother, destroying the front half of the house and driving the reverend, his wife, and five children out of their beds and into the night. The following day, the Klan struck again, blowing up the black-owned Gaston Motel, targeting room 30, the one that Martin Luther King used as his Birmingham headquarters. The bombs destroyed a chunk of the hotel but again missed their intended target—King was in Atlanta at the time. The attacks brought more demonstrators, more cops, more police dogs, more fire hoses, and more armored cars to Birmingham.

Despite death threats, Robinson and Patterson spent the night in the portion of the Gaston that had been spared. In the morning, at a rally in front of the First Street Baptist Church, Robinson lambasted Bull Connor in front of two thousand cheering demonstrators. At a second gathering, this one at the Pilgrim Baptist Church, the two athletes addressed a throng of young, admiring fans who hailed them with the kind of gusto reserved for returning war heroes.

Nearly a month later, on June 11, Governor George Wallace, who'd won election on his pledge of "segregation now, segregation tomorrow, segregation forever," stood in the doorway of Foster Auditorium at the University of Alabama in Tuscaloosa. He was there for one reason: to block two black students, Vivian Malone and James Hood, from enrolling at the college. Camera bulbs flashed and tape recorders rolled as Wallace, flanked by state troopers, proclaimed that he represented thousands of other Alabamians in his refusal to "submit to illegal usurpation of power by the Central Government." Moments later, President Kennedy federalized the National Guard to forcibly remove Wallace from the premises—and the governor stepped aside without incident.

That evening, Kennedy addressed the country on national television.

> Today we are committed to a worldwide struggle to promote and protect the rights of all who wish to be free. And when Americans are sent to Vietnam or West Berlin we do not ask for whites only. It ought to be possible therefore for American students of any color to attend any public institution they select, without having to be backed up by troops. It ought to be possible for American consumers of any color to receive equal service in places of public accommodation, such as hotels and restaurants and theaters and retail stores without being forced to resort to demonstrations in the street. And it ought to be possible for American citizens of any color to register and to vote in a free election, without interference or fear of reprisal. It ought to be possible in short for every American to enjoy the privileges of being American, without regard to his race or his color. In short, every American ought to have the right to be treated, as he or she would wish to be treated. . . . Next week, I shall ask the Congress of the Unites States to act, to make a commitment it has not fully made in this century to the proposition that race has no place in American life or law.

In praise of Kennedy's efforts, Martin Luther King sent the president a telegram, calling his speech "one of the most eloquent, profound and unequivocal pleas for justice and the freedom of all men ever made by any president."

King later met with the other "Big Six" leaders of the civil rights movement—A. Philip Randolph, Whitney M. Young Jr., James Farmer, Roy Wilkins, Bayard Rustin, and John Lewis—to draw plans for pressuring Congress into signing Kennedy's civil rights package into law. Their strategy called for a mass demonstration starting at the Washington Monument and ending at the Lincoln Memorial. Scheduled to take place on August 28, the "March on Washington for Jobs and Freedom" would demand the integration of public schools, training programs for the nation's unemployed, and an end to job discrimination.

Word of the march spread—and Washington, fearing violence from outsiders, made tactical plans to protect the demonstrators. On the morning of the rally, 4,000 soldiers and marines stood at the ready, as did 500 reserves and 1,700 National Guard troops. Nearly 50 ambulances were parked nearby. The police put all of its resources into securing the eight-tenths of a mile route—and thus left other parts of the nation's capital unprotected.

Liquor stores locked their doors. Bars did the same. Retail marts cleared all valuables from their windows and shelves. The Washington Senators, advised that there'd be no police in DC Stadium, canceled two games with the Twins, scheduling a makeup doubleheader later in the week.

Sportswriter Sam Lacy, of the *Baltimore Afro-American*, used his column to galvanize professional athletes into taking part in the march.

"What about the colored ballplayers of the Senators and Twins?" he wrote. "The faces of [the Washington Senators'] Chuck Hinton . . . and [Minnesota Twins'] Earl Battey and Lenny Green certainly belong here. [The Senators' Minnie] Minoso could not have won a place in major league baseball, no matter what his talent, before earlier civil rights battles were fought. [The Twins' Zoilo Versalles and Vic Power] are required to accept segregated housing during spring training in Orlando, Florida."

Lacy also called on the black members of the Washington Redskins: "Not one of these fellows would dare question the merits of a civil rights demonstration, remembering, as they must, that they are members of the Redskins only because a twenty-five-year fight on their behalf was finally won."

When the day arrived, in spite of the withering heat and humidity, 250,000 protesters—the largest such turnout the country had ever seen—poured into Washington DC. Sidney Poitier and Dick Gregory were there. So were Lena Horne, Marlon Brando, and Judy Garland. Josephine Baker and James Baldwin flew in from Paris. Sammy Davis Jr. did the same from Toronto.

But to Sam Lacy's dismay, not one active baseball player could be found. Perhaps they feared retaliation from the owners or their schedules didn't allow. A smattering of players from other sports did attend, though. Bill Russell of the Boston Celtics was there (having met with Martin Luther King the night before), as was Jackie Robinson, who brought his eleven-year-old son, David.

"I think this proves that the Negro can meet in peaceful assembly," Robinson told reporters. "Congress had better take heed. If this demonstration doesn't do the job, we will come back, again and again, until we can gain unqualified civil rights."

From a podium on the steps of the Lincoln Memorial, the "Big Six" spoke to the immense crowd, religious leaders delivered homilies, and musicians, including Mahalia Jackson, Bob Dylan, and Joan Baez, performed protest songs. Black and white demonstrators stood shoulder to shoulder, dressed in their Sunday best, listening, praying, cheering.

John Lewis, the young chairman of the Student Nonviolent Coordinating Committee (SNCC), prepared a speech critical of the slow pace of change.

"In good conscience we cannot support the administration's civil rights bill, for it is too little, too late," he'd written. "There's not one thing in the bill that will protect our people from police brutality."

But Washington's Archbishop Patrick O'Boyle, upon seeing a draft of the speech, refused to deliver the opening invocation unless Lewis softened the language. Other leaders reacted similarly and forced Lewis to tone down his rhetoric. Still, Lewis poured out fiery words, vowing to "splinter the segregated South into a thousand pieces and put them back together again in the image of God and democracy."

Late in the day, Martin Luther King stepped to the podium to deliver the closing speech. He had agreed to go last because no other speakers wanted that final slot; they all assumed the news media would be long gone by then.

Over staticky loudspeakers, his voice carried only so far. Many in the crowd listened on transistor radios.

A few minutes into King's prepared script, Mahalia Jackson called out from the crowd.

"Tell them about the dream, Martin," she shouted, referring to a theme that King had flirted with during a speech two months earlier in Detroit.

Like the preacher that he was, King elevated his delivery to a passionate and fiery climax, with words so inspiring that nobody seemed to notice—or care—when he bulldozed past his four-minute allotment.

> I have a dream that one day this nation will rise up and live out the true meaning of its creed: "We hold these truths to be self-evident, that all men are created equal."
>
> I have a dream that one day on the red hills of Georgia, the sons of former slaves and the sons of former slave owners will be able to sit down together at the table of brotherhood.
>
> I have a dream that one day even the state of Mississippi, a state sweltering with the heat of injustice, sweltering with the heat of oppression, will be transformed into an oasis of freedom and justice.
>
> I have a dream that my four little children will one day live in a nation where they will not be judged by the color of their skin but by the content of their character.
>
> I have a dream today.
>
> I have a dream that one day, down in Alabama, with its vicious racists, with its governor having his lips dripping with the words of "interposition" and "nullification," one day right there in Alabama little black boys and black girls will be able to join hands with little white boys and white girls as sisters and brothers.
>
> I have a dream today.

Two weeks later, in the wake of a federal court order mandating the integration of Alabama's public schools, four members of the Ku Klux

Klan planted nineteen sticks of dynamite in the basement of the 16th Street Baptist Church in Birmingham—and set them off as services were about to begin. It was the city's third bombing in eleven days. The explosion tore large pieces of stone from the church façade and blew a passing motorist out of his car. It shattered stained glass windows, flattened parked cars, and injured twenty-two bystanders.

The greatest devastation took place in the ladies' lounge, where four young girls had gathered during Youth Day activities. Carole Robertson, Addie Mae Collins, and Denise McNair, all fourteen years old, and Cynthia Wesley, eleven, died instantly. Robertson was buried in a private ceremony; Collins, McNair, and Wesley were given a public service. The funeral drew more than eight thousand mourners, one of whom was Dr. King.

"[These girls] are the martyred heroines of a holy crusade for freedom and human dignity," King said, addressing the mourners. "And so this afternoon in a real sense they have something to say to each of us in their death. . . . They have something to say to every politician who has fed his constituents with the stale bread of hatred and the spoiled meat of racism."

Convinced that Wallace's pro-segregation rhetoric had incited the violence, King sent the governor a telegram that read, "The blood of our little children is on your hands."

Wallace didn't reply.

In the fall of 1963, Mudcat Grant and his wife, Lucille, were living in the Cleveland suburb of Shaker Heights. Despite a disappointing season—Grant had gone 13-14 and the Indians had finished twenty-five and a half games behind the Yankees—his mailbox was full of offers to speak at churches, businesses, and colleges. He was even fielding requests to perform with his singing act, Mudcat and the Kittens.

On Friday, November 22, Grant ate lunch at home and then got in his blue Cadillac and drove to the automotive store for new tires. He was unsure of which brand to buy, so he stopped outside the shop to call his father-in-law from a pay phone. When Bo answered, his voice was shaking.

"Your president has been assassinated," he said.

Grant couldn't grasp what he'd just heard. The president? President Kennedy? How could that be? He figured his father-in-law had somehow gotten it wrong, but when he hung up the phone and walked into the store, he could no longer hide from the truth. The place was empty except for a cluster of shoppers crowded around a television, many crying, as Walter Cronkite shared the news.

It had been three years since Grant's unforgettable breakfast with Kennedy, back when Kennedy was a senator, when he was campaigning for president, when he was selling his civil rights agenda to the electorate.

Grant forgot about the tires; he got back in his car and headed home. He needed to gather his thoughts, to try to make sense of what had happened to the politician who had shown such interest in him. The news reports on the radio were sketchy. Apparently, the president had been sitting beside Jackie as their motorcade made its way through downtown Dallas. They'd been in the back seat of the Lincoln Continental—*with the top down*—when a sniper fired from a building nearby. A lone gunman had been arrested. No name was given. (The suspect would soon be identified as ex-marine Lee Harvey Oswald.)

Grant was so distraught he drove right past his house. When he turned the car around and parked in front, he couldn't bring himself to go inside. Instead, he held the wheel and wept, letting out a soulful wail that expressed his pain better than any words he could have strung together.

He watched as neighbors ran out of their houses, congregating on front lawns, talking, hugging, crying, grieving. He didn't join them.

As Grant slowly digested the news, his thoughts shifted back to reality and he asked himself the same question that was surely on the lips of those around him: what now?

The Wallace standoff. The Birmingham bombings. The Kennedy assassination. America was coming to grips with a new wave of hatred—and publications like *Esquire* were putting it front and center.

With 1963 coming to a close, the magazine's muse became world heavyweight champion Sonny Liston, a mob-connected hood generally considered the embodiment of mankind's darkest urges, a Beelzebub in trunks.

Liston was so reviled that, a year earlier, President Kennedy had urged Floyd Patterson not to risk giving him a shot at the title, hoping to stop the former bagman from becoming the face of American sports. Patterson hadn't complied, and that September he lost the title to Liston. Ten months later, after his goodwill trip to Birmingham, Patterson lost to Liston again. Two fights. Two defeats. Two first-round knockouts.

For good or bad, Sonny Liston was the world heavyweight champ. And in December 1963, his face filled the cover of *Esquire*. The brown-skinned fighter, the "bad Negro," stared down America with his trademark dead-eyed, soulless gaze—dressed as Santa. It may have been the most sarcastic holiday greeting in American history.

Cassius Clay, the young, ebullient Olympic gold medalist, took one look at the cover and said to its creator, *Esquire*'s art director, George Lois, "That's the last black motherfucker America wants to see coming down their chimney."

Clay knew of what he spoke. The photograph instantly became one of the most provocative images of the era.

Esquire editor Harold Hayes recalled the photo many years later.

"[It was] a single, textless image that measured our lives and the time we lived them in," he wrote in *Adweek* magazine. "[The] angry icon insisted on several things: the split in our culture was showing; the notion of racial equality was a bad joke; the felicitations of the season—goodwill to all men, etc.—carried irony more than sentiment."

The man who shot the photo, Carl Fischer, had to do a fair amount of cajoling to get Liston to agree to the pose.

"That photo," he recalls, "attracted a lot of attention, and it had people thinking about what it was all about. And it was interesting to have people during those segregationist times realize that Liston disliked putting on a Santa Claus hat as much as white people disliked the fact that we made Santa Claus black."

By the close of 1963, America was more divided, more chaotic, and more traumatized than ever before.

The president was dead.

The leader of the civil rights movement had been the target of repeated bombings.

And Santa Claus was a black man who'd earned his living by smashing kneecaps.

Something had to give.

The Giants' Willie Mays had finished the 1963 season with a .314 batting average, 38 home runs, and 103 RBIs. For most players, numbers like those would be cause for celebration. For Mays, they were standard fare. Since earning Rookie of the Year honors in 1951, he'd won an MVP award and two home run titles. The perennial All-Star had also hit over .300 nine times and topped 100 RBIs seven times.

So it wasn't surprising when, in January 1964, Giants owner Horace Stoneham made Mays the highest-paid player in the game—at an eye-popping $105,000 per season.

As Wendell Smith wrote in the *Pittsburgh Courier*, "there are certified public accountants who will tell you, 'No baseball player is worth that much money. In fact, no *two* baseball players are worth $105,000.'"

But Smith went on to quote Stoneham: "[Mays] is worth every penny of it. In fact, he might be worth more, but that's all I can afford."

Actually, it may have been more than Stoneham wanted to spend. He'd originally intended on paying Mays one hundred thousand dollars, but when he heard Mickey Mantle was getting six figures, he'd opened his wallet and given Mays an additional five thousand dollars. In Stoneham's words, "Willie is not second."

The Giants' owner wasn't alone in his evaluation of Mays. Most baseball insiders—including the players themselves—acknowledged that Mays was the consummate athlete.

As Smith saw it, "Mickey Mantle, often advertised as the 'game's greatest player,' gets more publicity than Willie, but it must be remembered that the Yankee star is 'sold' by the game's greatest propaganda machinery. Madison Avenue's famous advertising agencies have nothing on the Yankees' publicity factory."

Stoneham was smitten with Mays right from the start. When the team called him up from the Triple-A Minneapolis Millers in 1951, the twenty-year-old center fielder had been hitting .477. Baseball-loving Minnesotans had been so upset at losing Mays that Stoneham felt compelled to run ads in the local papers explaining why the team had promoted its budding star.

Even the Giants' manager at the time, Leo Durocher, had gushed over Mays, saying, "I'll marry him so no one will ever get him."

Durocher had little to worry about. As *Ebony* magazine pointed out, even if Mays wanted to test the waters—to see whether another team such as the Yankees would up the Giants' offer—he was stuck.

"Why not wait until the contract runs out and then sign with another team?" *Ebony* asked. "There is the rub. The contract never runs out."

Willie Mays, the best player on planet earth, was owned by the San Francisco Giants.

On February 7, 1964, four days after hitting the top of the American music charts with "*I Want To Hold Your Hand*," the Beatles arrived in the United States. The four British musicians—John Lennon, twenty-three, Paul McCartney, twenty-one, George Harrison, twenty, and Ringo Starr, twenty-three—landed at New York's Kennedy Airport on Pan Am flight 101 from London. Wearing matching suits and sporting their trademark soup-bowl haircuts, they stepped off the plane and into a throng of screaming fans.

"We heard about [the welcoming committee] in midair," McCartney said years later. "There were journalists on the plane, and the pilot had rang ahead and said, 'Tell the boys there's a big crowd waiting for them.' We thought, 'God, we really have made it.'"

The Beatles were due to appear on the *Ed Sullivan Show* two days later and would be starting their American tour in Washington DC soon after that. Harry Benson was traveling with the group, shooting photos for the *London Daily Express*, and he needed to come up with some photo ops on non-performance days. His first idea was to shoot the boys with Sonny Liston. The British-born Beatles couldn't have picked Liston out of a lineup—and Liston, as Benson soon found out, had even less interest in the Beatles. Apparently, when a handler showed Liston a picture of the four mop-tops, Liston called them a bunch of sissies and said he wouldn't waste his time posing with them. (He did, however, go to the studio taping of the *Ed Sullivan Show*. His critique went as follows: "My dog plays drums better than that kid with the big nose.")

Benson, in a jam without Liston, had another idea. He decided to take the band to meet Cassius Clay, who was training to fight Liston later that month. Clay was also unaware of the Beatles—and the Beatles unaware of Clay—but there was little doubt the boxer would go along with the photo shoot. At twenty-two, Clay had yet to meet a publicity stunt he didn't like. Despite being a 7–1 underdog against Liston, he'd been taunting the champion in the press for months. At one point, he'd purchased a 1953 Flexible thirty-passenger bus, had the sides decorated with a sign that read, "World's Most Colorful Fighter: Liston Must Go in Eight," and after notifying the press to swing by "for a good show" drove it to Liston's home in Denver in the middle of night. There, in front of reporters and photographers, he'd baited the sleeping Liston, "Come on out of there. I'm gonna whup you right now."

As David Remnick tells it in *King of the World*, Clay also sabotaged Liston when the champion arrived in Miami to train for their upcoming fight. While Liston was making his way onto the tarmac, Clay showed up, shouting, "Chump! Big ugly bear! I'm gonna whup you right now!"

Benson took the Beatles to a rundown area in Miami Beach. At the corner of Washington Avenue and Fifth Street, one creaky flight up from the liquor store, was the hardcore boxing gym where Clay trained. The room was lined with open windows, one of which displayed a hand-painted sign that read "5th St Gym." Dead, sticky air filtered in from the street below. A boxing ring took up one half of the room; chairs, tourists, and boxing writers filled the other half.

Robert Lipsyte of the *New York Times* was one such journalist. Unlike the older generation, who'd written off Clay as a waste of time, Lipsyte, at twenty-six, figured the event had potential and stopped by the gym.

Ringo Starr said hello to Lipsyte, then introduced him to the other Beatles.

"They kept looking at their watches," Lipsyte says. "They were really mad because [Clay] was late and they decided they weren't gonna wait."

Clay finally showed up.

Lipyste recounted the story in *At the Fights: American Writers on Boxing*:

> Suddenly, the door burst open and this voice said, "Hey, Beatles. Let's make some money!" At first, the Beatles gasped, and so did I because that first glimpse of Cassius Clay was thrilling. . . . He filled the doorway, six foot three and over 200 pounds, the most beautiful creature any of us had ever seen. He glowed. . . . He was perfect. . . . And then—if I hadn't known better I would have sworn it was choreographed—he turned and the Beatles followed him . . . out to the ring and they began capering around the room. They lined up. He tapped Ringo. They all went down like dominoes. It was a marvelous, antic set piece. Then a few minutes later, he called me over and said, "So, who were those little faggots?"

Ivor Davis, a correspondent for the *London Daily Express*, was traveling with the Beatles—and was privy to conversations that Lipsyte wasn't.

> [The Beatles went in] expecting to meet Sonny Liston, and instead they met Cassius Clay. They couldn't very well walk out. And Harry [Benson] got these great iconic pictures of Clay sticking his fist out, lying down on the canvas. At the end of it all, John [Lennon] was very upset because, he said, "first of all, this isn't the champion. And second of all, when we got into the ring with Clay he told us what to do, he choreographed the pictures." So at the end of about fifteen minutes of larking around they had these wonderful pictures. When they were leaving the gym, John felt very upset and said, "Harry, you cheated us, and not only did you cheat us, but this guy Clay made fun of us, he used us."

In all likelihood, Lennon had no idea just how polarizing a figure Clay was becoming. The Baptist-born fighter had been associating with members of the Nation of Islam since 1962 and had gotten close to Malcolm X, the group's main spokesman, who was second in command to its leader, Elijah Muhammad. Like Malcolm X, whose denunciation of whites had alarmed many in the mainstream press, Clay had been speaking up. He'd recently appeared at a Nation of Islam rally in New York City and was being condemned for adopting the organization's agenda: to create a nation of black Americans, separate and apart from whites.

In a profile that ran in the *Saturday Evening Post*, Clay explained his views to the writer Myron Cope. Downplaying the notion of the "white devil," Clay said, "They blow up all these little colored people in church, wash down people in the street with water hoses. It's not the color that makes you a devil, just the deeds that you do. . . . It's as our leader Elijah Muhammad teaches us. Couldn't nobody argue it. I'm no authority on Islam. I am just a follower. If you be a blue race, and you do the works of the devil, then we call you a devil. You got white people who died under demonstrations, died under tractor wheels for colored people. I wouldn't call them no devil."

Bill McDonald, promoter of the Liston-Clay fight, was afraid that word of Clay's affiliation with the Nation of Islam would affect ticket sales; he'd threatened to cancel the fight unless Clay renounced the group. Eventually, the promoter and the fighter reached a compromise—Malcolm X would leave Miami before the event, and Clay would wait until after the fight to announce his religious conversion.

As for the fighter's braggadocio style, Clay would later admit he'd borrowed his "script" from the wrestler Gorgeous George. The act paid off. He'd already made close to a million dollars, and his fight against Liston would add another $600,000 to his total worth. (Liston would earn $1,360,500.) Before the fight, Clay spoke with *Sports Illustrated*.

> That's how much money my fists and my mouth will have earned by the time my fight with Liston is over. Think about that. A southern colored boy has made one million dollars just as he turns twenty-two. I don't think it's bragging to say I'm something a little special. Where do you think I would be next week if I didn't know how to shout and holler and make the public sit up and take notice? I would be poor, for one thing, and I would probably be down in Louisville, Kentucky, my hometown, washing windows or running an elevator and saying "yes, suh" and "no, suh" and knowing my place. Instead of that, I'm saying I'm one of the highest-paid athletes in the world, which is true, and that I'm the greatest fighter in the world, which I hope and pray is true.

The Beatles left America three days before Clay took on Liston at Miami's Convention Hall. They didn't see the challenger outbox Liston, they didn't see him duck Liston's punches, throw lightning quick jabs, and in the fifth round—with his vision blurred by an astringent that Liston had allegedly put on his gloves to temporarily blind his challenger—dance and avoid the hulking, brutish ex-bagman. They didn't catch Clay open a cut under Liston's eye, a gash that required six stitches; they missed the sight of Liston sitting on his stool before the start of the seventh round, spitting out his mouthpiece, unable to answer the bell, the first time a heavyweight champion had lost the title in such a fashion since 1919. Nor did they see Clay run across the ring with his gloved hands in the air, justifiably shouting, "I shook up the world."

At the press conference the next day, a reporter asked Clay whether he was a "card-carrying member of the Black Muslims." Given the negative association with the phrase "card-carrying" (recalling, as it did, America's anti-Communist paranoia during the '50s), Clay took offense. But he did make clear that he was no longer a Christian, and that he believed in Allah.

"Card-carrying, what does that mean?" the outspoken fighter said. "I know where I'm going, and I know the truth, and I don't have to be what you want me to be. I'm free to be what I want to be."

The sportswriting demigod Jimmy Cannon, losing patience with a country that was changing around him, had a predictable reaction. Going after Clay, Cannon wrote in the *New York Journal-American*, "The fight racket, since its rotten beginnings, has been the red-light district of sports. But this is the first time it has been turned into an instrument of hate. . . . Now, as one of Elijah Muhammad's missionaries, Clay is using it as a weapon of wickedness in an attack on the spirit. I pity Clay and abhor what he represents."

Lipsyte recognized Cannon's bitterness as raining down from the elder generation. He told Remnick in *King of the World*, "For Jimmy Cannon, [Clay] was, pardon the expression, an 'uppity nigger' and Cannon could never handle that. The blacks he liked were the blacks of the '30s and '40s, they knew their place. Joe Louis called Jimmy Cannon 'Mr. Cannon' for a long time. He was a humble kid. Now here comes Cassius Clay popping off and abrasive and loud and it was a jolt for a lot of sportswriters, like Cannon. That was a transition period. What [Clay] did was make guys stand up and decide which side of the fence they were on."

On March 6, radios across America broadcast a statement recorded by Elijah Muhammad. In it, the leader of the Nation of Islam said that Cassius Clay would be renamed Muhammad Ali—Muhammad meaning "worthy of all praise," Ali meaning "most high."

When the Beatles found out that Clay, now Ali, had beaten Liston and become the world heavyweight champion, they quickly forgot how he'd treated them at the 5th Street Gym. And John Lennon forgave Harry Benson for pulling the bait-and-switch.

The four musicians had had their pictures taken—and disseminated throughout the world—with an American athlete who was quickly becoming one of the most recognized faces in sports.

7

With the end of World War II, America had rolled into the Golden Age of Capitalism, an era of economic expansion that affected all industries. New cars rolled off Detroit's assembly lines and onto freshly paved roads at the rate of seven million vehicles per day. In 1956 President Eisenhower signed into law the National Interstate and Defense Highways Act, thereby approving the construction of more than forty-one thousand miles of highways—and providing homeowners with clear paths out of the cities and into the suburbs. Real estate developers encouraged the flight, especially of white urban dwellers, sending them a simple message: living near a black or Hispanic family will kill your real estate investment—and, possibly, your family members.

Perhaps no suburb was guiltier of such sin than Levittown, a hamlet located at the western end of New York's Long Island. Built in assembly-line style, Levittown owned the distinction of being the country's first mass-produced suburb. Its two-bedroom homes were erected on concrete slabs with precut lumber and nails shipped from the company's warehouse in California. When the packaged community was completed in 1951, its seventeen thousand affordable homes caught the eye of World War II veterans looking to start new lives. This was the American dream just as William Levitt had envisioned it: a home, a front lawn, swimming pools, green space, and no blacks.

The color restriction was more than a backroom handshake. It was written in bold, capital letters in the 1947 standard lease-to-buy agreement in the first Levittown homes. Clause 25 read as follows: "The tenant agrees not to permit the premises to be used or occupied by any person other than members of the Caucasian race."

The clause was removed a year later when the Supreme Court, ruling on a separate case, declared such restrictions "unenforceable as law and contrary to public policy."

But William Levitt chose to ignore the law of the land. The fear-mongering developer simply put into practice an unwritten Jim Crow covenant that was as strict as any codified one—and defended it with a self-fulfilling warning in the *Saturday Evening Post*: "If we sell one house to a Negro family, then 90 to 95% of our white customers will not buy into the community. This is their attitude, not ours."

Levitt's tactics worked, and as late as 1960, only fifty-seven of Levittown's more than sixty-five thousand residents were black.

President Kennedy had addressed the issue, not only as it pertained to Levittown but also as part of a housing trend in suburban communities throughout the country. In 1962 he signed into law Executive Order 11063, banning discrimination in the sale, leasing, or rent of federally owned or operated properties.

But Levitt's attitude was so deeply ingrained in Levittown—and throughout Long Island—there was little any law could do. CORE, the Congress of Racial Equality, spent the '60s fighting to end housing discrimination, but the walls were too strong to tear down.

While Long Island was attracting young white families, its city neighbor, Queens, was undergoing its own population explosion—filling up with immigrants, many from Asia and Latin America. The borough's population grew from 1.5 million in 1950 to 1.8 million in 1960. Long Island's Nassau County, the suburban area closest to New York City, nearly doubled from 672,000 to 1.3 million residents over the same period.

That was a lot of fans without a baseball team.

When Shea Stadium opened in 1964, it was seen by many as a marvel of engineering, the future of public architecture, and a harbinger of multisport venues. Built on the former ash dump known as Flushing Meadows, Shea was home to two teams: the four-year-old football Jets and the two-year-old baseball Mets. (Both clubs had spent their early years playing in Manhattan's Polo Grounds.)

By now, Major League Baseball was no longer a regional sport anchored to the Northeast. Like so much industry in the United States, it was growing and expanding.

In 1961 Washington Senators owner Calvin Griffith had uprooted his team to the northern Midwest city of Bloomington, Minnesota, and renamed it the Twins. In return, the American League had given DC a new Senators team and installed a second franchise on the West Coast, the Los Angeles Angels.

The National League followed suit in 1962, putting the Colt .45s in Houston (they would soon become the Astros) and the Mets in New York.

Joan Whitney Payson, a high-society heiress with narrow eyes, a high forehead, and a fleshy face, had cofounded the Mets, thus becoming the first woman to own a Major League franchise without inheriting it. Unfortunately, Payson's patronage of the arts and love of horseracing hadn't translated into building a successful baseball team. The '62 Mets were, in anybody's view, a ragtag collection of castoffs and refugees who'd spent their finest hours elsewhere. Run by ex-Yankees general manager George Weiss and managed by ex-Yankees skipper Casey Stengel, the team's inaugural roster included ex-Yankee Marv Throneberry, ex-Dodgers Don Zimmer and Gil Hodges, and ex-nobody Clarence "Choo-Choo" Coleman. Their first seasons at the Polo Grounds had been abysmal. They'd lost 120 games in their inaugural year and 111 the next.

It hardly mattered.

From the moment the Mets had taken the field, they'd been embraced by bereft Dodgers and Giants fans. That's one reason why Flushing Meadows, which had scared off O'Malley a decade earlier, was such an ideal home for the team. Shea Stadium was conveniently situated for those who were moving out of the decaying urban areas around Ebbets Field, Yankee Stadium, and the Polo Grounds and trading up to the blossoming borough of Queens and nearby suburbs of Long Island.

As *Sports Illustrated* put it, Shea was "smack in the eye of a population hurricane."

Marty Appel, former public relations director for the Yankees and author of several books on the team, remembers the arrival of the Mets.

"Demographically, the Mets had the Brooklyn fans who'd migrated out to Long Island," he says. "Shea Stadium had the big parking lot around it, which the Polo Grounds didn't have, Ebbets Field didn't have. So now you could say 'Come out, it's easy. It's right off the highway.' And the Yankees were still getting the subway crowd."

Michael Feinberg, a teenage vendor at Shea in the early '60s, traveled to the ballpark from his family's apartment in Rockaway, a peninsula on Long Island designated part of Queens but geographically separated from the city.

"A lot of [white] people back then were moving out of Brooklyn and into Nassau County, and Rockaway was a natural place to go," Feinberg says. "I remember my grandmother lived in Bed-Stuy and there were black families all around her. And when we'd go to visit her I'd say these black kids are the only kids on the block."

The *Times*'s Robert Lipsyte views the popularity of the new Mets as tied to the booming immigrant population in Queens. "There was a really big market for the Mets. The idea that they were underdogs appealed to a lot of minority people," he says. "And the National League was also seen as kind of an heir to the Negro Leagues."

Walter O'Malley would have loved the futuristic Shea. It was the first ballpark built in the city since Yankee Stadium opened in 1923, and there was no denying that it was a product of the modern era. Surrounded by a web of highways and paved parking lots for seven thousand cars, Shea featured twenty-one state-of-the-art escalators, a 175-foot-wide electronic scoreboard, concessions on every level, a symmetrical field, color-coded seating tiers, and an absence of visible posts—which meant no obstructed views. Ebbets Field couldn't have made any of these claims, nor could Yankee Stadium or the Polo Grounds.

The Mets debuted at Shea on April 17, 1964. They were already 0-2, having lost their first two games in Philadelphia. But that didn't stop fifty thousand fans from converging on the stadium to see their new team host the Pittsburgh Pirates. The highways were so backed up, New York City traffic commissioner Henry A. Barnes got in a helicopter and, as it looped around the stadium, sent orders to the traffic cops below.

Pirates manager Danny Murtaugh marveled at the new facility. "This has to be a showplace, one that every visitor to New York will want to see," he said. "It's a beautiful stadium, well planned, a fine place to play baseball. I like everything about it."

Casey Stengel, well aware that his team had little dazzle on the field, gushed over the place. "With these escalators you won't get a heart attack going to your seats," he said. "Anybody can come out and see us, women, men and children, because we got fifty bathrooms all over the place."

By all accounts, the stadium was a success. Shea not only won over fans but it would also set the trend for the many cookie-cutter multipurpose stadiums that would spring up over the next dozen years.

As for the home opener, the Mets had a two-run lead in the fourth but then proceeded to do what they did best—blow the lead. The death knell was a tie-breaking single in the ninth off the bat of Bill Mazeroski. The Mets, now 0-and-3, would lose 106 more games by the time the season was over.

Robert Moses's dream of developing Flushing Meadows didn't stop with Shea. His handiwork was on spectacular display a hard line drive away from the stadium. There, sprouting up from the former ash dump, were hundreds of futuristic pavilions, not to mention a 140-foot high, seven-hundred-thousand-pound stainless steel globe known as the Unisphere. This was the 1964 World's Fair.

As its president and chief organizer, Moses had done all he could to create an event that would reap a large return—and reveal Flushing Meadows in all its glory. He'd even installed a new infrastructure despite the still-functional grid that remained on the site from his previous masterwork, the 1939 fair. According to Moses's calculations, the fair, which was scheduled to run for two six-month periods in 1964 and 1965, would ultimately refill the city and state coffers.

But on the day of the grand opening (five days after the Mets had dropped their home opener to the Pirates), the crowds were disappointing—and those who came found the pavilions to be lackluster, more dedicated to corporate bragging than to the future of technology, transportation, and government.

What's more, the event was marred by controversy.

Sonny Carson, a radical activist with the Brooklyn chapter of CORE, the Congress of Racial Equality, planned to protest lingering Jim Crow practices throughout America with an opening day "stall-in." He envisioned a thousand CORE members stalling their cars on the highways surrounding Flushing Meadows, creating massive traffic jams that would bring the fair to its knees.

"We wanted to put the city in the position that black people always find themselves in," Carson later said. "Those people needed to suffer some indignities that we were in control of."

James Farmer, CORE's national director, opposed Carson's plan, feeling the Brooklyn chapter was less concerned with civil disobedience and more concerned with creating public spectacles.

Instead of engaging Carson, Farmer suspended the Brooklyn chapter from the national organization and arranged his own demonstration, one in keeping with Martin Luther King's pacifist philosophy. His sit-in would take place inside the fairgrounds but leave the highways untouched.

Dick Gregory, the comedian and civil rights activist, backed Carson, who, presumably, was still going ahead with his own plans.

In an interview with *Playboy*, Gregory said, "If the duly elected senior citizens of this country, the United States Senators, can hold a stall-in in the sacred halls of Congress, a second-class citizen ought to be able to hold one on a bloody American highway."

Nonetheless, the expected stall-in failed to materialize. Farmer's protest, on the other hand, did. On the first day of the fair, 750 demonstrators—blacks and whites—showed up at nine in the morning, and, much like the Greensboro Four in Woolworth's, went about their protest peacefully. They marched with picket signs in front of the New York City Pavilion, which featured one of the fair's biggest draws, a small-scale model of the city's eight hundred thousand buildings. They also targeted other high-trafficked areas. They scaled the Schaefer Beer Pavilion to expose the company's discriminatory hiring practices; they also blocked the entrance to the Ford Motor exhibit, leaving the company little option but to shut down for the day.

When confronted by police, the protesters went limp and dropped to the ground—at which point they were dragged off the premises. By the end of the day, police had arrested more than two hundred demonstrators, including civil rights leader Bayard Rustin, who had been the chief organizer of the March on Washington.

President Johnson had flown by helicopter from Kennedy Airport to the fairgrounds, where he was scheduled to deliver the keynote address.

Robert Moses was there to greet him. So were New York senators Jacob Javits and Kenneth Keating, as well as Jackie Robinson.

To avoid the protest—and in light of John F. Kennedy's assassination only five months earlier—Johnson delivered his speech inside the Singer Bowl to ten thousand invited guests. He spoke about "Peace through Understanding" without ever mentioning the issues that the protesters were targeting—dilapidated housing, lack of jobs, inferior public schools, and police brutality. He also made no mention of the escalating conflict in Vietnam.

Instead, Johnson said, "I prophesy peace is not only possible in our generation, I predict it is coming much earlier."

His words, broadcast through a public address system outside of the pavilion, were no match for the protesters' vocal cords, which were straining to the chants of, "Freedom now! Freedom Now! Jim Crow must go!"

The president's closing line, which included his dream of an America "in which all men are equal," was drowned out by a chorus of boos.

August 1964. First place in the National League belonged solely to Philadelphia, as it had since mid-July. Baseball fans were starting to take notice. Could the Phillies actually win the pennant? In the city's eighty-one-year history, the franchise had been to the World Series only twice, in 1915 and 1950, and had lost both times. Yet September was less than a week away and the Phillies had a healthy seven-game lead on the Reds. Even their most disenchanted fans had to be growing hopeful.

But on August 28, as the Phillies were losing a road game to the Pirates, Philadelphia was dealt a blow nobody could have seen coming: the streets around Connie Mack Stadium were under siege.

The poor, predominantly black neighborhood of North Philly had long had the worst living conditions in the city. For months, reports of police brutality had filled the pages of the city's black newspaper, the *Philadelphia Tribune*. Earlier in the month, Andrew G. Freeman, the head of the advocacy organization, the National Urban League, told a gathering of civil rights leaders that Philadelphia "was a racial tinderbox" with "all the ingredients for disaster." He cited unemployment among sixteen- to twenty-four-year-olds as the city's biggest problem and warned that young blacks were "building up a store of frustration and resentment."

The 1964 Civil Rights Act had passed nearly two months earlier, but North Philly was a bubbling cauldron of frustration, anger, and tension—and on this hot, muggy summer night, it boiled over.

The trouble began when Odessa Bradford and her husband, Rush, were driving along Columbia Avenue, past the pool halls, jazz clubs, and retail shops lining the commercial strip known as Jump Street. They were drunk. They were angry. They were bickering.

When they reached 22nd Street, right in the center of the strip, their squabbling escalated into a full-blown argument. To make matters worse, their car stalled.

Two police officers, the white John Hoff and the black Robert Wells, pulled their cruiser up to the Bradfords' maroon Buick. Wells walked over to Odessa, who was behind the wheel. He tried to calm the situation down, but instead of quieting Odessa, he fired her up—and she turned her vitriol on him.

Traffic backed up. Drivers honked their horns. Residents gathered, shouting obscenities at the cops. One onlooker, forty-one-year-old James Mettles, darted out of the crowed, ran over to Hoff, punched him to the ground, and then went at Wells.

Somebody flung a brick. Somebody else threw a bottle.

All hell broke loose.

Now, hundreds of people—most of them responding to a rumor that the police had gunned down a pregnant black woman—began rushing to Columbia Avenue, looting the strip's white-owned businesses and burning the empty shells to the ground. In minutes, the heart of black Philadelphia became a war zone.

By midnight, six hundred officers were at the scene. On orders from Police Commissioner Howard Leary to withhold their weapons unless directly threatened, the police did little more than watch North Philly spiral into chaos.

The next morning, with the streets still in an uproar, Dick Gregory met with local NAACP leader Cecil B. Moore, who'd driven to Philly from the Democratic National Convention sixty miles away in Atlantic City. (There, President Kennedy's successor, Lyndon Johnson, had just received the nomination for the presidency in his own right.) Moore had a fair share of "street cred" in Philadelphia; he'd taken on the local merchants—fighting against their "rancid meat and cardboard shoes"—and had squared off against the cops, accusing them of using excessive force against black residents. Gregory and Moore had a plan to end the violence: track down Odessa Bradford and show that she wasn't pregnant or harmed in any way. They found her at her mother's house and by mid-afternoon had her perched on the back seat of a white Cadillac convertible, waving at the rioting crowd. Odessa later said the experience made her feel like a homecoming queen.

Moore shouted from a bullhorn, "Here she is! She's alive. She's not dead. She's not pregnant. She's not even hurt!"

Seeing a healthy Odessa did little to appease the crowd. Rioters destroyed Columbia Avenue, looting whatever stores were still standing. By Saturday evening, 1,800 cops strained to respond to reports of burglary, vandalism, and violence.

Philadelphia Mayor James Tate imposed a curfew on the roughly 410-block area. All bars and liquor stores were ordered to close under threat of arrest.

On Sunday, the streets finally quieted, and by Monday, seventy-two hours after it began, the melee was all but over.

The damage was quantified as hundreds hurt, three hundred plus arrested, and one dead. (Twenty-one-year-old Robert Green was shot after trying to knife a policeman.) More than six hundred businesses were damaged or looted, at a cost estimated at several million dollars.

But there was no way of measuring the emotional setbacks the riot had imposed on its own city and no way of predicting whether North Philadelphia's wounds would heal.

The Beatles arrived in Philadelphia on September 2, two days after the riots ended. In sharp contrast to the grim atmosphere on Columbia Avenue, where burned-out retail shops still smoldered, the mood in downtown Philly was surprisingly upbeat—at least for the thirteen thousand teens awaiting the Beatles' arrival. The fans were so hysterical, so eager to touch, kiss, grab, or maul any one of the four musicians, that the group had to be smuggled into the city by way of a Hackney's fish truck.

The band members were well aware of the rioting in North Philly. Sitting in their hotel rooms, they read the local papers and watched the TV, particularly sensitive to the social issues at hand. All four had come from Liverpool, a working-class city that was experiencing many of the same racial tensions festering in Philadelphia and the rest of America. They also felt a kinship with black culture. When the Beatles were starting out they'd performed at Liverpool's Cavern Club—as did a number of American blues acts, such as Big Bill Broonzy, Sonny Terry, and Brownie McGhee. The group had often invited young black artists to join them on stage—and now, in America, they'd brought black musicians, including the Exciters and Clarence "Frogman" Henry, with them on tour.

Shortly after playing in Philadelphia, the Beatles were scheduled to perform in Florida's Gator Bowl, which sat in the heart of the segregated South. Following local Jim Crow laws, the stadium was to be segregated, thus confining black fans to the balconies and upper tiers.

Larry Kane, an American journalist traveling with the group, remembers Paul McCartney as the first to respond.

"We're not playing there," McCartney said upon hearing the news.

John Lennon was even more blunt. "No fuckin' chance of that happening."

The band then released a statement to the press: "We will not appear unless Negroes are allowed to sit anywhere."

The Gator Bowl had yet to respond when the Beatles got on a plane for Jacksonville. As it happened, Hurricane Dora was wreaking havoc in South Florida and had already left thousands of homes without power. The band's plane was diverted to Key West, and the group waited out the storm at the Key Wester, near the airport.

John Trusty, a navy corpsman stationed at a nearby naval hospital, ventured over to the motel hoping to catch a glimpse of the Beatles. What he found was a dozen policemen face-to-face with a crowd of teenyboppers in bikinis. In Trusty's words, the cops were, basically, "trying to keep a colony of ants from getting to a sugar cube."

Trusty made his way to the back of the property, near the entrance to the motel's restaurant, and was let in by a friend who worked there.

When showing his ID to security, he was given only one warning: no cameras.

But even without photographs, he has a vivid recollection of the scene.

> I saw Ringo having a great time in the pool, just him and the females from the black vocal group, the Exciters. I am telling you the sight was very avant-garde given race relations in the U.S. and Florida in 1964. I had never seen a black woman in a bathing suit in my life, let alone three of them in the same pool. Here, in the segregated South, this was even more shocking. They were sitting near the div-

ing board dangling their feet in the water while Ringo repeatedly dove off the board to everyone's delight. Ringo would waddle down the diving board like Charlie Chaplin and then dive in[,] . . . and he would get out of the pool and make another goofy dive. The [Exciters] were just giggling and laughing. It was just not done in America in 1964—blacks in a swimming pool with white folk—not in Illinois, where I'm from, nor in Florida. It just didn't happen. The scene was very surreal to me.

The next day, the Beatles learned that the Gator Bowl had capitulated. For the first time in history, it would permit integrated seating.

So, on September 11, with Hurricane Dora still blowing—the gusts were so strong that the Beatles' road managers had to nail Ringo Starr's drums to the floor—the group took the stage at the Florida stadium.

And for one evening, despite the raging winds swirling around it, the Gator Bowl was a scene of racial harmony.

Three weeks after the Columbia Avenue riot, the Phillies were doing their best to revive their smoldering city. With twelve games left to play, they were still on top—leading both the Reds and the Cardinals by six and a half games. If nothing else, a trip to the World Series might breathe some life back into the city's deflated spirit.

On September 21, the Phillies hosted the Reds in the first game of a three-game homestand. It was a squeaker. Through five innings, neither team scored a run.

In the sixth, after allowing only three hits, Phillies starter Art Mahaffey gave up a single to rookie third baseman Chico Ruiz and then another to Vada Pinson that sent Ruiz to third. Right fielder Johnny Callison pegged out the speedy Pinson trying to take second—but nobody could imagine what was coming next.

With two outs, and two strikes on the dangerous Frank Robinson, Mahaffey went into his windup—and Ruiz sprinted for home. Flummoxed, Mahaffey rushed his delivery and threw wide.

Ruiz was safe. The kid had stolen home.

As Mahaffey would later tell reporters, Ruiz's surprise dash made no sense.

"You must realize that with two outs and two strikes, if you throw a strike, [the right-handed] Frank Robinson swings and knocks Chico Ruiz's head off," he said. "It was just so stupid."

Stupid or not, Ruiz had given the Reds the only run of the game. With the loss, the Phillies dropped a game in the standings.

But the play did more than beat the Phillies. It rattled them. Badly.

After the game, Manager Gene Mauch went into a tirade. "Chico Fucking Ruiz beats us on a bonehead play of the year. Chico Fucking Ruiz steals home with Frank Robinson up! Can you believe it?"

Desperate to restore order, Mauch came up with a curious plan: use his two winningest pitchers, Jim Bunning and Chris Short, on two days' rest for the remainder of the season. The following night, the Reds capitalized on Short's wildness and beat him, 9–2. The Phillies' side of the box score showed seven walks, one throwing error, and two passed balls.

The night after that, September 23, twenty-three-thousand fans came out for "Richie Allen Night," an event organized by local black and Jewish merchants to honor the team's sensational rookie. Allen, whom the baseball world insisted on calling Richie even though he'd repeatedly said his name was Dick, had already racked up twenty-six homers, eighty RBIs, and a .309 average.

"I won't say like Cassius Clay that I'm the greatest," he told the *Los Angeles Sentinel*. "But if a pitcher makes a mistake against me I might drop one out of the park."

The rookie wisely didn't bring up his fielding. In spring training, Mauch had moved Allen to third, a position he'd never played professionally. The results were disastrous. He'd already made thirty-nine errors and there were still ten games left in the season.

Regardless, before the game, Allen's admirers presented him with a TV set, snow tires, luggage, and a stereo. For the Phillies, the ceremony was the highlight of the evening. They blew a 3–2 lead in the seventh inning and lost their third in a row.

The next night, Bunning lost to the Braves, cutting the Phils' lead to three games.

The night after that, the noose got even tighter. Chris Short had a 1–0 lead over the Braves in the seventh inning when catcher Clay Dalrymple accidentally tipped Dennis Menke's bat with his mitt—sending

Menke to first on interference. Short promptly gave up two runs on a sacrifice fly and an RBI-single. In the twelfth, after the game had seesawed to a 5–5 tie, Dalrymple made his second error of the game and the Phillies lost again. Their lead was down to a game and a half.

After the loss, Mauch held a team meeting: "You're letting it slip away, letting somebody take it from you," he shouted. "Go start a fight. Do something."

Mauch's diatribe only made things worse. As Dick Allen said in his book, *Crash*, "Mauch was wrapped so tight we were afraid to open our mouths."

On September 27, the Phillies lost their seventh in a row, a 14–8 drubbing at the hands of the Braves. Bunning lasted all of three innings, and the Phillies found themselves in second place for the first time since July 15.

Then they lost the next game.

And the one after that.

On September 30, the nightmare continued. The Phillies lost their tenth straight, this one against the rampaging Cardinals, who'd now won eight in a row and were in first place. The Phillies were two and a half games back—but weren't dead yet. Despite their agonizing fall, they still had a shot at the pennant.

They did what they could by winning their last two games. Then they watched the scoreboard. If the Cardinals lost to the Mets, the season would come down to a one-game playoff between the Phils and the Cards.

But that playoff game would never come to pass. St. Louis trounced the Mets 11–5, won the pennant, and would go on to play the Yankees in the World Series.

The record books would show the Phillies losing the pennant by one game—and suffering the worst collapse baseball had ever seen.

As Larry Merchant wrote in the *Philadelphia Daily News*, "Future generations will be told this incredible horror story September after September, that the Phillies of Philadelphia led the league by six-and-a-half games—and couldn't win another game. Children will shriek, adults will shiver, managers will faint."

Philadelphians had been hit in the gut again. They had lost what had seemed so safely in their grasp. Emotionally, the city was still crawling on Columbia Avenue, struggling to get back on its feet.

The 1964 World Series was a barnburner between the Yankees and the red-hot Cardinals. After alternately lifting and dashing the hopes of fans in both cities, the seven-game rollercoaster came down to nine innings in St. Louis.

Yankees rookie Mel Stottlemyre shut out the Cardinals in the early innings before giving up three runs in the fourth. Relievers Al Downing and Rollie Sheldon allowed three more in the fifth—and despite home runs by Mickey Mantle, Clete Boyer, and Phil Linz, the Yankees couldn't claw their way out of the hole. The Cardinals were soon celebrating their seventh world championship.

Still, the Yankees had finished the season with ninety-nine wins and lifted another banner over the roof of their stadium. In the twenty seasons since Dan Topping and Del Webb had taken control, the Yankees had won fifteen pennants and ten World Series.

But those who were watching closely could see signs of wear. The team was relying on an aging core of stars—Mantle, Roger Maris, Elston Howard, and Whitey Ford—and the farm system was doing little to help out. Joe Pepitone and Tom Tresh, while talented, were not championship-caliber players. What's more, the Mets, who'd spent all but eight days of the '64 season in dead last, had attracted 1,732,597 fans to Shea, outdrawing the Yankees by a half-million.

Topping and Webb saw the writing on the wall. It read, "Sell."

Two weeks after losing the Series, they did. They turned over 80 percent of the club to CBS (the Columbia Broadcasting System) for $11.2 million. Over the next two years, they'd sell to the network the remaining 20 percent of the team for an additional $3.2 million.

With the Yankees slipping in the standings, and in relevance, the city's young sportswriters gravitated to the new team in town. The Mets offered the writers fresh, candid stories and a clubhouse with a decidedly un-stodgy, un-Yankees-like attitude.

Jimmy Cannon, the marquee sports name at the *New York Journal-American*, came from a school even older than Dick Young's. Having joined the newspaper business in 1926 as a copy boy with the *Daily News*, the self-taught Cannon showed particular disdain for the way the new breed of writers flouted convention. They wore fashionable clothes, grew their hair, asked rude questions, and refused to kowtow to elders in the press box.

Steve Jacobson was one of the newcomers. He had joined *Long Island Newsday* in 1960, two years after graduating from Indiana University.

"The new breed was down in the clubhouse asking the players and manager not just what they did, but why," Jacobson says. "These writers covered sports the way they would have covered politics or a fire, looking not just for news, but for an interesting angle. Inevitably, the atmosphere in locker rooms grew tense."

What Cannon didn't see (but would eventually admit) was that these writers were revolutionizing sports journalism. During one especially bitter moment in the press box, while listening to their incessant chatter, Cannon snarled, "You sound like small, furry animals. You're making that kind of noise. You sound like a goddamn lot of chipmunks."

Chipmunks. The name dripped with sarcasm and scorn, but the young writers adopted it as a badge of honor. They were proud to be set apart from the stodgy veterans, to be college-educated liberals who were printing stories the old guard wouldn't touch. Jacobson even remembers making up shirts with a Chipmunks logo and his fellow writers wearing them "like the green jacket of the Masters."

To use Cannon's phrase, the tribe's "inappropriate behavior" was simply the result of changing times. In the '60s, baseball was usually played in the afternoon, so the morning writers would submit their stories around eight o'clock in the evening. But many Chipmunks wrote for afternoon papers, giving them deadlines of midnight or later—and plenty of time to interview players, coaches, and managers after the game.

The *Times*'s Robert Lipsyte remembers it this way: "The morning paper guy wrote about the pitcher's no-hitter, the afternoon guy wrote about the fact that he pitched that no-hitter knowing that his father was about to die or his wife was about to give birth. [The afternoon guys] might have been covering the same news but they were covering it in a feature-y type way. They were looking for angles, and that was one. They tended to be quicker, livelier, smarter—and younger."

Oddly enough, Phil Pepe, who arrived at the *New York World-Telegram & Sun* in 1961, credited Chipmunk-style sports journalism to the most unlikely of gurus: Dick Young. (The old-school Young, of course, wanted no part of the Chipmunks.)

"It was Dick Young working at an a.m. paper who recognized that television was now giving the readers exactly what the morning papers were supposed to be giving them—what happened in the game," said Pepe. "[Morning readers] no longer needed the papers to tell them that. So Young took that extra step by becoming the first known a.m. writer to go into the clubhouse and to augment his game story with quotes and analysis and so on."

Geographically, Young's disciples were mostly East Coast writers. Besides Jacobson and Pepe, there was Stan Isaacs of *Long Island Newsday*, Vic Ziegel and Leonard Shecter of the *New York Post*, George Vecsey of the *New York Times*, Bud Collins of the *Boston Globe*, Roy McHugh and George Kiseda of the *Pittsburgh Press*, John Crittenden of the *Miami News*, and Larry Merchant, Stan Hochman, and Jack McKinney of the *Philadelphia Daily News*.

The most famous Chipmunk story involves Stan Isaacs. After a 1962 World Series game, Isaacs was interviewing the Yankees' winning pitcher, Ralph Terry. When Terry said his wife had been up late feeding their baby, Isaacs quipped, "Breast or bottle?"

The question never made it into the paper, but it spread through the pressroom like spilled ink.

Former Yankees PR director Marty Appel still remembers the incident. "The 'breast or bottle' thing was never going to be in the newspaper," he says. "It was just a smartass guy, which was what Stan Isaacs was. So [the Chipmunks] were sort of showing off for each other—trying to outdo each other. He would say anything and he had a self-assurance about him that he was going to get away with anything. They were feeding off each other."

It was only natural that the Chipmunks would find their way to the Mets. The Yankees were professional, buttoned-up. Covering the team after a loss was akin to attending the wake of a first cousin. The Mets were the opposite. They were a loose, fun bunch that didn't mind sharing personal stories. The Chipmunks, and many New York baseball fans, saw the Mets as a reflection of themselves. The hapless players were not all that different from real people facing real struggles—and dealing with the inevitable curveballs of life.

As Steve Jacobson remembers it, "The Mets were ideal for the Chipmunks. They were funny. They were ours. And it wasn't the end of civilization as we knew it when they were bad. The Mets lost all too often, but some of the ways they lost were extraordinary. Marv Throneberry going to the coaching lines and then coming back to pinch hit and getting a rousing hit and missing first base and Stengel going out to argue with the ump, and Cookie Lavagetto, the first base coach, telling him, 'Don't bother, Casey, he missed second base too.' Those were classic stories."

Then, too, there was the story of the Mets losing a game on a comebacker to the mound that managed to get by the pitcher, two infielders, and the center fielder.

Jimmy Cannon failed to see the humor in such ineptitude; he couldn't understand why anybody would want to follow a bunch of losers. As Jacobson remembers it, Cannon saw the Mets as "some kind of lower grade of human being. To him, the Yankees were still the empire."

In one of his columns Cannon couldn't resist ripping into those shameless New Yorkers who chose the Mets over the Yankees.

"A Mets fan," Cannon wrote, "is the kind of guy who buys a winning sweepstakes ticket, but it turns out to be counterfeit. . . . A Mets fan stops paying his insurance the day before he's run over by a cab crossing the street against the light."

So as Cannon and the old guard clung to the crumbling Yankees, the Chipmunks embraced the Mets, and their quote machine, Casey Stengel. Marty Appel sees Stengel's managing of the Mets as "one of the greatest things to happen to baseball in the 20th century."

Jay Hook pitched for the Mets from 1962 to 1964. He remembers Stengel holding court.

> At the end of a game, no matter what happened, Casey would call the writers into his office, and he'd give them a beer or whatever, and spend time talking about the game, or past history, or some totally new subject. And I think what he was doing, whether he planned it or not, he was making their job easier, because they'd always come out of that with something to write about. . . . And because we lost so many games the writers had to be creative in how they came up with stories, because how do you keep writing about losing teams, you know? And so the situation probably helped create those Chipmunks because they were having to come up with things that might be interesting for their readers.

Perhaps no Chipmunk rankled Cannon and his cronies more than the *Post*'s Leonard Shecter. Reverence had no place in Shecter's view of sports. He routinely knocked heroes off their pedestals—and was more than happy to pull back the curtain to expose stars like Mickey Mantle and Roger Maris.

Jacobson saw Shecter as his guiding light. "Lenny didn't take shit from anybody, and he didn't sugarcoat stuff. Mantle would say on occasion, 'Go ahead, Lenny, rip me,' when he had a bad day. Maris never understood that. A lot of players on the Yankees didn't understand that Lenny didn't work for them."

George Vecsey remembers Shecter as one of the first sportswriters to ask the players verboten questions—like how much money they were making.

"Len was more brash than any of us," Vecsey says. "He was fearless. He had his own Dick Young armor and went out to do battle with that armor. [He was] the iconoclast, the [sportswriter] that hated sports. If he heard something, he would write about it as long as he knew it to be true and he could back it up. He made people uncomfortable. To the Yankees, he was 'Fucking Shecter.'"

The Yankees' front office made it clear they didn't want players talking with the inquisitive Shecter. Many listened. But a few dissidents—Jim Bouton for one—shared Fucking Shecter's irreverence. Bouton even developed a friendship with him, often meeting for lunch or dinner when their schedules allowed. It's no surprise that Shecter wrote lengthy articles about Bouton, including one that featured the pitcher's adopting a child from Korea.

As for Jimmy Cannon, as much as he railed against the changing nature of his profession, it was evolving, and there was little he could do about it. The hinge on the clubhouse door had been oiled—and TV reporters were now charging their way through. Cannon's approach to sportswriting, an approach that had once broken ground and turned him into an icon, was disappearing as quickly as Yankee championship flags.

Lipsyte agrees. "[The Chipmunks] were a group of people who were in tune with their times. They reflected the changes. And [this] new generation of sportswriters encouraged and exulted in the new fan, went down and talked to the fan. They made the fan part of the panorama of baseball.

"What we're really talking about is the revolution of the '60s."

For some writers, the New York newspaper strike had been a chance to forge a new path and get away from the grind of the daily deadline. They'd survived those one hundred fourteen dark days by freelancing for magazines—and like spouses who found new lovers during trial separations, they never returned to their former lives.

Gay Talese, the literary journalist who started out as a copyboy at the *New York Times* before moving to the sports department, pointed to the strike as the event that kicked off, rather than ended, his career.

"The freedom," Talese told *Vanity Fair*, "made me, for the first time, know what it was like to be a writer rather than a reporter whose life was owned by the *Times*."

Talese wasn't alone. Writers like Tom Wolfe and Nora Ephron also joined the exodus out of the newsroom and into a new world, one in which they were free to write without worrying about column inches and journalistic formulas. Perhaps a bit high from their newfound independence, they used every bit of latitude they were given. Combining their storytelling skills and writing chops, they produced fresh, irreverent, genre-busting articles, many of which were told in the first person—a no-rules style of writing that would soon be referred to as "New Journalism."

Ironically, the first of these groundbreaking articles had been the direct result of writer's block. In 1963 Wolfe had come up with the idea of doing a piece on the hotrod culture of Southern California but was stumped for an angle on how to approach it. He wrote a note to his editor, Byron Dobell, at *Esquire*. The memo, which described what he'd seen on his trip to California, took him all night to write—and went on for nearly fifty pages. Wolfe dropped off the memo at *Esquire* first thing in the morning and got a call from Dobell at four in the afternoon. Dobell recognized Wolfe's notes as awkward and somewhat choppy but also saw them as a compelling first-person account of the custom car scene. Dobell told Wolfe he'd be removing the "Dear Byron" at the top of the memo and running the rest of the note verbatim—including Wolfe's colloquial phrases and onomatopoeia—under the title "There Goes (Varoom Varoom!) That Kandy-Kolored (Thphhhhhh!) Tangerine-Flake Streamline Baby (Rahghhh!) Around the Bend (Brummmmmmmmmmmmmmmmm)."

The piece was a natural for *Esquire*.

"[We] reflected what was going on in the world," says Carl Fischer, who shot the magazine's cover photo of Sonny Liston and dozens of others. "It became a political revolution, a sexual revolution, a cultural revolution in many ways. A lot of things came together at the same time[,] . . . and there were some very talented and clever people who accented it, who made a lot of great comments about everything going on."

Of the many pioneering journalists found in the pages of *Esquire*, none tackled the sports world in quite the same way as Gay Talese did. The former *Times* reporter found his muse in antiheroes—the losers, the benchwarmers, the mop-up guys. In 1964 one such fallen idol was Floyd Patterson, who'd lost the heavyweight title to Sonny Liston two years earlier. Perhaps more than any other athlete, Patterson was ashamed of losing. He was so embarrassed by his first-round knockout at the hands of Liston that he'd left the arena in a phony beard so as not to be recognized.

Talese's account of Patterson, "The Loser," ran in *Esquire* in 1964.

> You realize where you are, and what you're doing there, and what has just happened to you. And what follows is a hurt, a confused

hurt—not a physical hurt—it's a hurt combined with anger; it's a what-will-people-think hurt; it's an ashamed-of-my-own-ability hurt. . . . And all you want then is a hatch door in the middle of the ring—a hatch door that will open and let you fall through and land in your dressing room instead of having to get out of the ring and face those people. The worst thing about losing is having to walk out of the ring and face those people.

Talese continued showing the vulnerable side of the country's sports legends, the human frailties hiding behind the newsprint. He went on to dismantle Joe DiMaggio, revealing the Yankees' star to be a sullen, bitter man—a far cry from the icon the publishing industry had spent years creating.

Until Talese's *Esquire* profile, the DiMaggio myth had been constructed by a mind-numbing canon: *Lucky to be a Yankee*, *My Greatest Day in Baseball*, and *Baseball's Immortals: The Story of Joe DiMaggio*. It had been hard not to marvel at the man, the son of an Italian immigrant, a magnificent athlete whose skills had catapulted him to fame and dropped him squarely in the lap of the American dream—alongside Hollywood sex kitten Marilyn Monroe.

But Talese tore down the misconceptions, revealing the post-Monroe DiMaggio—exposing his pettiness regarding the heir to his throne, Mickey Mantle, and the soul-torturing depression he'd been courting since Monroe committed suicide four years earlier.

In the following excerpt from *The Silent Season of a Hero*, DiMaggio is fifty-one. As Talese describes it, his gray hair is slightly thinning at the crown, he's sporting a tailored suit and manicured nails, and he's chain smoking. He has just peered out of a restaurant window and spotted a guy he was hoping to avoid.

The man had met DiMaggio in New York. This week he had come to San Francisco and had telephoned several times, but none of the calls had been returned because DiMaggio suspected that the man, who had said he was doing research on some vague sociological project, really wanted to delve into DiMaggio's private life and that of DiMaggio's former wife, Marilyn Monroe. DiMaggio would never tolerate this. The memory of her death is still very painful to him, and yet, because he keeps it to himself, some people are not sensitive to it. One night in a supper club, a woman who had been drinking approached his table, and when he did not ask her to join him, she snapped:

"All right, I guess I'm *not* Marilyn Monroe."

He ignored her remark, but when she repeated it, he replied, barely controlling his anger, "No—I wish you were, but you're not."

The tone of his voice softened her, and she asked, "Am I saying something wrong?"

"You already have," he said. "Now will you please leave me alone?"

By the mid-'60s, "New Journalism" was going full throttle. In part to rival television, *Esquire* continued to feed the genre, releasing long-form pieces that compelled readers to pick up the magazine—and refrain from putting it down.

In the same summer in which he deconstructed DiMaggio, Talese also set his sights on another Italian American idol, Frank Sinatra.

In "Frank Sinatra Has a Cold," Talese captured a slice of the singer's life, a moment when the reclusive star was under the weather, unable to sing, looking morose, and sipping bourbon in favor of cough medicine. When Talese couldn't land an interview with the singer, he spoke with hundreds of Sinatra's friends and associates, recreating the man's story down to the finest details. Where was he standing? What was his posture?

Of the iconic singer Talese wrote, "This is the Sicilian in Sinatra; he permits his friends, if they wish to remain that, none of the easy Anglo-Saxon outs. But if they remain loyal, then there is nothing Sinatra will not do in turn—fabulous gifts, personal kindnesses, encouragement when they're down, adulation when they're up. They are wise to remember, however, one thing. He is Sinatra. The boss. Il Padrone."

Tom Wolfe took the genre a step further, releasing *The Electric Kool-Aid Acid Test*, an eyewitness, book-length account of novelist Ken Kesey's psychedelic, drug-addled life. Most likely taking his lead from Truman Capote's masterwork, *In Cold Blood*, Wolfe's *Electric Kool-Aid Acid Test* read like fiction, complete with recreated scenes and dialogue.

Because of *Esquire*—specifically Wolfe, Talese, and other new journalists—the public was beginning to see its heroes as flawed human beings.

In July 1965, Philadelphia sportswriters had a juicy story on their hands. It involved Dick Allen, the Phillies' young black superstar, and Frank Thomas, the white veteran first baseman picked up in a trade with the Mets the previous season.

Allen was, by far, the better ballplayer. At 5'11" and 187 pounds, he had a tight, muscular physique—and enough upper-body strength to swing a forty-two-ounce bat with authority. He'd run away with the 1964 National League Rookie of the Year award, and, after holding out for more money in the beginning of '65 (he wound up settling for twenty thousand dollars), he'd started the season in grand fashion. In May, he hit a 510-foot homer off the Cubs' Larry Jackson—the ball landed in a tree on Woodstock Street, a full city block from Connie Mack. In July, he was leading the league with a .335 average, was a lock to start the All-Star game, and was even showing signs of becoming more comfortable at third base.

But on July 3, everything changed.

Late that afternoon, Allen stood by the batting cage watching Frank Thomas take practice swings as the team got ready to host the Reds. Phillies right fielder Johnny Callison was razzing Thomas, mostly about a botched bunt the previous night. Thomas, assuming the comments were coming from Allen, fired a racially charged wisecrack at the black star.

"Who are you trying to be, another Muhammad Clay?"

This was nothing new; Thomas was famous for insulting his teammates, especially younger black players who were too shy, or too intimidated, to say anything. According to Stan Hochman, a Chipmunk who covered the baseball beat for the *Philadelphia Daily News*, Thomas particularly liked needling the guys who he thought "couldn't take it" and sensed Allen fell into that category.

Thomas was right. Allen did have a short fuse, and with good reason.

He'd grown up in racially integrated Wampum, Pennsylvania, but in 1963, at the age of twenty, was sent to the Phillies' farm club in Little

Rock, Arkansas—the same city where Governor Orval Faubus had ordered the National Guard to stop black students from entering Central High School.

Arkansas fans had greeted Allen—the Phillies' first black minor leaguer in Little Rock—with racial slurs, placards reading, "Don't Negroize our Baseball," and handwritten death threats.

In his memoir, *Crash*, Allen wrote, "There might be something more terrifying than being black and holding a note that says, 'Nigger,' in an empty parking lot in Little Rock, Arkansas, in 1963, but if there is, it hasn't crossed my path yet."

The bigotry in Little Rock was so pervasive that Allen considered quitting baseball until his older brother, Coy, reminded him that his only alternative was working in a Wampum steel mill.

So Allen stuck it out, and he was called up the following year to the Phillies—a franchise universally considered one of the most racist in baseball.

Years earlier, Phillies general manager Herb Pennock had insisted that Branch Rickey leave his rookie, Jackie Robinson, back in Brooklyn when the Dodgers played in Philadelphia. Rickey would have none of it, and when Robinson took the field, he endured a constant string of abuse from the Phillies' dugout. At one point players stood on the dugout steps, raised their bats like rifles, and pretended to fire.

When the Phillies grudgingly integrated in 1957—the last NL team to do so—for the most part they passed over black players in favor of Latinos. It wasn't until Wes Covington arrived in 1961 that they had a black player of significance, and it wasn't until Allen had joined the team three years later that they had a legitimate black star.

On the afternoon that Allen and Thomas went at it, racial tension in Philadelphia was still high. So it was no big surprise that Allen reacted to Thomas's insults by socking him across the jaw. The shocker was that Thomas, a 6'3", two-hundred-pound galoot known as "The Big Donkey," retaliated by picking up a bat and swinging it at Allen, bashing the star's right shoulder. Teammates separated the two, but the damage had been done—and it wasn't only to Allen's body.

After the game, the Phillies placed Thomas on irrevocable waivers—not because they felt he'd instigated the fight but because he was hitting

.260, playing part-time, nearing the end of his career, and was on the trading block anyway.

Manager Gene Mauch, on orders from above, instructed his players not to speak about the incident to the press, threatening a one-thousand-dollar fine to anyone who opened his mouth. He doubled-down with Allen, warning him that if he said a word, he'd be charged two thousand dollars.

So when reporters asked Allen about the incident, he simply replied, "What fight?"

But Thomas, no longer a Philly, had less to lose. He waged an all-out PR campaign, a transparent attempt to save his reputation and attract potential suitors. He spoke openly to the press, most notably to radio station WFIL-AM. The following is his account of his showdown with Allen:

> I was in the batting cage and Allen and they were kidding me. Allen said, "Do what you did last night," referring to my striking out in the seventh with runners at first and third. We were behind at the time, 3–2. [So, then, during BP,] I dropped a bunt down the third base line and [Allen] hollered, "That's 21 hours too late." I shouted back, "You're running off at the mouth like Muhammad Cassius Clay." Allen threatened to come in the cage after me, and I told him if he wanted to I'd be there. He came down the line and I told him I was sorry if I hurt his feelings. "That don't go with me," Allen said and he hit me in the chest. I had a bat in my hand and I hit him on the shoulder. It was a reflex action. I told him if I hadn't had the bat in my hand I would have hit him with my fist.

The Philadelphia sportswriters, already on the hunt for off-the-field stories, gave the fight nearly as much ink as they had given the team's historic collapse the previous season.

Chipmunk Larry Merchant claimed the incident had nothing to do with race. "When Thomas told [Allen] he was mouthing off, it was a fatal putdown, a kick in the gut," he wrote in the *Philadelphia Daily News*. "It was like telling him he was still a punk kid, mind your manners. But Thomas's release only exposes Allen as a kid who caused a veteran to lose his job."

Ray Kelly Jr., who had just started covering the Phillies for the *Courier-Post*, remembers Merchant's article. "Larry Merchant was more in tune with the New York guys when the Chipmunk wars broke out," he says. "Allen was convenient; he was news. There was nobody else that was news, that was worth writing about."

So what really happened? According to Kelly, the real story is worlds apart from Thomas's—and Merchant's—version.

> When I got to the team and started covering it, an old-timer who worked at the *Courier-Post*, Bill Duncan, told me that Thomas was baiting these guys forever, and that basically Dick Allen was sticking up for Johnny Briggs, who was a softhearted (black) kid who wasn't gonna make any waves. And Thomas was continually giving him the business. "Hey, boy, get over here and shine my shoes." Crap like that. And Allen had told him "Knock it off, knock that crap off." So that built up and up. It wasn't like the way Thomas portrayed it, that some chatting around the batting cage had gotten out of hand. That's a bunch of baloney. [Allen] had basically warned Thomas, and Thomas just pushed harder and harder. . . . Allen knew the guy wasn't gonna stop. And so he stepped toward Thomas, and Thomas used a bat.

Whether or not Kelly's version is accurate—and most baseball insiders, including players on the field at the time, support it—the anti-Allen campaign had begun.

Allen Lewis, a veteran beat writer for the *Philadelphia Inquirer*, would say two years later that Dick Allen had duped a lot of people, that he'd managed to convince them he'd been treated unfairly. In Lewis's view, Allen wasn't ready for the responsibility of being a superstar; he wasn't willing to make the sacrifices that came with such fame, even though he'd demanded the money that came with such status.

Many Phillies fans—to nobody's surprise—took Thomas's side. Within twenty-four hours of the incident, Allen seemed to have more enemies than supporters.

"I stuck my head out of the dugout and I'd never heard such booing," he told *Life* magazine years after the incident. "People yelled, 'Nigger' and 'Go back to South Street with the monkeys.'"

On the field, Allen continued to knock the cover off the ball. Off the field, he stayed out of sight, spending hours riding his horse "Old Blaze" in Fairmount Park.

But he couldn't lay low enough.

He'd demanded more money, insisted the writers call him Dick, and was trouble in the clubhouse.

In Philadelphia, that meant only one thing. He was "uppity."

10

In 1965 the Mets lost 112 games. A desperate fan might have seen this as an improvement. In their inaugural season of 1962, they'd lost a record 120.

Yet since moving to Shea the perennial losers were consistently outdrawing their crosstown rivals. If CBS, the new Yankees owners, wondered why fans would sooner follow the Mets than they would a team with twenty-nine pennants and twenty world championships, the answer wasn't on the field—it was in the stands.

Mets fans giddily flocked to Shea as if they were off to a neighborhood block party. They showed up with tambourines, hoisted flags on fishing poles, hung banners, blew trumpets, and lit firecrackers. Forget Yankee Stadium; when it came to hosting a mass jubilee, Shea was outdoing even the World's Fair.

As Chipmunk Leonard Shecter wrote, "the Mets are a lively example of this being an age for zaniness. Look for another word to explain why the bedraggled Mets are, in this age of sleekness—in women, cars, and filter tips—so much more popular than the ultra-sleek Yankees. Zany is the only word that describes it."

Perhaps no player symbolized the team's ineptitude more than first baseman Dick Stuart, who went by any number of nicknames, the two most famous being "The Man with the Iron Glove" and "Dr. Strangeglove."

Stuart couldn't field—and for the brief time he was in New York, he couldn't hit either. But he was popular, so much so that he had his own pregame TV show, "Stump Stuart." The show, sponsored by Thom McAn shoes, consisted of Stuart going into the stands and answering questions posed by the fans. The basic premise was that any fan who stumped him would walk away with a new pair of Thom McAn's.

Michael Feinberg, the young vendor from Shea, tells the story.

They taped the show hours before they opened the gates. So a whole group of vendors would take off their outfits, put on their regular clothes again, fill up a couple of rows of seats in the stands, and the camera would zoom in and make it look like a big crowd. But, if anybody watched this show, they would see that the same guys were sitting there day after day, winning pairs of shoes. I must've had forty pairs because I would always ask [Dick] the same question: "What was your batting average in the World Series?" It was terrible and Dick would always come up with some ridiculous answer.

Feinberg also took part in another Mets tradition. Banner Day, a holdover from the Polo Grounds, put the spotlight on the fans, inviting them to march their homemade signs across the field in a sort of ragamuffin parade, the kind you might expect to see in a small town on Halloween. The winners took home a year's worth of bragging rights, along with a prize package roughly comparable in value to a pair of Thom McAns.

The competition was stiff, mostly because the fans had so much fertile material to work with.

One banner read, "We Don't Want to Set the World on Fire, We Just Want to Finish Ninth."

Another called out to President Johnson: "Thanks for Medicare, LBJ. Apply it to the Mets Right Away."

Yet another played on a popular ad campaign: "I Dreamed I Won the Pennant in My Maidenform Bra."

The year that Feinberg and his friend, Roy, entered the contest, they made a sign out of cloth stretched over a giant wooden frame. They covered the cloth with a picture of the team's mascot, Mr. Met, holding a get-well card to Casey Stengel, who was recovering from a broken hip.

Feinberg's story illustrates just how homespun the entire operation was.

We had two-by-fours and we were trying to build a frame during the first game of a doubleheader. We get all the wood lined up and we don't have a hammer. So I run through the bullpen and I get [Mets pitcher] Tug McGraw to get me a hammer. Tug McGraw gets me a hammer and we finish making the sign. It was a two-man sign and the gates open and the parade starts and we start bringing it out, and it's too windy, and the thing is twisting all over the place. So we call people from the stands on the third-base side to jump over and help us. We had about eight people helping us carry it. But when we got to the infield we told them to leave, because [we were in the two-person competition and] that's when you walk past the judges. And we were picked as one of the finalists. The banner covered basically half the infield. It was huge. When the parade finally ended, they called all the finalists together.

And they said, "And now for first prize in the two-man category is the big banner . . ."

And me and Roy started running up.

"Casey Stengel!"

We stopped short. Oh my god, that's not us, our banner's not Casey Stengel, ours is Mr. Met.

And Tug McGraw jumps up from the top step of the dugout screaming at us, "That's you, idiot! That's you!"

Banner Day was one of the season's biggest draws, but ironically, Mets ownership couldn't stand the signs—or the circus-like atmosphere that came with them. As George Vecsey explains, "The Mets were run by a stuffy old WASP owner, Mrs. Payson. . . . It was a grim organization that somehow produced a funny team. Mets management wanted nothing to do with banners; they wanted to get those things out of the ballpark."

One of the club's biggest nuisances was Karl Ehrhardt, a Mets-aholic who'd worked as a German translator for the Allies during World War II. When the Mets arrived at Shea, Ehrhardt was a commercial artist who designed ads for American Home Foods. It wasn't long before he was creating banners at his home in Glen Oaks, Queens, and driving to Shea to hold them up during Mets games.

One of Ehrhardt's early banners referred to the team's losing record and its chairman and minority owner, M. Donald Grant. The sign read,

"Welcome to Grant's Tomb." Stadium security guards confiscated it, slicing it to pieces on the charge that it was an insult to the team's ownership.

Seeing the Mets as the people's team, and the action of the guards as an affront to free speech, Ehrhardt brought his case to the press box, telling the writers that he'd just been censored. The Chipmunks rallied around him, and Ehrhardt was quickly back in his seat, his Mets derby on his head, holding up the sharp-witted placards that would make him a local celebrity and give him the nickname "The Sign Man."

After one of many José Cardenal strikeouts, Ehrhardt raised his sign, "José, Can You See?" When Frank Tavares made an error, he proclaimed, "Look Ma, No Hands!"

Robert Lipsyte sees those years at Shea as the point of inflection during a decade of change. "What was really happening in baseball, and at arenas everywhere, was the sensibilities of the rock generation infiltrating sports," he says. "And that was reflected by the banners, by the fact that the crowd now became more engaged, expressing themselves in ways they never did before. You weren't going to church, but there [had been] a certain kind of respect and dignity in ballparks. By the '60s, people were dancing in the aisles at concerts, expressing themselves in the ballpark."

The rock generation invaded Shea in more ways than one.

In August of '65, the Beatles were back in the United States, kicking off their two-week tour with a stop at Shea. The group was already enjoying unprecedented fame, having sold a hundred million singles and more than twenty-five million albums worldwide.

Afraid that Beatles fans would clog the tunnels from Manhattan to Queens, the police escorted the four pop stars from their midtown Manhattan hotel to the East 34th Street Heliport. There, they put them into a helicopter and flew them to a rooftop landing at the World's Fair, where a Wells Fargo armored van was waiting to bring them to the ballpark.

Michael Feinberg worked that evening and remembers wandering the ballpark's underground passages hoping to find the rock stars: "I was walking toward what I figured would be the Beatles' dressing room . . . and there's nobody there and I hear an argument, and the argument is between Sid Bernstein, the guy who promoted the concert, and Brian Epstein, the Beatles' manager. And Brian Epstein is livid because there are no refreshments in the Beatles' dressing room. And I'm listening to this. So I walk in wearing my vendor's uniform, and I say, 'Excuse me, I was just at the commissary and I was wondering if you guys need any food.'"

When Feinberg received a resounding "Yes," he rushed upstairs, grabbed a bunch of sandwiches and drinks, and brought them back to the dressing room. Minutes later, he was joined by the four Beatles. Feinberg elaborates as follows:

> The Lovin' Spoonful were in there, the Mamas and the Papas were in there, the Stones came after the Beatles were already on the stage. There were these girls who had baked heart-shaped cakes for the Beatles, and they were crying and begging to bring them into the dressing room. . . . I had never smoked marijuana in my life, and they were smoking marijuana. And I had just sat down next to John Lennon when the pot was going around, and my first marijuana experience was John Lennon handing me a joint, and going, "Here." The only person in the room *not* smoking pot was Ed Sullivan [the sixty-three-year-old television personality, who was the evening's emcee].

The Beatles took the stage at 9:17 after being introduced by Sullivan. The crowd noise was so deafening that the police plugged their ears with cotton. The band's three front men—Lennon, McCartney, and Harrison—were forced to look at each other for musical cues, since they couldn't hear the beat coming from their drummer, Starr, who was stationed immediately behind them.

The *New York Times* reported, "Several of the fans in the first row of the grandstands moaned, wept, and called to the special police on the field, 'Please, please, give us some blades of grass. They walked on the grass.'"

It was the first time a rock concert had been staged in an outdoor sports stadium, and it brought in record numbers—not only the $304,000 in ticket sales but also the Beatles' take of $160,000.

It was doubtful any of the fifty-five thousand fans could hear the band over their own screams. But one thing was certain: the rumble could be felt across America.

By the fall of 1965, the Dodgers' Sandy Koufax was thriving in Los Angeles. Not yet thirty years old, he'd thrown four no-hitters (one a perfect game), won two Cy Young awards, and collected an MVP trophy.

As Pittsburgh Pirates slugger Willie Stargell said, batting against Koufax was "like eating soup with a fork."

Koufax was the most dominant left-hander in the game—and with that title came celebrity status. Yet, the reluctant star guarded his privacy to the point of reclusiveness. For most celebrities, the paradox would be unmanageable, but Koufax handled it brilliantly.

He realized his name was feeding his retirement account, so he leveraged it whenever possible, figuring he'd relax when his playing days were over. The young star also recognized that time was working against him, that there were only a finite number of innings left in his arthritic elbow. His left arm was nearly always in pain. He'd already taken to plunging it into ice water after games; he'd also been downing codeine pills and Butazolidin, a non-steroidal anti-inflammatory used on racehorses. Koufax was even known to slather his arm with capsaicin, the compound found in the world's hottest chili peppers. The stuff was so harsh that ballplayers called it "atomic balm." (One teammate, who'd innocently donned one of Koufax's long-sleeve workout shirts, came in contact with the cream; his skin was soon blistering, and he was doubled over, vomiting.)

It was to Koufax's advantage that he was in Los Angeles—even better, that he was in Hollywood. When word reached entertainment producers that the handsome, raven-haired athlete was available, they began calling, often to inject life into a sagging television series. (They also called the Dodgers' ace right-hander, California-blond Don Drysdale, and the team's fiery third-base coach, Leo Durocher.) Koufax played a cop in *77 Sunset Strip*, a doorman in *Bourbon Street Beat*, and a soldier in *Colt .45*.

The pitcher's moneymaking ventures also extended to Santa Monica Boulevard, just south of the Sunset Strip and a short walk from the legendary Troubadour nightclub. There stood the Tropicana, a modest motel that Koufax had purchased in 1962, renaming it Sandy Koufax's Tropicana Motor Inn and promoting it with advertisements that touted air-conditioned rooms and friendly prices.

By the mid-'60s, the Trop had become a second home to musicians performing at the Troubadour—up-and-comers like Bob Marley, the Mamas and the Papas, the Byrds, Van Morrison, and Janis Joplin. Jim Morrison also stayed there, spending his nights hanging out at the Palms, a lesbian dive across the street, before returning to the Trop in the wee hours to crash and write songs, many of which became hits for his group, the Doors.

"The rooms looked like Little Richard decorated them with somebody's Midwestern grandma on a lost weekend, and they were continually being trashed," writes Iris Berry, a musician and pop culture historian. "[The Trop] was the Chelsea Hotel with poolside AstroTurf. Parties sometimes lasted for months and often ended in mayhem. There was a constant parade of groupies, photographers, and drug dealers."

Despite the cultural history being made at his motel, Koufax was seldom if ever there. Instead, he was focused on baseball. With two months left in the '65 season, the Dodgers were in first place—with the Braves, the Giants, and the Reds nipping at their tail. On August 10, they came back to Dodger Stadium for an eight-game homestand. Koufax started it off by striking out fourteen and beating the Mets for his twentieth win.

But just as Dodger fans were getting excited about their team's chances, the real world suddenly intruded, casting a giant pall over the city and the rest of the country.

On Wednesday, August 11, as Don Drysdale stood under the lights at Dodger Stadium and traded zeroes with Mets starter Larry Miller, a skirmish was breaking out only twelve miles south. Two police officers, both white, had stopped a black motorist suspected of drunk driving—and were soon surrounded by a crowd of angry, fired-up locals. This was Watts, a black neighborhood in South Central Los Angeles with a history of simmering resentment, a community plagued by high unemployment, inadequate schools, and a tense relationship with a mostly white police force. The scene became all too familiar. Words were exchanged. Punches were thrown. A bottle crashed by the cops' feet. Blood was spilled. Out came more bottles. And more cops. And more spectators. And a gun.

By the time the Dodgers game ended around 10:30—Drysdale beat the Mets 1–0—the situation in Watts had escalated into a full-blown riot. Enraged residents were shooting at the police and firefighters, torching buildings, and looting stores. When the Dodgers took the field two nights later, plumes of black smoke drifted over the crowd of 32,551, hovering like storm clouds as Claude Osteen beat the Pirates 3–1.

Forty-six square miles of South Central LA had turned into a war zone. The city called for a curfew and declared martial law, dispatching fifteen thousand National Guard troops to the area. Yet the Dodgers continued to play. On Saturday night, Koufax nailed down his twenty-first win, a ten-inning, 1–0 masterpiece against the Pirates. After the game, Dodgers outfielder Willie Crawford, who lived in the curfew zone, couldn't go home. Instead, he stayed with teammate Johnny Roseboro.

The melee finally calmed on Tuesday, but the week of violence had left thirty-four dead, more than a thousand people injured, four thousand arrested, and forty million dollars' worth of property destroyed.

Five days later, on August 22, the Dodgers were in San Francisco, closing out a four-game series with their archrivals, the Giants. Only one and a half games separated the two teams, and tempers had been running high all weekend.

Dodgers catcher Johnny Roseboro and Giants pitcher Juan Marichal were especially on edge.

The Watts riot had rattled Roseboro. He lived on the fringes of Watts and feared that the violence would spread to his street. On more than one occasion, he spent the night on his front stoop, clutching a gun, guarding his home and his family.

Marichal was deeply troubled by the news coming from his homeland, the Dominican Republic. The country, where he was born and raised, was in the midst of a civil war and the twenty-seven-year-old pitcher hadn't been able to reach family members.

Fans poured into Candlestick Park, filling it to near capacity. Not only were the Dodgers and Giants fighting for the pennant, but the game's matchup was a beauty: Sandy Koufax was squaring off against Marichal, who'd already won nineteen games.

When the Dodgers jumped out to a 2–0 lead—on a Ron Fairly double in the first and a Roseboro single in the second—Marichal went looking for a fight. His first target was Maury Wills. He threw an inside fastball that sent the shortstop sprawling to the dirt.

The next inning, Koufax responded by whizzing a fastball over Willie Mays's head.

In the top of the third, Marichal knocked down Fairly.

In the bottom of the inning, with the Dodgers clinging to a 2–1 lead and Juan Marichal at the plate, Roseboro called for an inside pitch. Koufax threw a heater, and Roseboro intentionally dropped it. When he picked it up, he threw a laser back to Koufax, barely missing Marichal's face.

Marichal confronted Roseboro, who came out of his crouch and threw his glove to the ground. Before anybody could intercede, the two were going at it. In the heat of the moment, Marichal raised his bat and brought it down on Roseboro's head—opening a gash that would require fourteen stitches.

Both benches emptied. The players ran onto the field and vented their frustrations on one another, brawling for fourteen minutes. Two of the teams' biggest stars, Koufax and Mays, did their best to make peace—with little success.

Roseboro wound up missing two games in the thick of the pennant race. Marichal, the ace of the Giants' staff, was suspended, missing two outings.

As for the game, Koufax, who'd started the day with a 21-4 record, was clearly shaken. He promptly served up a three-run homer to Mays, lost 4–3, and dropped his next two starts.

By September, though, he was back in form and doing what he could to get the Dodgers into the World Series. He threw a perfect game against the Cubs, silencing a lineup that featured All-Stars Ernie Banks, Billy Williams, and Ron Santo. On the second-to-last day of the season, he struck out thirteen Braves en route to a 3–1 victory.

The Dodgers clinched the pennant, beating out the Giants by two games.

Koufax was ready for the Series. The only issue would be his religion.

It was no surprise that Dodgers manager Walter Alston had slated Koufax to pitch the Series opener. Not only would Koufax give the Dodgers their best chance against the Twins, but he'd also be available to face them three times.

Unfortunately for Alston and the Dodgers, the '65 World Series would open on October 6. That day happened to be Yom Kippur—and Koufax happened to be Jewish. Although not overly observant, Koufax had said earlier that he wouldn't work on the religion's holiest day. For eleven seasons, the Dodgers had respected his wishes, although Yom Kippur had yet to conflict with the postseason. For the record, Koufax was not the first player to make such a request. In 1934 future Hall of Fame first baseman Hank Greenberg, also Jewish, had asked for, and received, a similar concession from the Detroit Tigers during the team's drive for the American League pennant.

Alston had no choice. In place of Koufax he sent his second best arm, Don Drysdale, to the mound. The right-hander gave up three earned runs in 2⅔ innings. When Alston walked to the mound to pull him in the third inning, Drysdale reportedly said, "I bet right now you wish I was Jewish, too."

All concerned agree that Koufax in no way wanted to be the face of Hollywood, baseball, or Judaism. Yet he immediately became the poster-child for a generation of Jewish Americans. Newspapers wrote about him. Television commentators spoke about him. Jewish baseball fans deified him. Rabbis praised him.

Writer Jane Leavy covered the issue in *Sandy Koufax: A Lefty's Legacy*. "By refusing to pitch that day," she wrote, "Koufax became inextricably linked with the American Jewish experience. He was the New Patriarch: Abraham, Isaac, Jacob and Sandy. A moral exemplar, and single, too! (Such a catch!)"

According to Jonathan Sarna, a professor of American Jewish history at Brandeis University, "a generation of young Jews considered [Koufax] the greatest Jew in America. In an era when lots of Jews thought it was best to keep their Judaism quiet, he gave some Jews courage to be outwardly Jewish in other ways—by wearing a Jewish symbol, demonstrating for Soviet Jews, or the like."

Mitchell Wohlberg, a Baltimore-based rabbi, remembers how, before Koufax sat out that Series opener, Jews would often keep their religious beliefs to themselves. "And along came Sandy Koufax," he said in a sermon, "the Jewish kid from Borough Park, Brooklyn, who announced to all the world, 'I'm not pitching. It is Yom Kippur, my holy day.' On every Bar and Bat Mitzvah questionnaire, I ask the young man or young lady who their three favorite Jewish people are. . . . To this day, the most frequent answer is Sandy Koufax."

Years later, Koufax would meet with Steve Lipman, a writer for the newspaper *Jewish Week*, at the Dodgers' spring training headquarters in Arizona. Koufax would tell Lipman the incident drew more notice simply because it coincided with the World Series.

The following exchange is from Lipman's article, published shortly after the interview:

> Why didn't he play that game?
>
> "Respect."
>
> It's as simple as that?
>
> "It's as simple as that," Koufax said.
>
> He wasn't trying to make a statement about Jewish pride?
>
> "Absolutely not."
>
> Did anyone—owners, management, teammates—pressure him to start the Series, a pitcher's most prestigious assignment?
>
> He shook his head. "No pressure."
>
> Was it a risk—could he have endangered his standing with the team?
>
> "No."
>
> When did he start to realize that, for many Jewish fans, he would become more famous for the one game he didn't pitch than for the hundreds he did?
>
> "The buzz began, a little, the next year; the momentum built after that."

When Koufax did take the mound, in game two, he was sharp, throwing five scoreless innings before giving up a pair of runs in the sixth.

The Twins, a hungry bunch that hadn't been to the World Series since 1933 when they were still the Washington Senators, jumped on reliever Ron Perranoski for three runs and beat the Dodgers, 5–1.

Los Angeles won the middle three games at home but dropped the sixth at Metropolitan Stadium to Mudcat Grant, who pitched a gem for his second Series win.

The Series came down to the final game. Alston had a decision to make: go with a rested Drysdale or give the ball to Koufax, who'd thrown nine innings of shutout ball only two days earlier.

He went with Koufax. How could he not? Koufax had gone 26-8 during the season, striking out 382 batters and posting a 2.04 ERA.

Pitching on two days' rest, Koufax made Alston seem prescient.

On October 14, the most famous Jew in America reduced the headlines over his skipped start to wasted ink. He threw a complete-game, two-nothing shutout, clinched World Series MVP honors, and ensured that yet another championship trophy would be delivered to the Dodgers' clubhouse.

Mudcat Grant, like Koufax, had gone 2-1 in the Series. But while Koufax scored all the gifts and accolades one would expect—not to mention a long list of high-paying national endorsements—Grant had received little more than the standard World Series bonus.

Steve Jacobson commented on the disparity in *Newsday*: "[Grant] won two games and lost one, just as Koufax did. But there were other things even a victory in the seventh game wouldn't have brought Grant. For one thing, he's married. For another, he's a Negro. He won twenty-one games, pitched two complete games in the Series and wears clothes as well as anybody around. But nobody has been around yet to ask him to endorse a product. Being the biggest winner in the American League won't get those fringe benefits for him."

Phil Pepe had this to say in the *New York World-Telegram and Sun*: "Jim Grant is a Negro and the world is not quite ready for Negro heroes, and so Jim must struggle because nobody is breaking his neck to sign him for movies and endorsements. He is handsome and he is famous, but he is black. . . . Sandy [Koufax] could get $100,000 just for demonstrating the way he soaks his arm in a bucket of ice after he pitches.

Jim Grant has the kind of pleasant face that would look good in a television commercial . . . if television was ready for his kind of face."

Grant wasn't surprised by the lack of endorsement offers, but he did expect a sizeable raise from the $21,500 he'd earned that season. Anybody could see he was worth more, even the famously insensitive Twins owner, Calvin Griffith. (Years after moving the Senators to Minnesota, Griffith spoke at a Lion's Club, saying he'd brought the team to Bloomington when he realized the area had only fifteen thousand black residents. "Black people don't go to ball games, but they'll fill up a rasslin' ring and put up such a chant it'll scare you to death," he said. "It's unbelievable. We came here because you've got good, hardworking, white people here.")

Grant met with Griffith after the '65 season. He wanted to raise his salary to fifty thousand dollars.

"How much money you guys get from the World Series?" Griffith asked him.

"Forty-five hundred dollars."

"How many games did you win?" Griffith said.

"Twenty-one."

"Yeah, you won two games in the World Series. I'll tell you what I'm gonna do. I'm gonna give you a $2,000 raise, and you take that two thousand, and you put it with the forty-five hundred, and you've got a lot of money."

Grant stared back in disbelief. "You can take that offer, cut it up into little bitty pieces, and shove it . . ."

Griffith started laughing. At which point he had the pitcher removed from his office.

In the end, Griffith agreed to thirty-five thousand dollars.

Luckily for Grant, he had another talent besides baseball. When the World Series ended, he flew to New York, where he cut a record with his singing group, the Kittens. His agent, Bob Messenger, had booked him on a national tour, and after seeing Grant's heroic performance in the Series, raised his client's performance fee.

Mudcat and the Kittens hit the club circuit; they played the Holiday Inn in Groton, Connecticut; Steelman's Steak House in Cherokee, Iowa; and the Winona Winter Carnival in Minnesota. And they performed everything from show tunes to rock-and-roll standards. Grant donned white Mohair suits, told jokes, and danced; the Kittens sang and shimmied behind him, at times purring in their feline getups. One performance puts Grant in New York's Basin Street East nightclub the same night Maury Wills was crooning folk songs and spirituals. The two played together between sets.

For one performance, in Minnesota, Twins fans received free tickets from a local automobile dealer.

One music critic, reviewing the act, said that Grant was at his best singing or joking with the audience. "Mudcat Grant," he wrote, "is unquestionably the best singer in the area to have won two World Series games this year."

It hardly mattered. Only two hundred people had shown up to support the man who'd brought their team within one victory of a world championship.

11

In the winter following the 1965 World Series, Sandy Koufax met Don Drysdale and his wife, Ginger, at a Russian restaurant in the San Fernando Valley. The two pitchers, both twenty-nine, had become friendly when they went through basic training in Fort Dix, New Jersey, in the late '50s. They hit it off, despite coming from wildly different backgrounds. The Brooklyn-born Koufax had attended the University of Cincinnati and taken night classes in architecture at Columbia University. He was studious and humble—and most comfortable at home, listening to classical music or reading. The blue-eyed Drysdale was a product of Van Nuys High School in Southern California; he looked as though he'd been plucked off a surfboard and was usually trailed by admiring teammates and hangers-on.

As heroes of the world championship Dodgers, Koufax and Drysdale were the toasts of LA. They'd won a combined forty-nine regular-season games, more than half the team's total, and three more in the Series. Everyone knew the Dodgers would have been a middling bunch without them.

Which is why Koufax was so irritable at dinner.

He'd spent the morning in general manager Buzzie Bavasi's office, negotiating his salary for the '66 season. The meeting hadn't gone well. Despite being a unanimous choice for the NL Cy Young award and taking World Series MVP honors, Koufax hadn't been able to squeeze more than ninety-five thousand dollars out of Bavasi.

"You walk in there and give them a figure that you want to earn," Koufax said to Drysdale. "And they tell you, 'How come you want that much when Drysdale only wants this much?'"

The story irked Drysdale, mainly because Bavasi had pulled the same stunt on him, offering a mid-nineties salary and telling him Koufax was happy with less.

Bavasi had obviously been playing one pitcher against the other. Justifiable or not, he'd had his reasons. For starters, he prided himself on signing players for as little as possible. He also felt that starting pitchers were worth less than, say, shortstops, since starters worked every fourth day. Most important, though, was that Koufax and Drysdale were looking to top one hundred thousand dollars. Like all general managers, Bavasi saw that mark as an informal barrier, a glass ceiling that, once shattered for an elite athlete, would become meaningless when negotiating with lower-caliber players. The six-figure category was hallowed ground, strictly reserved for Willie Mays and Mickey Mantle.

Knowing Koufax and Drysdale had little choice but to sign, Bavasi hadn't worried that he was screwing with box office gold, that his figures showed the two stars generating as much as six hundred thousand dollars in ticket sales. He also hadn't concerned himself with another obvious truth: without the dynamic duo, the Dodgers wouldn't have made it to the World Series, which turned out to be the most lucrative in history. The Dodgers and Twins had brought in nearly three million dollars from those seven games alone.

Ginger Drysdale listened as her husband and Koufax compared notes. Having worked as a model and an actress, and having been a member of the Screen Actors Guild, she couldn't understand why ballplayers didn't have agents. This wasn't the first time the issue had come up. In 1962, when Mickey Mantle and Roger Maris made cameo appearances in the Hollywood movie *Safe at Home*, the film's star Patricia Barry was surprised to learn that neither player had an agent. She casually mentioned as much to the Yankees' general manager, Roy Hamey, who responded with an invective-laced diatribe.

In the case of Koufax and Drysdale, Ginger offered some unsolicited advice: "Why don't you just walk in there and hold out together?"

A bell went off. Go in together? As a pair? Like a union? It had never been done before. But there was no denying it would give them more leverage.

According to Ginger, the two committed to a joint holdout right then and there.

"The only thing that was left for them to figure out was the representation," she recalls. "Sandy had a business manager that was also an agent for some very big stars, and he suggested that J. William Hayes manage the negotiations for the both of them. So they made a pact that they were going to deal through this man only."

The two pitchers met with Hayes, who recommended they go in with a package deal: $1 million for three years, or $166,666 per pitcher per year.

Following Hayes's advice, the pair walked into Bavasi's office, together, and gave him their proposal. Then they told the GM that all negotiations would go through Hayes.

Bavasi, no doubt thrown that he was suddenly dealing with a union, albeit a small one, reached for one of his most tried-and-true tactics.

"Why don't you head down to spring training?" he suggested. "We'll straighten it out there."

But Koufax and Drysdale had made a pact—with Hayes, and with each other.

"Speak to Hayes," they said.

Ginger remembers hearing about Bavasi's reaction. "[The Dodgers] were absolutely shocked that Don and Sandy both said to the front office, 'We're not negotiating these contracts. We have an agent, and he will be handling our affairs.' And at first, the front office took the position, 'Well, we don't talk to agents; you boys are gonna be out on the street because we just don't operate that way.' And so there was a long period of time that there was nothing said between the two parties."

Eventually, though, Bavasi suggested the gang of two meet him at the Hollywood Roosevelt Hotel. Soon, the three were sitting at a table in the corner of the empty room, trying to settle on a number that would satisfy everybody.

Koufax scribbled a figure on a piece of paper. Bavasi took one look and grimaced.

Koufax tried again, this time lowering the total package price to $900,000, but Bavasi still scoffed at the number. He also made it clear that he wouldn't agree to a multiyear deal and that he was through negotiating with Koufax and Drysdale as a unit.

The three left the hotel as they'd walked in: at a stalemate.

In the spring of 1966, nearly one out of every four American wage earners belonged to a union. That statistic included professional baseball players, even though their union was financed by the owners and came with virtually no bargaining power. It existed almost solely to run the pension fund.

Since the late 1800s, baseball players had tried, periodically, to organize themselves into an independent union—mainly to fight the reserve clause. But the courts had repeatedly sided with the league. It didn't help the players that there were no rival leagues, no threats to dangle over an owner's head. That is, until 1946—which is when outfielder Danny Gardella refused to re-up with the Giants, choosing instead to double his salary by joining the Mexican League.

When he returned to the States, Gardella found that no team would hire him, so he sued baseball for running what he argued was an illegal monopoly. His lawsuit raised the question, since teams were receiving income from radio and TV broadcasts, and doing business in several states, weren't they subject to antitrust laws?

The league had little time for such distinctions.

Baseball officials badmouthed Gardella in the press. Branch Rickey called him a communist. But the league must have felt it was on shaky ground, because it settled with Gardella—and gave amnesty to any other players who'd joined the Mexican League. Moreover, to ward off any further rebellion, the owners had conceded to a minimum salary of five thousand dollars, a maximum pay cut of 25 percent, and a weekly spring training allowance of twenty-five dollars.

As the 1966 season was getting underway, many players were again growing dissatisfied, this time because their pension fund was malnourished. They'd seen too many retired players, broke and without any job prospects, scraping by on miniscule retirement checks.

According to the Uniform Player's Contract, the owners were to contribute to the pension fund 60 percent of TV and radio revenue from the All-Star game and World Series, plus 60 percent of the box office receipts from the All-Star game. In 1966 that equation yielded $2.5 million, a paltry sum for a pension plan of that size. Still, the rumor mill was rife with speculation that the owners, particularly Walter O'Malley, were out to revise the agreement when it expired the following year. All indicators pointed toward TV revenue growing exponentially and the owners trying to freeze their payments by agreeing to a flat fee instead of a percentage-based figure. The deal would greatly benefit the owners.

A trio of veterans—Robin Roberts, Jim Bunning, and Harvey Kuenn—formed a search committee to find a new director for the Players Association, one that would help turn it into a bona fide union. Surprisingly, the committee's biggest hurdle was the group it represented. The new executive director would have to be elected by the players, and many of them—not to mention managers and coaches, who also had a vote—came from the South. To them, "union" was a dirty word.

With that in mind, the committee's first choice had been Robert Cannon, a Milwaukee district court judge who'd been serving as the Association's de facto director for years, taking no pay, raising no ire, and championing no causes. While hardly an ideal choice, Cannon had one significant check in the plus column: he'd get votes from conservative players and the blessing of owners, who'd be signing his fifty-thousand-dollar paycheck. How could he not? He'd shown a decidedly hands-off approach, and if anything he had sided with management on most major disputes. John Galbreath, the owner of the Pirates, had been so keen on the candidate, he'd promised to include him in the players' pension fund. But it turned out that Judge Cannon had no interest in leaving his courtroom, let alone moving his family to New York.

And so the committee turned to its second choice: a highly respected, mustached, silver-haired labor attorney named Marvin Miller.

Employee disputes had been in Miller's blood for most of his forty-nine years. As a youngster in Brooklyn, he'd joined his father on the garment workers' picket lines; he'd also watched his mother become one of the first members of the New York City teachers' union. Miller had gone on to earn economics and law degrees from New York University, after which he'd spent sixteen years serving as the chief economist and contract negotiator for the United Steelworkers, a union of more than a million members.

Miller was largely responsible for turning the steelworkers into the biggest and most powerful industrial union in the country. To sell the staunchly pro-labor Miller to the players, Robin Roberts suggested bringing on former Republican vice president, Richard Nixon, as general counsel.

To Miller, the idea was practically laughable. He discussed the proposal in his book, *A Whole Different Ball Game*.

"Work shoulder to shoulder with Tricky Dick?" he wrote. "After twenty-five years in labor relations—on the side of labor—I could scarcely think of anyone I would have liked less to work with. . . . [He was] the neophyte congressional candidate from California who won election by slandering his opponent, Jerry Voorhis. I knew him as the senatorial candidate who weaseled into office using rotten Red Scare tactics against Congresswoman Helen Gahagan Douglas . . . [as] a politician who consistently supported antiunion legislation."

Miller told the committee that if Nixon was in, he was out; he called the politician an "owners' man" with "no background whatsoever in representing employees and wouldn't know the difference between a pension plan and a pitcher's mound." Besides, Miller had said, Nixon was already putting together a run at the presidency in 1968.

The owners, wanting no part of an agitator like Miller, proceeded to assault him with an unfettered smear campaign, painting him out to be a club-wielding labor boss, a head-banger straight out of *On the Waterfront*. Soon, a petition—allegedly written by players—appeared in the *Herald Examiner*. It read, "Our feeling is that [the new director of the Players Association] should have a legal background that the owners can respect. We have progressed a great deal in the past few years and we think this relationship between the owners and the players should continue."

Miller ignored the attacks, as did the committee. Robin Roberts and his crew approved him, and Miller set out to gain votes by visiting all twenty spring training camps in Arizona and Florida.

"There were six hundred major league players. I could meet with and talk with every team," Miller said to Major League Baseball years later. "That's the essence of being an effective union president, to be able to communicate, and I don't mean in writing. I mean to meet with one-on-one, and talk, and [share] ideas."

By all accounts, Miller was an excellent listener, and what he heard in those meetings was that most players had no concept of trade unionism. He sought to point out that the steelworkers had used collective bargaining to improve wages and working conditions—as the industry's profits soared. But convincing pro ballplayers of what they could accomplish was a whole different matter.

"To my dismay," Miller said, "when I started talking about the reserve clause, I found that players had been so brainwashed they had extreme doubts. I had players mouthing the management line—that the owners would take their bats and balls and go home. It would be impossible to have competitive leagues."

At one point, Miller had stood in the New York Yankees' locker room, addressing the team and explaining why players had to get rid of the reserve clause. When he finished, Yankees pitcher Jim Bouton pulled him aside. Having attended a year and a half of college at Western Michigan University, Bouton had a deeper education than many players. He also had a keen interest in baseball's labor situation.

Bouton questioned Miller about his vision. How could baseball work without a reserve clause? If players could move freely from team to team, wouldn't the richest teams get the best players?

"You mean like the Yankees do now?" Miller asked him.

Bouton considered Miller's response. For years, small-market teams like the Kansas City A's had become, essentially, farm systems for the Yankees, often trading their best players for cash.

"I never thought about it like that," Bouton said.

Miller recalled the conversation years later. "If one of the brightest players had been brainwashed to that extent, I knew that the task ahead was a very large one, indeed."

When the time came to cast their ballots, players in Arizona's Cactus League rejected Miller, 102–17. But in Florida's Grapefruit League, where the rosters of the Dodgers, Cardinals, Phillies, Braves, Twins, and Pirates were fully integrated, Miller won a sweeping victory, 472–34.

"You now had a great many black and Latino players," Miller told *Counterpunch*, looking back at that fateful spring. "You now had a much more diverse sampling of the American people than in the '40s. You now had at least some people who were able to think in terms of what was wrong with the society, what was wrong with the conditions, people much more accustomed to thinking about these things."

And so Miller became the first full-time executive director of the Major League Baseball Players Association. On day one he picked up the phone and called the owners to set a meeting. He didn't expect the warmest of greetings, but he surely assumed his calls would be returned.

He was wrong.

While the Dodgers were working out in Vero Beach, Koufax and Drysdale were sitting at home, following the advice of J. William Hayes. They hadn't shown up at spring training. They were being firm. They were ready to walk away.

For Koufax, the advice was easy to follow. He was making plenty in endorsements and had just signed to write his life story with author Ed Linn for a reported advance of $160,000. He also couldn't stand the stronghold the owners had on players. This was his chance to even the score. Most important, though, was the deterioration of his arthritic elbow. There was little doubt that continuing to pitch would leave him permanently disabled. Even if he signed, the 1966 season would probably be his last.

The negotiations were tougher on Drysdale. He had plenty of life left on his arm and was just starting to raise a family. He was part-owner of a restaurant in Van Nuys, Don Drysdale's Dugout, but as Ginger remembers it, "it was scary. We had just moved into a bigger house; we had expenses. We were two kids without a lot of investments because we were just learning how to operate in the big world."

To make matters worse, all signs pointed to an extended holdout.

Walter O'Malley, by now accustomed to the role of Machiavelli, took his case to the press. "I admire the boys' strategy, and we can't do without them, even for a little while," he said. "But we can't give in to them. There are too many agents hanging around Hollywood looking for clients."

Unlike O'Malley, Koufax and Drysdale stayed clear of the press. They held out in silence, surely aware of the stakes at hand. Thanks to their stratospheric seasons, they were in a position to fight for every player in the league. And the timing couldn't have been better.

As Michael D'Antonio wrote in *Forever Blue*, his biography of O'Malley, "in California especially, the '60s counterculture was in full bloom and it was hardly the time to stand in the way of anyone seeking to assert their rights."

According to the *New York Times*, "Both Koufax and Drysdale . . . are amply aware of the economic implications of their negotiations, though they flatly refuse to talk about them. They know collective bargaining is anathema to baseball. They know that if they succeed in blowing the top off baseball pay scales the whole salary structure inevitably will rise. They know that the sort of hard-nosed bargaining they are conducting is unknown to a sport in which the players have traditionally been the pawns."

Players around the league were divided in their opinions of the holdout.

Leon Wagner, left fielder for the Cleveland Indians, said, "Fifty percent of [players] probably feel that [Koufax and Drysdale] are classing themselves as twenty times better than the average player and this hurts their pride. The other fifty percent feel the guys should get all they can. I make $35,000 a year. Koufax is good, all right, but I don't think he's a five-times better ballplayer than I am."

The Yankees' Elston Howard worried about the long-term impact of the holdout. "It could get out of hand," he told the press. "I think the best method is the individual going in before management and bargaining his own salary."

Vic Power, the onetime Yankees prospect who had recently retired from the Angels, said, "Never in my life have I been a holdout. I told all my general managers, 'You pay me what you think I'm worth. If you think I'm worth ten cents, pay me ten cents—but don't expect me to play like a twenty-cent ballplayer.'"

As for the Dodgers, they were in full support of the striking pitchers, squashing any notion that they resented either one.

Reliever Ron Perranoski had been with the Dodgers since 1961. "Knowing Sandy the way I do," he told the press, "I'm sure he's concerned about what the rest of us think. I can tell him, though, we're behind him one hundred percent. I hope he shows up, though. I'd hate to have to pitch 162 of those games by myself."

Dodgers outfielder Lou Johnson was equally sympathetic. "I hope they get [the money]. I only wish I was in a position to negotiate like that. Us resent what they're asking? Baloney. More power to them both. I'd love both of them to get what they want."

One player, who spoke anonymously, was quoted as saying, "Anyone of us who's resentful of what [Koufax] is asking ought to have his head examined. We ought to get down on our knees and thank him. He's sticking his neck out for all of us. The way I understand it, he feels, 'Why should the top baseball salary be arbitrarily set at $100,000?' I know I'll never get that much, or anywhere near that, but what Koufax is doing now is bound to help us all."

What few players asked, but what *Sports Illustrated* wanted to know, was what made some players worth more than others.

The following is from the magazine during the stalemate: "What are Koufax and Drysdale worth to the Dodgers? In terms of standings, the Dodgers are world champs with them, second-division bums without them and their 49 wins. A second-division finish means at least a 300,000 attendance drop, and at $4.50 per fan that is a loss of $1.35 million. What's more, Koufax draws an extra 10,000 fans when he pitches, and he starts twenty times at home. So there is another $900,000, making the total loss $2.25 million, not counting road receipts. Walter, give Buzzie the money."

Koufax and Drysdale hoped O'Malley was reading. In the meantime, they stayed in shape—Drysdale worked out at Pierce College in Los Angeles—but they also started planning careers outside of baseball. They signed to act in a movie, *Warning Shot*, which was to star David Janssen, and they told Hayes to accept any offers that paid well. Hayes listened, lining up more television deals, plus an exhibition tour in Japan.

It was around this time that Hayes unearthed a state law making it illegal to extend personal service contracts in California beyond seven years. The result of a 1944 lawsuit brought by actress Olivia de Havilland against Warner Brothers, the law had been enacted to break the stranglehold Hollywood studios had on their actors and actresses. As Hayes saw it, the same law could be applied to the Koufax-Drysdale holdout.

He began preparing a lawsuit against the Dodgers. He kept his findings under wraps but did tell the press that if the two pitchers were to successfully challenge baseball's reserve clause, they'd be "the Abraham Lincolns of the game."

Someone, very possibly movie producer Mervin LeRoy, tipped off Walter O'Malley as to Hayes's strategy—and softened the Dodgers' stance.

On March 30, Chuck Connors, the star of TV's hit show *The Rifleman*, and a onetime Dodgers prospect, stepped in and set up a meeting between Bavasi and the two pitchers.

Koufax was unable to attend, but Drysdale kept the appointment and met with Bavasi at Nikola's, a restaurant near Dodger Stadium. They drank coffee and talked numbers. According to Drysdale, Bavasi agreed to pay him $115,000 and Koufax $125,000. Drysdale called Koufax on the phone and relayed the offer while Bavasi called O'Malley. Both came back to the table with a green light, ending a holdout that had lasted thirty-two days.

When the deal was announced to the press at Dodger Stadium, O'Malley immediately kicked into damage control, making it clear that the two pitchers were signed as individuals, not as a unit. They were being paid different salaries, he said. They were signed for one year, and they'd represented themselves. No agent.

Koufax kept the focus on baseball. "Thank god I don't have to act in that movie," he said.

He would never again act in any movie but would turn in another superb pitching performance. In 1966 he'd go 27-9 and lead the Dodgers to another pennant. He'd also take home his third Cy Young award, again by a unanimous vote.

As for Don Drysdale, the $115,000 pitcher would go 13-16 during the regular season and lose two games in the World Series.

The Dodgers would be swept by the Orioles in four games.

And Sandy Koufax, as he'd planned, would retire after the World Series, finally resting his blessed, arthritic elbow.

Fig. 1. (*top*) Presidential candidate John F. Kennedy speaks to supporters in Detroit's Cadillac Square on Labor Day, 1960. Hours earlier, he had breakfast with Indians pitcher Mudcat Grant. (The Tony Spina Collection, Walter P. Reuther Library, Archives of Labor and Urban Affairs, Wayne State University.)

Fig. 2. (*bottom*) In the 1960s Jim Crow was alive and well in the South. Black ballplayers who traveled to Florida for spring training were subjected to segregation in all aspects of society. (LOOK Magazine Photograph Collection, Library of Congress, Prints & Photographs Division [LC-L9-51-54-L].)

Fig. 3. Curt Flood suits up before a game, 1959. Flood had been traded to St. Louis by the Reds, who apparently weren't ready for an all-black outfield. (The State Historical Society of Missouri Research Center, St. Louis.)

Fig. 4. The Cardinals' Bill White was one of the first Major Leaguers to speak out against Florida's Jim Crow laws. Here, he reads his fan mail after a game. (From the collections of the St. Louis Mercantile Library at the University of Missouri–St. Louis.)

ON STRIKE
AGAINST
THE
NEW YORK TIMES

Fig. 5. (*opposite top*) In December 1962, hundreds of members of the International Typographical Union walked off the job at the *New York Times*. Within hours, all seven of the city's major dailies would shut down. (Library of Congress, Prints & Photographs Division, *U.S. News & World Report* Magazine Collection [LC-U9-8921].)

Fig. 6. (*opposite bottom*) Desks sit empty at the *New York Times* during the 114-day newspaper strike of 1962–63. (Library of Congress, Prints & Photographs Division, *U.S. News & World Report* Magazine Collection [LC-U9-8925].)

Fig. 7. (*above*) Chavez Ravine was cleared to make room for Dodger Stadium. More than one thousand residents, mostly Mexican American, were evicted from their homes. (*Herald-Examiner* Collection/Los Angeles Public Library.)

Fig. 8. Walter O'Malley stands in front of a nearly completed Dodger Stadium. His dream park would accommodate sixteen thousand cars. (Joe Rustan, *Herald-Examiner* Collection/Los Angeles Public Library.)

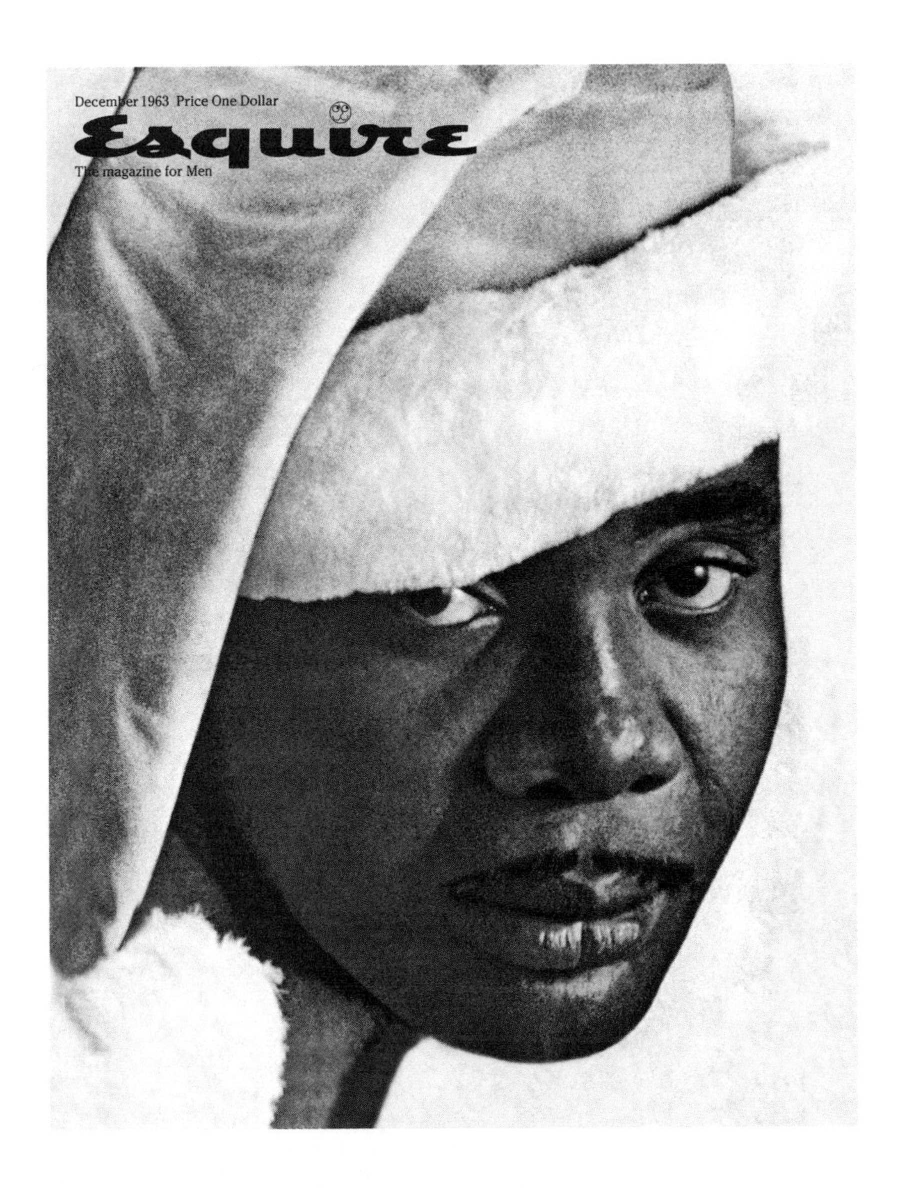

Fig. 9. Sonny Liston graces the cover of *Esquire*, December 1963. Cassius Clay said of the photo, "That's the last black motherfucker America wants to see coming down their chimney." (*Esquire*, George Lois, creative director; Carl Fischer, photographer.)

NEW
THUNDERBIRDS
AND FORDS
SE HABLA ESPAÑOL
FORD
City
THERE IS NO GOD

Fig. 10. (*opposite top*) Muhammad Ali, formerly Cassius Clay (*center*), with Elijah Muhammad (*left*), in 1964. Ali was one of the first public figures in America to openly embrace the Nation of Islam. (*Herald-Examiner* Collection/Los Angeles Public Library.)

Fig. 11. (*opposite bottom*) President Lyndon Johnson is greeted by World's Fair organizer Thomas J. Deegan Jr. at the 1964–65 New York World's Fair. Mayor Robert Wagner looks on (*left*). CORE protesters roundly booed the president's remarks. (*LOOK* Magazine Photograph Collection, Library of Congress, Prints & Photographs Division.)

Fig. 12. (*above*) CORE protesters at the 1964–65 World's Fair demand an end to job discrimination, police brutality, and slum housing. (*LOOK* Magazine Photograph Collection, Library of Congress, Prints & Photographs Division.)

Ye Olde
King Kole
COMPTON
FOR
WE
WANT
SCRANTON

WASH
LAUNDRY
QUALITY
PENN
BEEF
CO.
MEATS

Fig. 13. (*opposite top*) Jackie Robinson (*fourth from right*) was a familiar figure at civil rights rallies throughout the '60s. (Photograph by David Johnson, 1963.)

Fig. 14. (*opposite bottom*) Rioters loot retail stores along Columbia Avenue in North Philadelphia, August 1964. A month later, the Phillies collapsed in historic fashion. (Special Collections Research Center, Temple University Libraries, Philadelphia PA.)

Fig. 15. (*above*) The Beatles kick off their 1965 U.S. tour at Shea Stadium. The crowd noise was so deafening security guards had to cover their ears. (Library of Congress, Prints & Photographs Division, NYWT&S Collection [LC-DIG-ds-08257].)

Fig. 16. Beatlemania at Shea Stadium, 1965. By the mid-'60s, the sensibilities of the rock generation had infiltrated sports. (Library of Congress, Prints & Photographs Division, NYWT&S Collection [LC-DIG-ds-08258].)

12

On April 12, 1966, the sun broke through the clouds and flooded the streets of Atlanta. It was a Tuesday—a workday, according to the calendar—but local offices and schools had closed early. Instead of tending to business, homework, and doctor visits, two hundred fifty thousand Atlantans jammed the sidewalks of downtown, jockeying for good vantage points along the city's most celebrated street, Peachtree.

The city had come out to cheer its new Major League Baseball team, the Braves. Throngs of black and white children waved pennants and climbed on their parents' shoulders—a few shimmied up street lamps—to catch a glimpse of the stars. Players sat in open convertibles, wearing their new home uniforms, their names taped to the sides of the cars (Atlanta fans had yet to see a scorecard). They rolled slowly along Peachtree behind a queue of military vehicles, waving, many of them seeing downtown Atlanta for the first time. Butler Shoes. Wormser Hats. H. L. Green's.

The moment had been years in the making.

As early as 1960, the city's leaders—local politicians, college presidents, bankers, and CEOs—had been working together to transform the city into a commercial and cultural hub, a nationally ranked metropolis that dissociated itself from the Jim Crow South. In short, they were out to create the anti-Birmingham. Their goal was to desegregate from the top-down by opening up schools and public facilities, and appointing blacks to political positions. As part of the remaking of the city, they'd set their sights on attracting major sports franchises, believing that pro sports teams would further legitimize Atlanta as a world-class hub. Now, six years later, they were seeing their collective dream come to fruition.

Andrew Young, executive director of the Southern Christian Leadership Conference, and one of Martin Luther King's top advisors, remembers the efforts made by the city's politicians and businesses—especially the local giant, Coca-Cola—to create a color-blind city.

> I think Atlanta was different in large measure because of Coca-Cola. . . . In the 1960s, the CEO of Coca-Cola, J. Paul Austin, had just come back from South Africa. He'd been there fourteen years and he saw what apartheid had done to the economy. He was a native Southerner, but he became a progressive because of his experiences in South Africa. So one of the first things Austin did when he came back was to push to keep the public schools open [to both races]. They formed a committee of distinguished elders, the Sibley Commission. The Commission went around and held hearings, basically, with white businessmen, and let them know why it was important to have school desegregation without a lot of violence and upheaval. The economy of the South depended on us being able to get along.

Young credits Mayor Ivan Allen Jr. as being one of the main catalysts of change. Allen, a former segregationist, had heeded the advice of his father, who'd been the head of the Chamber of Commerce. Allen Sr. told his son the city had to tackle racism in order to be truly effective.

Allen took the mandate to heart. After narrowly defeating pro-segregationist (and future governor) Lester Maddox in 1961, Allen fought to integrate the city. He took down the "colored" and "white" signs from city hall, appointed the city's first black firemen, and ordered the desegregation of public swimming pools. And in a move that nearly cost him reelection, he became the only prominent southern politician to appear before Congress in support of the bill that would become the Civil Rights Act of 1964.

As Andrew Young tells it,

> It was really under Ivan Allen that [city and business leaders] began to *force* communication between the races. Allen used to tell the story of saying in the Chamber of Commerce when he was president, "Look, everybody else in the South has put the burden of segregation on the backs of their children. Atlanta can't do that. Atlanta

has to stand up. We have to be the leaders. We have to take the burden of this problem on our shoulders because it's the manly thing to do."

And then he introduced a motion that the Chamber be integrated, and that Herman Russell be invited to join the board. Herman Russell was a black contractor.

After the motion, there was a thunder of silence until [Robert Woodruff, the former president of Coca-Cola] leaned over, and in his raspy whisper, took his cigar out of his mouth and said, "You're right, Ivan."

And once he said that, everybody voted for it.

Coca-Cola wasn't the only company prospering in Atlanta. Allen had attracted private businesses by using federal urban renewal money and other public funds to build the city's infrastructure. The plan worked; in a two-year period, the city built 1.7 million square feet of downtown office space. Up went the thirty-one-story Bank of Georgia, the twenty-story Georgia Power Company, and the twenty-three-story Peachtree Towers Condominiums. When all was said and done, more than one hundred million dollars were poured into the city's skyline. And as the beams of steel went up, the walls of segregation trembled.

In the minds of many, no construction project was more significant than that of the new baseball park. Mayor Allen, along with Mills B. Lane of the Citizens and Southern National Bank, had lured the Braves with the promise of a new stadium—and even though they hadn't gotten the okay from the city council or the financing from the bank, they'd gone ahead with the eighteen-million-dollar project.

Writing for ESPN, Howard Bryant examined the social issues driving Allen's decision to build the facility, despite having no support for the project.

> One of the first concessions Allen made (with the backing of the city's corporate leaders) was to prohibit segregated seating and facilities for sporting events—a sweeping victory in contrast to the two decades it took to desegregate spring training facilities in Florida.

It would be at a sporting event that many people, black and white, first shared public restrooms, sat in the same sections of public events or drank at the same water fountain. It would be through sports that national business leaders came to believe that the South now offered viable business opportunities, that it was a safer place to invest. Allen was so confident that sports could be a unifier to a segregated city that he began construction on what would be Atlanta-Fulton County Stadium before the Braves had even agreed to move.

Atlanta, while still dealing with sit-ins and other forms of civil rights protests, was quickly becoming the cultural capital of the South. Artists were already settling there, and entertainers were including it on national tours. When the Braves arrived, followed by the NFL Falcons a few months later, and the NBA Hawks two years after that, Metro Atlanta had a population of 1.25 million and was growing by 35,000 residents a year. It was also 44 percent black and had a new slogan: "Atlanta, the city too busy to hate."

But turning the city into a showpiece had come at a steep cost. Atlanta's version of urban renewal had required the demolition of thousands of low-income housing units. According to Charles Rutheiser, author of *Imagineering Atlanta*, the city displaced more than sixty-five thousand residents, or one in every seven residents. Most of the displaced were poor blacks, victims of the city's success.

Henry Aaron made his way along the parade route in his bright #44 Braves jersey, a smile on his boyish, thirty-two-year-old face. The slugger was new to the city, but his reputation had reached all the way from the Upper Midwest. For starters, his .320 batting average was the highest among active National Leaguers. He also had 398 career homers, putting him fifth among active players and twelfth on the all-time list. The perennial All-Star had already collected two batting titles, a home run crown, an MVP, two pennants, and a World Series ring.

Andrew Young watched from the sidewalk in front of the American Hotel.

"I was standing behind these two good old boys," he says. "When Hank came by they were saying, 'We're a big league town now. He's gonna have to live anywhere in this town he wants to live.' I was shocked and I thought, 'They said that? This must mean something.'"

Even with Atlanta's shiny new reputation, Aaron had had little desire to move his family back to the South. He'd been living in Mequon, a Milwaukee suburb on the western shore of Lake Michigan. His four children and his wife, Barbara, lived free of harassment. That wouldn't be the case in the Deep South. Aaron could remember, as a child in Mobile, Alabama, hiding under his bed from the Ku Klux Klan. He also had painful memories of playing minor league ball with the Jacksonville Braves in Florida. He and three black teammates had broken the color line in the South Atlantic League—and in return received a steady diet of threats and intimidation.

As Young says now, "Hank Aaron, in many ways, had a more difficult road than Jackie Robinson, because Aaron played minor league ball in the Southern League."

The indignities served to Aaron had extended as far north as DC. After eating in a restaurant near Griffith Stadium with his teammates on the Negro League Indianapolis Clowns, Aaron could hear their dinner plates being smashed in the kitchen.

"Here we were in the capital, in the land of freedom and equality," Aaron wrote in his autobiography, *I Had a Hammer*. "They had to destroy the plates that had touched the forks that had been in the mouths of black men. If dogs had eaten off those plates, they'd have washed them."

Braves center fielder Lee Maye was equally vocal, but while Aaron had been too talented to trade, the same couldn't be said for Maye. He'd had his best season in 1964, batting .304, but was injured in the beginning of the '65 season. When he returned from the disabled list, he found out he'd been traded to the Astros and would have to play in the segregated city of Houston.

Aaron received a different treatment—mostly because he could help the Braves compete in the National League. City officials had appealed for his support, explaining that Atlanta Stadium would be integrated, as would the city's restaurants, movie theaters, and public accommodations. They'd surely added that Aaron's children would be able to choose from a wealth of local colleges and universities, including a consortium of six historically black colleges. Dick Cecil, then the Braves' business manager, had driven Aaron around Atlanta, showing off the city's cosmopolitan charm.

Aaron was finally persuaded when he met with C. Miles Smith, the president of the local NAACP, and received letters from Whitney Young, the president of the National Urban League (no relation to Andrew Young). They both urged him to give the South another chance.

And so, on opening night, a few hours after the parade on Peachtree, Aaron took the field with the rest of the newly named Atlanta Braves, serenaded by fifty thousand cheering fans. The ballpark was everything it was cracked up to be. Like New York's Shea Stadium, the multipurpose venue was a round, concrete doughnut, complete with three tiers of seating, no supporting pillars, and no obstructed views. The playing field was symmetrical, although quite a distance from the stands. It also happened to be a thousand feet above sea level, which, as the minor league Crackers had discovered the previous season, helped batted balls fly out of the park. For this reason, it would soon be dubbed "The Launching Pad."

The Braves lost the opener, an extra-innings affair in which the Pirates' Willie Stargell delivered the deathblow, a two-run homer, in the top of the thirteenth. But Mayor Allen's vision had been realized in living color. Throughout the stadium, whites and blacks played together, sat together, and worked together. Of the seven hundred stadium employees, more than four hundred were black.

Jimmy Carter, then a Georgia state senator, spoke of the importance of having Aaron and the Braves in Atlanta. "Having sports teams legitimized us," he told Howard Bryant. "It gave us the opportunity to be known for something that was not going to be a national embarrassment. Henry Aaron was a big part of that because he integrated pro sports in the Deep South, which was no small thing. He was the first black man that white fans in the South cheered for."

It was equally important for black fans to have a hero who represented their race. As Andrew Young explains, "Sports was always a part of our growing up. We didn't have any political leaders that I knew of. But we knew Joe Louis, we knew Jack Johnson, we knew Satchel Paige, we knew Josh Gibson, we knew Jackie Robinson. Sports has always been the vehicle for self-esteem in the black community. It meant so much to me to see a black compete and win; it was a silent statement of equality."

Even with the Braves, however, racism in Atlanta didn't disappear overnight. Aaron moved his family into a ranch house in southwest Atlanta, where the iconic star would occasionally find hate letters in his mailbox—compounding the racial insults he heard at the ballpark.

As he told Sam Lacy of the *Baltimore Afro-American*, "I have participated in civil rights demonstrations and marches for over two years. I was one of the first players to join the Afro fight for one-roof housing in spring training. So I have absolutely no fear of anybody's revenge."

Aaron continued to speak out for civil rights in the most visible way he knew how: he hit home runs. Adjusting his swing to his new ballpark, he regularly drove balls deep into the leftfield stands.

As Milo Hamilton, the Braves' announcer put it, "Aaron had been a pretty good home run hitter before, but had a lot of opposite-field home runs in Milwaukee. When he got to Atlanta and saw [Atlanta Stadium], he became almost a dead-pull hitter. The ball just flew."

Aaron explained his new approach to hitting in his book, *I Had a Hammer*. "I knew that, as a black player, I would be on trial in Atlanta," he wrote. "I needed a decisive way to win over the white people before they thought of a reason to hate me. And I believed that the way to do all of this was with home runs."

The Braves would finish their first season in Atlanta in fifth place, ten games behind the Dodgers. Aaron would be one of the few bright spots; he'd lead the league with 44 homers and 127 RBIs. In so doing, he'd pass Duke Snider and Ernie Banks on the career home run list, moving up to fourth among active players, tenth all-time.

The Beatles returned to the United States in the summer of 1966. There was less fanfare this time. It's possible the public's attitude had shifted the previous month, when an American teen magazine reprinted an interview that John Lennon had given earlier in the year to the *London Evening Standard*.

The piece had run as a portrait of the private Lennon and was entitled *How Does a Beatle Live? John Lennon Lives Like This*. Lennon mused on an array of subjects, including religion.

"Christianity will go," he had told the interviewer. "It will vanish and shrink. I needn't argue with that; I'm right and I will be proved right. We're more popular than Jesus now. I don't know which will go first, rock-n-roll or Christianity. Jesus was all right but his disciples thick and ordinary."

The interview attracted little notice in the United Kingdom, but by the time it reached America, particularly the South, Lennon's remarks had morphed into his saying, "I'm bigger than Jesus."

The backlash was fueled, in part, by a shift in popular music. Over the previous few years, folk and rock musicians had been recording protest songs in reaction to political and social events taking place throughout the country. In 1963 Bob Dylan, then a young folk singer who had been writing social protest songs, paid tribute to slain civil rights leader Medgar Evers with his ballad "Only a Pawn in Their Game." Dylan performed the song at a voter registration drive in Greenwood, Mississippi, and a month later played it in front of a quarter-million civil rights protesters at the March on Washington.

In 1964 black soul singer Sam Cooke had penned a deeply personal song about the despair, and also the hope, he felt for black America. "A Change Is Gonna Come" was Cooke's response to years of mistreatment. He'd written it after being turned away from a hotel in Louisiana; he'd protested so vehemently that the police arrested him. Apparently, as big as a star as Cooke was, he couldn't escape being a black man in the segregated South.

By the time the Beatles returned to the States, Cooke's song was on its way to becoming an anthem of the civil rights movement. (Cooke didn't live to see it happen, though. He was shot and killed in a Los Angeles motel shortly before the song's release.)

The old-school establishment, already out of sorts with the swiftly changing times, pinned its rage on the most convenient target they could find: the non-American John Lennon.

Several Bible Belt disc jockeys, spurred on by WAQY radio hosts Doug Layton and Tommy Charles in Birmingham, Alabama, declared Lennon's remarks blasphemous and issued an "eternal" ban on all Beatles music. Listeners were urged to bring their Beatles records to any one of fourteen pickup locations in Birmingham so they could be burned in a public bonfire. When Lennon learned of the boycott, he decided to apologize, not for what he had said but for the way his message was received. As he'd say years later, "I couldn't go away knowing I'd created another little piece of hate in the world. So I apologized."

Lennon faced the press in Chicago. "I wasn't saying the Beatles are better than Jesus or God or Christianity," he said. "I was using the name Beatles. . . . But I could have said TV, or cinema, or anything else that's popular . . . or motorcars are bigger than Jesus. . . . I just never thought of repercussions. My views are only from what I've read or observed of Christianity and what it was, and what it has been, or what it could be—it just seems to me to be shrinking. I'm not knocking it or saying it's bad. I'm just saying it seems to be shrinking and losing contact."

Lennon's explanation seemed to assuage his critics, although the Ku Klux Klan showed up to protest the Beatles' concert in Memphis.

While the media focused on the Christianity brouhaha, it paid no attention to the remarks Lennon gave later on during the tour. When asked about the Vietnam conflict, he said, "We think of [the war] all the time. We don't like it. We don't agree with it. We think it's wrong."

It was certainly as antiestablishment as anything else the Beatles had said—and also the first time a rock musician had openly discussed politics with the press. Considering that President Johnson had just announced the systematic bombing of North Vietnam, it could certainly have been taken as a sign that antiwar sentiments were creeping into the public consciousness.

But the American public didn't seem to notice.

It just wanted to be sure that Lennon didn't think he was bigger than Christ.

In June 1967, Muhammad Ali was the heavyweight champion of the world. Since taking the title from Sonny Liston, he'd successfully defended it nine times—including a rematch with Liston and a twelve-round TKO of ex-champ Floyd Patterson.

As he stood in the crowded hallway of the Federal courthouse in Houston, Texas, dressed in a light grey suit and black alligator shoes, Ali signed autographs and chatted with fans, waiting for the jury to decide his fate. If he were to be found guilty, his run as heavyweight champ would end. If things went really badly, he'd never enter a professional boxing ring again.

Ali's legal troubles had begun when President Johnson had escalated American troop levels in Vietnam. The move had required expanding the draft; to do so, the military loosened its recruitment policies, including the qualifying score on its intelligence test. Ali, who had scored seventy-eight, was reclassified. He was no longer 1-Y, unqualified to serve, but 1-A, available for military service.

Upon word of Ali's revised status, reporters had descended on his rented home in Miami, Florida. They bombarded him with questions until they got a newsworthy response. Little did he realize, he'd delivered a doozy.

"Man," he'd finally said, "I ain't got no quarrel with them Vietcong."

Ali had shown the audacity to question America's presence in Vietnam—and his statement ricocheted through newsrooms around the country. Every sportswriter in America began weighing in on the champ's sense of patriotism.

According to Jerry Izenberg of the *Star-Ledger*, "the statement almost made Ali the patron saint of the antiwar movement. . . . Before that, none of the protesters could really articulate why they were against the war. He gave them the reason."

The old guard, of course, railed against Ali.

Jimmy Cannon wrote that the boxer was "part of the Beatle movement," that he "[fit] in with the famous singers no one can hear and the punks riding motorcycles with iron crosses pinned to their leather jackets and Batman and the boys with their long dirty hair and the girls with the unwashed look and the college kids dancing naked at secret proms held in apartments and the revolt of students who get a check from dad every first of the month and the painters who copy the labels off soup cans and the surf bums who refuse to work and the whole pampered style-making cult of the bored young."

Red Smith was more concise. The boxer, he wrote, "makes himself as sorry a spectacle as those unwashed punks who picket and demonstrate against the war."

Ali's troubles had multiplied the morning he was scheduled for induction into the armed forces. In the midst of a media frenzy, he'd steadfastly refused to take the oath.

"My conscience won't let me go shoot my brother or some darker people, some poor hungry people in the mud, for big, powerful America," he'd said. "Shoot them for what? They never called me nigger, they never lynched me, they didn't put no dogs on me."

The New York State Athletic Commission had promptly suspended Ali's boxing license and stripped him of his title. Within days, other state commissions had followed suit—leaving the champ with no means of income.

Now, inside Houston's Federal courthouse, the jury was back. After twenty minutes of deliberation, the six white men and six white women found Ali guilty of draft evasion.

No one was surprised. Ali's lawyers, Hayden Covington of New York and Quinnan Hodges of Houston, had never denied that their client refused induction. Rather, they maintained that the draft board had acted improperly in not granting their client a deferment as a minister.

All involved—even U.S. Attorney Morton Susman, who had prosecuted Ali—expected Judge Joe Ingraham to hand down a light sentence. Aside from a minor traffic offense, Ali's record was spotless, and the fighter was already paying a price by having his livelihood taken away. But Ingraham hit Ali with a ten-thousand-dollar fine and sentenced him to the maximum penalty: five years in prison. He surely knew that the verdict would be appealed.

He then ordered Ali to turn his passport over to the court.

The *New York Times* observed, "[Ali's] step was as jaunty as ever as he walked from the courtroom after being released on $5,000 bond. He held hands with two young women who had been with him during intermissions in the trial and he smiled at the crowd that gathered around. He allowed the television cameramen to surround him and shuffle him off down the street."

The government had spoken. But Ali was determined to have the last word.

In November 1967, five months after Ali's guilty verdict, Major League Baseball commissioner William Eckert made a point of telling the press about four ballplayers who'd gone on a goodwill tour throughout South Vietnam. Baseball supported the war, Eckert said, and the troops that were fighting in it.

"It was a thrill that many of our fighting men will never forget," Eckert told the *New York Times*. "Most of them had only read about such persons as Joe DiMaggio and Jerry Coleman, former New York Yankees stars, Tony Conigliaro of the Boston Red Sox, Pete Rose of the Cincinnati Reds, and Bob Fishel, vice president of the New York Yankees. All of this was made possible by baseball and the United Service Organization shows, which provide entertainment for the military around the world."

One player, the scrappy, twenty-five-year-old second baseman Pete Rose, was not pushing the same agenda. He and his delegation had ventured into areas that had been ignored by previous USO tours, and what he'd seen was enough to rattle the most patriotic American. In Cai Nhum, a village that had recently been attacked by Vietcong forces, Rose was engulfed by the smell of smoke and the sound of mortar shells. Most disturbing was the sight of body bags being readied for transport to the United States. Rose counted nineteen bags, each one containing a dead marine.

"You see that and you really know a war is going on," Rose later told reporters.

The previous year, four All-Stars—Henry Aaron, Joe Torre, Harmon Killebrew, and Brooks Robinson—had visited South Vietnam with retired baseball icon Stan Musial.

As Henry Aaron explained to the *Associated Press*, "we didn't sit back at the bases. We went right to the troops in the field and visited the men in the hospitals. That's what made the trip so good. They were so anxious to see us. We created a crowd wherever we went. We talked baseball and showed the movie of last year's All-Star game. We realized we were in the war zone, but we didn't think we were in any danger. They took every precaution whatsoever. I wasn't afraid."

While the goodwill tours were surefire morale boosters, they also raised a question: if Major League Baseball supported the war, why were so few players fighting in it? In 1967 the subject became a point of contention for Lucien Nedzi, a Democratic congressman from Michigan and a member of the House Armed Services Committee. To Nedzi, only one answer made sense: athletes had been receiving preferential treatment.

In response to Nedzi's allegations, the Defense Department released a set of figures that seemed only to support the congressman's position. Of the 360 professional athletes (145 baseball players) serving in the National Guard or reserves, more than 85 percent had joined *after* their teams had signed them, indicating that they may have been protected or, at the very least, encouraged to avoid the draft.

Commissioner Eckert did not discuss these numbers. Nor did team owners. They never admitted to any backroom deals, nor any conversations discouraging players from enlisting. What they did continue to say—loudly—was that baseball was in full support of the war and that the sport did its part by sending players on goodwill tours.

But the numbers didn't lie. During World War II, more than five hundred professional ballplayers had served in the military—and those included stars like Ted Williams and Joe DiMaggio. During the Vietnam era, when there were more teams and more players than ever before, only fifty or so players served—none of them stars.

Something was amiss.

As the pressure from Congressman Nedzi mounted, Robert McNamara, the U.S. secretary of defense under President Johnson, ordered that all National Guard vacancies be filled on a first-come, first-served basis.

His dictum had virtually no effect on whatever process had been put in place.

Consider the case of George Gmelch, a twenty-two-year-old prospect in the Detroit Tigers' organization. Gmelch was a student at Stanford and had continued his studies via correspondence courses in the off-season, thus extending his college deferment and keeping himself out of active duty.

In 1966, while playing for the Daytona Beach Islanders in the Florida State League, Gmelch had attended spring training with the Tigers.

One night, while studying in the team's executive offices, he meandered through the neighboring suites to stretch his legs. What he saw hanging on the wall of a conference room caught his attention.

"The names of all 125-odd players in the Tiger organization were posted," Gmelch recalls. "Each had a star by his name, color coded by draft status."

It was obvious the Tigers were keeping close tabs on their players. Gmelch wondered whether they were watching so closely that they were steering them into reserve units.

"Teams wanted to protect their players, especially their prospects," Gmelch says. "I think they were probably advising them on what they needed to do in terms of avoiding the draft. Teams let players stay in college. I knew players that were high draft picks and the organization would fly them to spring training and didn't require them to report until classes ended in June. And they did that because they wanted to protect them from being drafted."

But those maneuvers couldn't help Gmelch when he received a letter from his draft board in San Mateo, California. Apparently the military had expanded its call-up and no longer permitted correspondence courses to qualify for college deferments—a change that neither Gmelch nor the Tigers had seen coming.

Gmelch was told to report to the Armed Forces Examining and Entrance Station in Jacksonville for a pre-induction physical. It so happened that two of his teammates, Norm McRae and Rudy Burson, had received similar notices. On the bus ride, the three teammates conspired on ways to flunk their physicals. They considered eating soap to raise their blood pressure or downing excessive amounts of soda to raise their blood sugar.

"My memory is that it was certainly okay to do everything you could to get into a reserve unit and not have to be drafted," Gmelch says. "Nobody thought that was unpatriotic."

When Gmelch realized he didn't have any soap to eat or soda to drink—or time to kill—he changed tactics, choosing instead to cheat on his hearing test. First, he pretended not to hear his name when he was summoned in the waiting room; then he intentionally provided false responses to audio prompts during the exam.

“There was no way I was gonna go,” he says. “I would have gone to Canada rather than have served in the military. I don’t know what the other two guys did [to flunk the test], but we were all declared 4-F, so all three of us were able to avoid the draft.”

What Gmelch did know, though, was that Major League Baseball teams were helping to guide players into the National Guard and reserves—help that more than a half-million other young American men were seeking but couldn’t find.

13

In December 1967, the representatives of the Major League Baseball Players Association flew to baseball's annual winter meetings in Mexico City. They went there in the hope of sitting down with team owners to discuss, among other things, a new minimum salary. But the owners ducked the players at every turn, responding to their overtures with nothing but ill will.

"The owners gave the players the back of their hands," Marvin Miller wrote in his memoir, *A Whole New Ballgame*. "[They'd] been sidestepping our advances for almost a year. As 1968 drew near, the minimum salary for a major league player was still $6,000."

Aware of the reputation Miller had built as a negotiator for the United Steelworkers, Bowie Kuhn, assistant counsel to the National League, sought advice. One of his first calls was to Harvard industrial relations professor James Healy, who, upon hearing the name Marvin Miller, advised his client, "Bowie, you need lots of help."

Jim Bunning, a member of the players' executive board, told the press, "I know that baseball people resent our new leader[,] . . . [but] I have news for them. Marvin Miller will be around for a long time."

Bunning knew of what he spoke. In a show of support for Miller, the players extended his contract for three more years, locking him in through 1970. They also gave him a five-thousand-dollar raise, thus increasing his salary to fifty-five thousand dollars per year.

As for the Players Association, the central issues were not all salary-related. The union was still eager to fortify its meager pension plan. It also sought many of the same benefits won by industrial unions throughout the United States—most notably, the freedom to bring grievances to an impartial arbitrator.

The owners' chief negotiator, John Gaherin, advised his clients to concede on this issue, explaining that they couldn't present the commissioner as the final word on grievances, that no legitimate union would accept a partisan judge. The owners steadfastly refused and instructed Gaherin to duck the issue. Baseball, they maintained, was unlike other industries; it was its own entity and should continue running itself.

Gaherin did his best to sway his clients. In *The Lords of the Realm*, John Helyar quotes him: "I've worked in the railroad business. I've worked in the inland marine business. I've worked in the newspaper industry. And in each I've heard erudite presentations on how they're different. But since 1932 there hasn't been a labor union in this country [that] would go for a non-independent arbitrator."

But the owners insisted Gaherin quash the issue. According to Helyar, when Gaherin was leaving the conference room, Walter O'Malley took him by the elbow and pulled him aside.

"Tell that Jewish boy," O'Malley said, referring to Marvin Miller, "to go on back to Brooklyn."

The two sides finally returned to the negotiating table in January 1968. Again, the owners remained intractable. And again, Miller accused them of sabotage—though he now brought up the possibility of federal mediation.

From the *New York Times*: "At a time when football players have moved toward outright unionism, and when basketball players have obtained some of the points the baseball players still seek, Miller called attention to what he considered the unsatisfactory atmosphere of the negotiations."

As talks resumed, the owners—perhaps tired but more likely fearing federal intervention—began to bend a little. On February 22, 1968, the two sides agreed to a two-year labor contract, the first collective bargaining agreement in baseball or any other sport. (NFL players would need to strike before reaching a deal.)

Baseball's new agreement raised the minimum salary to ten thousand dollars and boosted spring training allowances to forty dollars from twenty-five dollars per week. Meal money was also raised, to fifteen dollars per day from twelve dollars.

One of the players' biggest victories came on the very issue the owners had been trying so hard to duck: arbitration. Going forward, grievances would be settled by an outside mediator. As Miller put it, "clubs could no longer play sheriff, judge, and jury with ballplayers."

The players also got the owners to agree to fly them first-class, a significant issue because players spent an inordinate amount of time in the air, and narrow coach seats were unsuitable for their oversized frames. This accommodation didn't sit well with some general managers. One of them, the Reds' Bob Howsam, simply ignored the mandate until veteran pitcher Milt Pappas, the Reds' player rep, complained to the union that the team was still flying coach. A month later, Howsam traded Pappas to the Braves.

It would take another year, and the threat of a players' strike, before the owners would agree to a new pension plan. With it, players would become eligible for pensions after four years instead of five. Plus, owner-contributions would increase to $5.45 million, a difference of more than a million dollars.

Still, the thorniest issue, the reserve system, would remain untouched. And it would stay that way for months, until the day the phone would ring in Marvin Miller's office.

14

On Sunday, March 31, 1968, President Johnson addressed the country on national television. Sitting behind his desk in the Oval Office, wearing a dark blue suit, brick-red tie, silver star lapel pin, and clear-framed, rectangular eyeglasses, Johnson delivered an announcement that stunned even his own administration: he would not run in the upcoming election.

There's little doubt Johnson's decision had to do with the public's growing dissatisfaction with the Vietnam War. Earlier that month, Minnesota senator Eugene McCarthy, the antiwar candidate, had catapulted into contention by winning a surprising 42 percent of the vote in the New Hampshire primary. Moreover, New York senator Robert Kennedy, the former attorney general, was about to enter the race. He, too, had an antiwar platform.

All along, Johnson had tried to distance himself from Vietnam, maintaining that he'd inherited the dilemma from his predecessors, Eisenhower and Kennedy, and that his agenda as president was to push for civil rights legislation. The following is from a speech he delivered three years earlier to Congress:

> This is the richest and most powerful country which ever occupied this globe. The might of past empires is little compared to ours. But I do not want to be the president who built empires, or sought grandeur, or extended dominion. I want to be the president who educated young children to the wonders of the world. I want to be the president who helped to feed the hungry and to prepare them to be taxpayers instead of tax-eaters. I want to be the president who helped the poor find their own way and who protected the right of every citizen to vote in every election. I want to be the president who helped to end hatred among his fellow men and who promoted love

among the people of all races, all religions and all parties. I want to be the president who helped to end war among the brothers of this earth.

What Johnson omitted from his speech was that he didn't want to be the president who allowed South Vietnam to fall to communism—which is why he'd brought the conflict to new heights. By 1968, more than half a million troops were dispatched to the region, a staggering number considering that only fifteen thousand were there when Johnson had taken office. What's more, Johnson had secretly authorized a program of sustained aerial bombardment, deceiving both Congress and the American public.

It's likely Johnson first realized he was in a no-win battle—in Vietnam and at the polls—on January 30, when seventy thousand North Vietnamese troops launched a series of mass attacks on more than a hundred cities in South Vietnam. The attacks shocked Americans into a new reality about the war and severely damaged the administration's credibility. For Johnson, the damage didn't come in the form of mortar shells—it came by way of broadcast signals. The TV networks, which had been parroting the generals' updates that U.S. forces were winning the war, canned the jingoism, replacing it with footage of helicopters transporting body bags and a tote board with nightly body counts.

The *New York Times* declared, "The American people have been pushed beyond the limits of gullibility."

Newsweek was equally blunt: "The U.S. must accept the fact that it will never be able to achieve decisive military superiority in Vietnam."

The final blow may have come when Walter Cronkite, one of the most respected news anchors on television, concluded a CBS special report on Vietnam by saying,

> For it seems now more certain than ever, that the bloody experience of Vietnam is to end in a stalemate. . . . To say that we are closer to victory today is to believe in the face of the evidence, the optimists who have been wrong in the past. . . . To say that we are mired in stalemate seems the only realistic, if unsatisfactory, conclusion. On the off chance that military and political analysts are right, in the

next few months we must test the enemy's intentions, in case this is indeed his last big gasp before negotiations.

Watching Cronkite's commentary, a defeated Johnson reportedly turned to his aides and said, "If I've lost Cronkite, I've lost Middle America."

By the time Johnson addressed the nation in late March, his approval rating had plummeted to 36 percent, a far cry from the robust 76 percent he'd had when he took office almost four and a half years earlier.

On April 3, days after Johnson's announcement, Martin Luther King arrived in Memphis, Tennessee. Along with fellow leaders of the Southern Christian Leadership Conference, King was in the troubled city to support 1,300 sanitation workers who had been on strike since early February. The garbage men, most of whom were black, earned so little money they relied on welfare and food stamps to feed their families.

King saw the struggles in Memphis as symbolic of the economic inequality and racial injustice he'd been fighting to end—and he made the strike a focus of his civil rights agenda. He had made two trips to Memphis, drawing national attention to the strike. And now on his third visit, he was again leading a march in support of the workers.

The demonstration turned violent when a small group of participants broke off from the marchers, shattering store windows and looting merchandise. When Memphis police shot and killed a black teenager, Mayor Henry Loeb, an avowed segregationist, called for a citywide curfew and imposed martial law—bringing in four thousand National Guard troops.

On April 3, King delivered a speech to the striking workers.

"We've got some difficult days ahead," he said. "But it really doesn't matter with me now, because I've been to the mountaintop. And I don't mind. Like anybody, I would like to live a long life; longevity has its place. But I'm not concerned about that now. . . . I've seen the Promised Land. I may not get there with you. But I want you to know tonight, that we, as a people, will get to the Promised Land."

King was staying in room 306 of the Lorraine Motel, at the corner of Butler and Mulberry, in downtown Memphis. The two-story building, advertised by a neon yellow sign, was a popular stop for black musicians performing at the jazz clubs along Beale Street. It was also home to barnstorming Negro League baseball teams that swung through town to play the Memphis Red Sox.

On April 4, just before six in the evening, King was getting dressed for dinner. When he stepped onto the second-floor balcony for some fresh air, he met what he and his advisors had long feared—a sniper's bullet.

King staggered backwards and fell onto the concrete walkway. Blood spurted from his neck.

Ralph Abernathy, a colleague and close friend of King's, ran out of his room when he heard the gunshot.

"Oh my god!" he shouted. "Martin's been shot."

Police officers patrolling the area rushed to the Lorraine. Within minutes, an ambulance arrived. Emergency medical technicians rushed to King's side; they placed his body on a stretcher, carried him into the ambulance, and sped off to St. Joseph's Hospital.

"Give me lights!" the driver shouted into his radio.

At once, all traffic lights on the one-and-a-half-mile route were set to green, but the ambulance couldn't travel fast enough to reverse time. The bullet had shattered King's jaw, traveled through his neck, and severed his spinal cord.

An hour after the shooting, doctors pronounced King dead. He was thirty-nine years old.

News of King's assassination set off a wave of rioting in cities across the nation—Baltimore, Chicago, Detroit, Kansas City, Washington DC. Statistics tied forty-six deaths to the riots.

In Memphis, local activists urged Mayor Loeb to honor King by settling with the sanitation workers. Loeb refused, and on April 8, forty-two thousand supporters demanded justice with a silent march through the city. Coretta Scott King, who would bury her husband the following day, led the march.

President Johnson sent Undersecretary of Labor James Reynolds to Memphis to mediate, and two weeks later, the strike was settled. The city agreed to recognize the union and raise wages fifteen cents per hour to $1.90, although it took the threat of a second strike before the money showed up in the workers' paychecks.

Within days of King's murder, Johnson pushed the Civil Rights Act of 1968 through Congress. A legacy to King, the legislation advanced Kennedy's Executive Order 11063, which had banned discrimination in federal housing. The new law forbade discrimination in the sale, rental, or financing of *any* homes based on buyers' or renters' religion, ethnicity, nationality, or sex. The so-called Fair Housing Act is generally considered the last great legislative achievement of the civil rights era.

Baseball Commissioner William Eckert seemed to have no idea how to honor King, or whether to acknowledge his death at all. Tired of waiting for a decision, many players showed their respect for the slain leader by sitting out the last few days of spring training—a gesture that prompted several owners to demand that the league penalize them.

Eckert didn't listen. This was nothing new; he had been at odds with the owners since taking the reins from Ford Frick three years earlier. It probably didn't help that Eckert, a retired air force lieutenant general, was hired by accident. Apparently, when the vote was taken, some owners thought they were casting their ballots for the distinguished Eugene Zuckert, former secretary of the air force. So few owners knew Eckert, he soon came to be known as "The Unknown Soldier."

On April 8, the day the season was scheduled to begin, Eckert was still struggling with how to proceed—and ultimately came up with the most spineless decision of all: He left it up to the teams to decide whether they wanted to play their home openers.

The Pittsburgh Pirates, whose roster included eleven minority players, faced a dilemma. Their hosts, the Houston Astros, had decided to play, and the Pirates, as the visiting team, were obligated to comply.

The team held a closed-door meeting.

Roberto Clemente, Pittsburgh's star right fielder, was especially vocal. He'd been so influenced by King that he'd begun performing goodwill missions of his own during the offseason—and was outraged by the commissioner's seeming lack of respect.

"When Martin Luther King died," he'd say years later, "they come and ask the Negro players if we should play. I say, 'If you have to ask the Negro players, then we do not have a great country.'"

Clemente was not alone. The Pirates voted overwhelmingly to sit out the opener. They also asked their GM, Joe L. Brown, to postpone the next game as well, since it would fall on the day of King's funeral.

Clemente and teammate Dave Wickersham, a white journeyman pitcher, issued a statement on behalf of the team that read, "We are doing this because we white and black players respect what Dr. King has done for mankind."

When black players on other teams—most notably Cardinals pitcher Bob Gibson—took a similar stance, Eckert finally took substantive action: opening day would be officially postponed until April 10, the day after the funeral.

Eckert had ostensibly acted out of respect for the slain civil rights leader, but Dick Young, writing in the *New York Daily News*, saw it another way:

> The commissioner of baseball was running around as though his head had been cut off. . . . He was calling up the club owners, not to tell them what to do, but to ask them. On the basis of his calls to the owners, and to some civic leaders, decisions were made . . . not out of any great compassion for the Rev. Mr. King, or for his family, or for what he stood for, but out of fear. If the commissioner was assured that a ballgame could be played without provoking a racial demonstration, it was not canceled. This was the prime motivating factor, and let us not kid ourselves, let us not pretend. Then came the most astonishing ruling of all. A Tuesday was to be the day of the Rev. King's funeral, and Tuesday was opening day for most ball clubs. It was decided that teams in the East and Midwest, which would be playing during the funeral hours, should postpone their games. It was decided that teams in California, which would be opening at an hour when the funeral had concluded, would play. It was as though someone was standing by the side of the bier with a stopwatch and a starter's gun.

On April 9, two funeral services were held for King: a private service at the Ebenezer Baptist Church and a public one at his alma mater, Morehouse College.

The 1968 baseball season began the following day.

With Lyndon Johnson out of the presidential race, Democrats sought a new nominee, Vice President Hubert Humphrey. But both Eugene McCarthy and Robert Kennedy were coming on strong, buoyed by a wave of support from antiwar factions.

"I do not run for the presidency merely to oppose any man," Kennedy had said when joining the race. "I run because I am convinced that this country is on a perilous course and because I have such strong feelings about what must be done, and I feel that I'm obliged to do all I can."

On June 4, Kennedy and his supporters celebrated a major victory—the California primary—in the ballroom of the Ambassador Hotel in downtown Los Angeles. The forty-two-year-old candidate bounded onto the stage at 11:30 p.m. and kicked off his speech by congratulating Don Drysdale, who had shut out the Pirates five miles away at Chavez Ravine. The win put the streaking right-hander on the verge of breaking Walter Johnson's mark of 55⅔ consecutive scoreless innings, set in 1913.

"I'd like to express my high regard to Don Drysdale for his six great shutouts," Kennedy told the packed room. "And I hope we have as good fortune in our campaign."

Minutes later, the presidential hopeful turned from the crowd, parted the gold curtains behind the platform, and left the ballroom. As he cut through the pantry to meet the press in the Colonial Room, he was stopped cold. Sirhan Sirhan, a twenty-four-year-old Palestinian nationalist embittered over Kennedy's support of Israel, stepped in front of him, held out a rolled-up campaign poster, and from under it, fired a twenty-two-caliber revolver, point-blank.

Roosevelt Grier, the former NFL defensive tackle, and Rafer Johnson, the former Olympic gold medal decathlete, were guarding the candidate. Both rushed the gunman, but Sirhan kept shooting, emptying the eight-round chamber into the air. *Pop! Pop! Pop!* Bullets ricocheted throughout the room, hitting five bystanders—and Kennedy.

As Kennedy dropped to the floor, Juan Romero, a seventeen-year-old busboy, knelt down beside him, cradling his head—but there was nothing he could do other than watch Kennedy's blood leak onto his white uniform jacket.

Pete Hamill, a journalist and close friend of Kennedy's, wrote an eyewitness account days later in the *Village Voice*. According to Hamill, Grier had his arm around the shooter's neck, choking him.

"Rosey, Rosey, don't kill him," Kennedy's bodyguards had shouted. "We want him alive. *Don't kill him, Rosey, don't kill him*."

"Kill the bastard," a Mexican busboy said. "Kill that son of a bitch bastard."

"*Don't kill him, Rosey*."

"Where's the doctor?" another voice cried out. "*Where in Christ's name is the doctor?*"

Kennedy was brought to Central Receiving Hospital and then transferred to Good Samaritan Hospital for surgery.

Don Drysdale heard the news of the shooting on the car radio while driving home to Hidden Hills from Dodger Stadium. A man who usually kept his emotions in check, Drysdale couldn't do so this time. The announcement was just too painful, not only because Kennedy had mentioned the pitcher in his speech but also because the two had had a personal connection. They'd met twice before, once at a Jobs Corps affair and then at Hickory Hill, Kennedy's estate in Virginia.

Drysdale, along with the rest of the country, spent the next twenty-four hours waiting anxiously for news of Kennedy's condition. Then, in the early hours of June 6, it arrived. Kennedy was gone. He died with his wife, Ethel, and sister-in-law, Jackie, at his side.

Two days later, Drysdale was getting ready to face the Phillies at Dodger Stadium. His focus was not on his pursuit of Walter Johnson's record but on the TV, where he watched the pallbearers at Arlington National Cemetery carry Robert Kennedy's body to rest, thirty yards from the grave of his older brother, John.

The news images were compounded by an announcement that investigators in London had captured the man suspected of assassinating Martin Luther King. After a nine-week manhunt, police had arrested small-time crook James Earl Ray at Heathrow Airport.

Drysdale took the mound at 2:30 that afternoon. In honor of his slain friend, he wore a black armband on his white uniform.

Dodgers announcer Vin Scully opened his broadcast with a heavy heart.

> They say the eye of the storm is the quiet part, and here, Dodger Stadium, has suddenly become the eye of the storm. A large crowd, approximately 50,000, and the winds of all kinds of emotions swirling around the ballpark. Certainly there are still the winds of sorrow; what a dreadful, drab and heartbreaking day it has been. But as the gray skies now slowly start to disappear tonight, so, too, the feelings in the ballpark are turning. And from almost the pits of despair, we concentrate on a child's game—a ball, a bat and some people hitting it, throwing it and catching it, and particularly Don Drysdale's big night in baseball.

Drysdale steeled himself for the job at hand. He broke Johnson's record in the second inning when he struck out Clay Dalrymple and continued to roll through the fourth inning. But in the fifth, with one out and runners on first and third, he gave up a sacrifice fly to pinch-hitter Howie Bedell that scored Tony Taylor. His record-setting streak had ended at 58⅔ innings.

But the horror that two days earlier had cast a pall over the country had by no means lifted. When Drysdale left the ballpark, with the pressure of the game behind him, he drove home, trying to figure out how the world had gone so terribly wrong.

15

The deaths of Martin Luther King and Robert Kennedy struck the Cardinals' Bob Gibson especially hard. He and millions of other black Americans had looked to the two leaders as their best hopes for achieving racial justice.

For Gibson, it had been a long time coming.

He'd grown up in the projects in Omaha, Nebraska, with his widowed mother and six siblings. Until Gibson's senior year at Omaha Technical High School, his skin color was considered too dark for the baseball team. So he turned to basketball, became the team's first black player, and showed so much promise that he set his sights on playing hoops at Indiana University. But prejudice cut him down again when Indiana informed him that the school had already reached its quota of black players: one. Undeterred, Gibson stayed in his hometown and became the first black athlete to receive a basketball scholarship from Creighton University. As a star at Creighton, he broke every school scoring record.

After college, Gibson was still undecided between basketball and baseball, so he signed with the Harlem Globetrotters and the St. Louis Cardinals. He eventually chose baseball and made the Majors in 1959, which is when he ran into Cardinals manager and unabashed bigot Solly Hemus.

Aside from calling Gibson and other black players "nigger" as a motivating tool, the thirty-six-year-old Hemus told the young Gibson he wasn't big-league material. He even suggested that going over opposing hitters was beyond his intellectual scope. Just when Gibson was on the verge of quitting, he got some career advice from batting coach Harry Walker.

"It wasn't much," Gibson recalled, "but it hit the right chord. [Walker told me], 'Hang in there, kid. Hemus will be gone long before you will.'"

Sure enough, Hemus was fired in the middle of the '61 season, replaced by coach Johnny Keane (who would be replaced by Red Schoendienst in 1965). Keane didn't give a damn about color. Upon taking over the reins, he gave his full support to black players, most notably Curt Flood, Bill White, and Gibson. With his manager's encouragement, Gibson steadily blossomed into one of the game's elite pitchers, finishing the 1963 season with an 18-9 record and 3.39 ERA. In the 1964 World Series, he beat the Yankees twice. In the 1967 Series against the Red Sox, he was nearly untouchable, hurling three complete-game victories and striking out twenty-six batters in twenty-seven innings.

But Gibson's elevated stature in baseball earned him little respect outside the game. Vandals still pelted his house with bottles and eggs in an effort to drive him and his wife, Charline, out of their West Omaha neighborhood. Which is why, on the day that Martin Luther King was assassinated, Gibson was inconsolable.

Cardinals catcher Tim McCarver was quoted in Gibson's 1996 memoir, *Stranger to the Game*.

> Probably the last person he wanted to talk to that morning was a white man from Memphis, of all places. But I confronted him on that. . . . I told him that I had grown up in an environment of severe prejudice, but if I were any indication, it was possible for people to change their attitudes. . . . He didn't really want to be calmed down and told me in so many words that it was plainly impossible for a white man to completely overcome prejudice. I said that he was taking a very nihilistic attitude and that just because some white people obviously maintained their hatred for blacks and considered them inferior, it was senseless to embrace a viewpoint that would lead nowhere.

The good news for the Cardinals was that Gibson channeled his fury into his pitches.

"You wouldn't see him talk to the other players at all," Schoendienst told *Sports Illustrated*. "It seemed like he just hated them. He said, 'I ain't going to get friendly with anybody.'"

The result was pure intimidation: a flamethrower with a scowl as nasty as his pitching arsenal.

"It was said that I threw, basically, five pitches," Gibson wrote in his memoir. "Fastball, slider, curve, change-up, and knockdown. I don't believe that assessment did me justice, though. I actually used about nine pitches—two different fastballs, two sliders, a curve, change-up, knockdown, brushback, and hit-batsman."

Gibson started the 1968 season strong but had so little run support that he soon found himself with a losing record (4-5) despite his 1.66 ERA. On June 6, against the Astros, his team's offense became a moot point. Gibson fired a shutout—and then did the same against the Braves, the Reds, and the Cubs.

"Without a doubt, I pitched better angry," Gibson wrote. "I suspect that the control of my slider had more to do with it than anything, but I can't completely dismiss the fact that nobody gave me any shit whatsoever for about two months after Bobby Kennedy died."

At the end of June, he four-hit the Pirates and ran his shutout streak to five, putting him one shy of Drysdale's mark. Sportswriters asked him whether he felt pressure trying to catch the Dodger ace.

"I face more pressure every day just being a Negro," he said.

Gibson wasn't alone. By the mid-'60s, black athletes were becoming increasingly vocal about racial inequality—and writing about it in autobiographies, such as Frank Robinson's *My Life in Baseball*, Orlando Cepeda's *My Ups and Downs in Baseball*, and Gibson's first, *From Ghetto to Glory*.

At the same time, *Sports Illustrated* came out with a special series on the black athlete, in which it exposed the inequalities lurking in boxing rings, baseball dugouts, basketball benches, football huddles—and just about every other playing field. Black athletes, the magazine reported, were excluded from social activities on college campuses, taunted with racial slurs in professional arenas, subjected to tokenism in most sports, and regarded as lacking intellect across the board.

The popular press—*Life*, *Time*, *Newsweek*, *U.S. News and World Report*—took up the issue as well, running stories on Harry Edwards, an instructor at San Jose State, who was mobilizing black athletes into boycotting the upcoming Olympics in Mexico City. The group's goal was to draw attention to the exploitation of black athletes in the United States and abroad. It called for, among other things, the reinstatement of Muhammad Ali's heavyweight title, the hiring of more black coaches, and the removal of Nazi sympathizer Avery Brundage as head of the International Olympic Committee.

According to founding Chipmunk George Vecsey, "the first generation of black players all had to be Sidney Poitier; they all had to be the good Negro, the man who came to dinner, Jackie Robinson included. But there was another generation of black players; the core of the Cardinals in the mid-'60s was black: Bob Gibson. Curt Flood. Lou Brock. They were all college guys. They had their opinions. These guys were taking on the role of teachers and shit-stirrers."

On July 1, Gibson took the mound looking to break Drysdale's scoreless-inning streak. The Cards were in Los Angeles, and Gibson was facing none other than Drysdale himself.

The suspense ended quickly. With two outs in the bottom of the first, Gibson gave up back-to-back singles. Then, with runners on first and third, he threw a fastball that tailed inside, surprising backup catcher Johnny Edwards. The ball skipped off Edwards's glove, allowing a run to score. It was the first run Gibson had surrendered in a month, and the only one he'd give up in the game. His streak had ended at forty-seven innings, but he beat the Dodgers and raised his record to 10-5.

Gibson wouldn't stop there. He'd go on to have one of the greatest seasons in baseball history. Displaying complete mastery of the craft of pitching—and riding his anger over the dual losses of King and Kennedy—he'd finish twenty-eight of his thirty-four starts. He'd compile a 22-9 record, 268 strikeouts, and a 1.12 ERA—the lowest in more than half a century.

"It was otherworldly," says Tim McCarver, looking back on Gibson's 1968 performance. "It staggered the imagination that during one stretch a guy pitched ninety-five innings and gave up two runs. He had eight shutouts in ten starts. . . . Keep in mind, every team had not only two or three, but in some cases four or five guys who could pummel you. . . . That season, [Gibson] could throw a ball to a spot no more than two balls wide, at will. Almost blindfolded. You can't make 1968 bigger than it was."

The Cardinals would ride Gibson's golden right arm to the National League pennant, nine games ahead of the San Francisco Giants.

On July 9, 1968, Denny McLain staggered across the infield in the Houston Astrodome, surrounded by nearly fifty thousand fans, plus another twenty million watching on television.

This was the 1968 All-Star Game, and McLain was hung over.

The hard-throwing right-hander figured he wouldn't see the lighter side of a pitching rubber for days—not after hurling a complete game two days earlier, when he beat the Athletics 5–4 in the first half of a doubleheader. Nobody would want to screw with his arm, especially since he was leading the Majors with sixteen wins. At that pace, he'd break Dizzy Dean's thirty-win mark set in 1934.

After Detroit had played the second half of that doubleheader against Oakland, McLain and his wife, Sharon, had scooted out of Tiger Stadium, climbed into a private Lear jet, and flown to Las Vegas. At the Riviera, McLain drank free booze, first while parked at the craps table, and then, once the sun came up, while playing blackjack. After folding his cards, he collected Sharon, got back into the rented jet, and took off for Disneyland, where they killed a few hours before hightailing it to Houston.

The All-Star Game was going into its fifth inning when American League manager Dick Williams called upon his weary pitcher. The game had been a nail-biter—the only run to cross the plate had been on a double play—and Williams had already used Luis Tiant and Blue Moon Odom. It was only natural that he'd turn to the winningest guy on his squad. A bedraggled McLain downed a few Pepsis and made his way to the mound. Undaunted—or perhaps too hung over to notice—McLain faced a lineup that included Henry Aaron, Willie Mays, and Willie McCovey. He survived, shutting out the National League for two innings.

With his pitching chores completed, McLain showered, grabbed Sharon, and flew back to Vegas for one last taste of the dice. Hours later, he dropped Sharon back home in Michigan and then took off for Minnesota, where the Tigers were set to begin the second half of the season. The three-day joyride had gone off without a hitch—until the door of the jet flew open at eighteen thousand feet. As the plane nosedived, McLain grabbed his oxygen mask, certain his luck had run out. But when the pilot deftly stabilized the aircraft at ten thousand feet, McLain's mind did a one-eighty: how could anything possibly go wrong the rest of this blessed season?

It wasn't the first time McLain had pushed the envelope. Rumors surrounding his oddball behavior had been circulating for years.

It was, for instance, popular knowledge that he had a habit of downing twenty-four bottles of Pepsi a day. Instead of causing concern, the addiction only tantalized. How could he pitch effectively on a diet of carbonated water and sugar? Did he have a magical waistline?

Ed Schober, a local merchandising director at Pepsi, didn't wait for answers. He knew a good thing when he saw one—and a twenty-four-bottle-drinking media-friendly pitchman qualified. He offered McLain an endorsement deal valued at fifteen thousand dollars per year and agreed to ship ten cases (240 bottles) of Pepsi a week to the pitcher's door. McLain accepted.

When it became known that McLain was an accomplished organist who performed in clubs in and around Michigan, the higher-ups at Hammond had the same reaction as Schober's. They offered the pitcher thirty thousand dollars per year in exchange for plugging their latest keyboard, the x-77. McLain gleefully cashed that check, too.

With all that endorsement money, McLain was making significantly more off the field than he was on it. But while most fans saw him as a harmless flake—an image he enhanced by sporting square, Clark-Kent-style eyeglasses, and pulling the brim of his cap low on his forehead—the young hurler was also gaining a reputation as a shady character.

In 1967 the Tigers had found themselves—along with the Twins, the White Sox, and the Red Sox—in one of the tightest pennant races in history. McLain had seventeen wins at the end of August but then suddenly lost his groove, turning in three subpar performances. On September 18, with a chance to redeem himself against Boston, he lasted only two innings, surrendering four runs—and Detroit's one-game lead in the standings.

After the loss, McLain told the press he'd been nursing a sore foot. One of the more popular explanations he'd given was that he'd fallen asleep on the couch while watching TV and then stubbed his toes jumping up to investigate a noise in the garage.

The story seemed a little farfetched.

Nonetheless, McLain was out for two weeks in late September. He came back just in time to face the Angels in the final game of the season. It was a must-win for the Tigers; if they lost, their season was over. If they won, they'd face Boston in a one-game playoff.

McLain wasn't sharp; he gave up a home run in the second and was gone before the end of the third. The Tigers lost the game, 8–5, and the pennant by one game.

A few years later, *Sports Illustrated* would publish a cover story on McLain, tying him to gamblers and loan sharks—and placing him with mobster Tony Giacalone at the time he'd hurt his foot. According to SI, Giacalone had strong-armed McLain into paying a forty-six-thousand-dollar gambling debt and, to make his point, slammed his heel down on the pitcher's instep—dislocating his toes.

McLain would deny the incident, but in his 2007 memoir, *I Told You I Wasn't Perfect*, he'd admit to having been "spooked" that September, constantly worried that a gambler would be looking for money owed by his partner. McLain identified his cohort as Ed Schober, the merchandising director from Pepsi. It seems the two had paired up in a bookmaking operation and gotten in over their heads. To darken the shadow over McLain, SI would also report that Giacalone had bet heavily on the Red Sox and the Twins to win the pennant and made a large bet on the Angels in McLain's final start.

Some people wondered whether trouble was in McLain's DNA. Growing up in a working-class suburb of Chicago, McLain had modeled himself after his chain-smoking, beer-guzzling, belt-swinging father. He'd even learned to play the organ to be like his keyboard-loving dad. But unlike Tom McLain, a Major League wannabe who never made it to the pros, Denny was talented. He was a standout on his Little League and Babe Ruth teams and a star at Mount Carmel High School, where he played short, pitched, and led his teams to three titles. The White Sox snatched him up out of school—whereupon McLain promptly screwed himself out of the job. In the words of his minor league manager Ira Hutchinson, "He thought he was king of everything. You couldn't talk to him."

The White Sox dumped the young McLain on the Tigers, and manager Chuck Dressen took the kid under his wing. The sixty-nine-year-old skipper taught his protégé everything he knew: the curve, the change-up, and the Dressen method of handicapping horses. McLain ran with the knowledge, showing talent on the mound and an equally impressive aptitude for the ponies. Unfortunately, he was soon in hot water with Tigers management after being found placing bets on the pressroom phone.

Now, five years later, in 1968, Mayo Smith was at the helm of the Tigers and McLain was blossoming into the ace of the staff. The front office, which had been looking to unload their headache of a pitcher over the winter, was suddenly featuring him in team promotions. And McLain was living up to the hype. After his All-Star performance, he went 9-1 before losing two games in a row for the first time all season.

On Sunday, August 25, the Tigers flew into McLain's hometown, Chicago, where the Democratic National Convention was set to begin the following day. It was no secret that delegates would be siding with Lyndon Johnson loyalists and nominating Hubert Humphrey as their presidential candidate.

The air was hot and sticky. The cab drivers were on strike. And thousands of antiwar activists were amassing in Grant Park.

Anticipating a week of protests, Mayor Richard Daley had put the city in a stranglehold. He installed bulletproof doors at the entrance to the convention center—the International Amphitheatre—and erected a barbed-wire fence around the building. He also deployed nearly twelve thousand police and fifteen thousand soldiers and National Guardsmen, insisting, "As long as I'm mayor of this town, there's going to be law and order in Chicago."

In a nod to Scott McKenzie's recent hit song "San Francisco (Be Sure to Wear Flowers in Your Hair)," the *Chicago Seed*, the city's most prominent underground newspaper, warned its readers, "If you're coming to Chicago, be sure to wear some armor in your hair."

It was good advice.

By the time the convention opened on Monday, the streets had become a battleground between police and protesters. Violence and chaos were the order of the day, with marches and rallies broken up by police wielding fists, nightsticks, and tear gas. At midweek, television cameras captured a melee in front of the Conrad Hilton Hotel. On the nightly news, the TV networks treated their national audiences to a full-scale riot, complete with out-of-control cops attacking unarmed demonstrators.

Watching inside the convention center on closed-circuit monitors, Senator Abraham Ribicoff of Connecticut condemned what he called "Gestapo tactics on the streets of Chicago."

Denny McLain, a proud product of Chicago, spoke about the event to *Sports Illustrated*.

"I had three uncles on the police force," McLain said. "Our family was as political as any family making under $10,000 could be. I remember one of my uncles, who went about six-five, 1,000 pounds . . . telling me what a great thrill it was to beat on people legally. You weren't allowed to be different in Chicago in those days."

After two days in Chicago, McLain had to leave his hometown behind—and in chaos. He flew with the Tigers back to Detroit, where he hurled a complete-game victory against the Angels. He then did the same against Baltimore and Minnesota.

On September 10, he beat the Angels in Anaheim. He now had twenty-nine wins—and a bulging appointment book. He hobnobbed with pop music star Glen Campbell, showed up at Disneyland to book some off-season appearances, stopped at Capitol Records to shoot publicity photos, lounged by Tommy Smothers's pool while going over a script for a Smothers Brothers TV special, and swung by Vine Street to tape an organ performance for an episode of *The Steve Allen Show*.

The following passage is from an article by Alfred Wright in *Sports Illustrated*:

> Denny McLain bathed happily in all the front-page fuss. . . . He managed to create a kind of ersatz Hollywood of his own right in his suburban Detroit split-level. From morning to night the place was choked with booking agents in sideburns and mod suits and their miniskirted chicks—all of them shouting at each other and over the long-distance phone while McLain, accompanied by the members of his four-piece combo, was down in the den, shattering neighbors' eardrums with his X-77 Hammond organ as ABC-TV cameras cranked away.

Detroit's daily papers, the *News* and the *Free Press*, out on strike for 267 days, restarted their presses in August and were running nonstop headlines about McLain, boosting circulation and resuscitating sales. As for the national sports media, it hadn't been this hyper-focused since Yankees slugger Roger Maris made his celebrated chase of Babe Ruth's single-season home run record in 1961. McLain's baby face was also popping up in *Time*, *Newsweek*, *and Life*.

"Me? Revel in the media? Damn right," McLain wrote in his memoir, looking back on the media circus he'd created. "Baseball was all show-biz, and that's why there were writers covering it in the first place. I wanted the attention of the writers so badly that I'd get depressed between starts because they weren't in front of my locker. I wanted to talk about anything and everything in grand fashion, and be the center of attention."

McLain got his wish. There was such a flood of media requests that his agent, Frank Scott, had taken to running interference between the pitching star and the press.

"A lot of things are contingent on his winning thirty," Scott told reporters. "We have eight to ten deals already, but twenty or so are waiting on his winning thirty."

On Saturday, September 14, McLain was scheduled to pitch before a packed house at Tiger Stadium and a national TV audience. As Jack Saylor wrote in the *Detroit Free Press*, "this was the World Series, Mardi Gras and the Academy Awards all wrapped up in one."

McLain started the morning with his customary breakfast: eggs, sausage, and Pepsi. When he got to the park, he saw that Detroit left-hander Mickey Lolich—whose solid 14-9 record had been lost in the McLain hoopla—had posted a sign in the clubhouse. "Attention sportswriters: Denny McLain's locker this way."

To add to the circus, Dizzy Dean himself showed up. "I'll tell ya, I think he's a great pitcher," he told the media horde in his thick Arkansas accent. "He pitches a lot like me . . . throws it hard and light, although he's not as fast as I was. He kicks up that left leg the same way I did."

McLain felt loose and ready, and chatted with reporters. When he stepped on the mound, though, he needed more than confidence, he needed his best stuff—and he didn't have it. He gave up a homer to Oakland's young slugger Reggie Jackson in the fourth, an RBI single to Bert Campaneris in the fifth, and another homer to Jackson in the sixth.

When the Tigers came to bat in the bottom of the ninth, they trailed 4–3. Their bats, which had supported McLain all season, came to his rescue again—first on a fielder's choice to tie it, then on a Willie Horton single to win it. When the ball jumped off Horton's bat, McLain got so excited he leapt up in the dugout and slammed his head against a concrete slab.

"I almost knocked myself out on the dugout ceiling," he said later. "I was absolutely, no question about it, out cold for a moment."

His next start may have lacked the drama of his record-tying win, but it had plenty of controversy. The Tigers were hosting the Yankees, who were well on the far side of greatness. Whitey Ford had retired. Roger Maris and Elston Howard had been traded. Mickey Mantle had moved to first base to save his broken-down legs. The team was in fifth place—eighteen games behind the Tigers. Since Detroit had already clinched the pennant and McLain's thirtieth was in the books, barely nine thousand fans showed up.

McLain had a commanding 6–1 lead and was all but assured of notching his thirty-first win when his childhood idol came to bat in the eighth. The thirty-six-year-old Mantle, limping slightly, had nine more games left to the season and, most likely, his career. The baseball universe knew that the aging star had been sitting on 534 home runs for almost a month—and still needed one more to pass Jimmie Foxx on the all-time list.

McLain called catcher Jim Price to the mound.

"I want Mantle to hit one," he said.

Price nodded, and as he got back to the catcher's box, relayed the message to Mantle.

McLain delivered as promised. His grooved his next two pitches—flat fastballs, right down Broadway—but Mantle took them both for strikes.

Price called time and went back to the mound. He told McLain that Mantle wanted to know whether another meatball was coming.

"*What the fuck? What are we missing here?*" McLain said. "*Yes!*"

Price went back to the plate and relayed the message to Mantle before going into his crouch.

McLain threw another fat one and Mantle gave it a healthy rip, but fouled it off.

Exasperated, McLain yelled to Mantle, "Mickey, where do you want the fucking ball?"

In McLain's words, "[Mantle] put his hand out about balls-high on the outside part of the plate. I nod my head and throw it there, and Mantle hits a line drive into the upper deck just inside the foul pole. . . . When he got to second he took his hat off and acknowledged the crowd. When he got to the plate, he looked at me, waved the cap again, and shouted, 'Thank you.'"

After the game, the Yankees retrieved the ball. Mantle signed it and gave it to McLain. According to Jane Leavy's *The Last Boy*, the inscription read, "Denny, thanks for one of the greatest moments in my entire career, Mickey."

One person who couldn't understand the gesture was Bob Gibson. "I would have dropped my pants on the mound before I would have deferred to an opposing player that way," he said when asked about the incident. "My method of showing respect for a guy like Mickey Mantle would have been to reach back for something extra with which to blow his ass away, if I could. But I guess that's why McLain was on the cover of *Time* and I was still borrowing money from insurance policies."

On September 28, in his last start of the season, McLain had a 1–0 lead against the Senators in the bottom of the seventh when Mayo Smith removed him for a pinch-hitter.

"You need a rest," Smith told McLain.

McLain had been a workhorse all season, throwing 28 complete games and 336 innings. But he still felt strong and thought he could secure his thirty-second win. He marched out of the dugout, furious, and broke every light bulb in the tunnel leading to the showers. The Tigers went on to lose 2–1, but the loss was credited to relief pitcher Don McMahon.

The Tigers would wind up with 103 wins, the most in the Majors.

As for McLain, he finished the season at 31-6—and was hurtling toward a showdown with the irascible, unhittable Bob Gibson.

16

On October 2, 1968, the World Series opened at Busch Stadium in St. Louis, and the matchup promised to be a classic.

UPI hyped the "supercool" Bob Gibson versus the "super-flake" Denny McLain.

Sports Illustrated wrote about the "ornery cuss" and the "garrulous Gus."

Arthur Daley, writing in the *New York Times*, summed it up this way: "Not since the two top gunslingers of the Old West blazed away at each other on a dusty street of some border town has there been a shootout to match the showdown . . . between Denny McLain with 31 notches on the handle of his trusty six-shooter and Bob Gibson with 22."

The night before game one, McLain held court in the lounge of the Sheraton-Jefferson Hotel in downtown St. Louis, where he played the organ until closing. He even dedicated "Sweet Georgia Brown," the Harlem Globetrotters' theme song, to former 'Trotter Bob Gibson.

Gibson spent the evening in seclusion.

The way Gibson saw it, he and McLain were simply cut from different flannel, and the differences in their personalities were heightened by the climate of the times.

"There's no way to gloss over the fact that racial perception contributed a great deal to my reputation," Gibson said years later. "I pitched in a period of civil unrest, of black power and clenched fists and burning buildings and assassinations and riots in the streets. There was a country full of angry black people in those days, and by extension—and by my demeanor on the mound—I was perceived to be one of them."

To no one's surprise, Gibson opened the Series in top form. He struck out seven of the first nine batters and mowed down Detroit's powerful lineup.

McLain struggled. His arm was killing him. He'd gotten an injection of cortisone before the game and popped a few greenies (amphetamines) to boost his energy. By the third inning his shoulder was throbbing, and when he was lifted for a pinch hitter in the sixth, the Tigers were down 3–0.

After eight innings, Gibson had fourteen strikeouts and was leading 4–0. Tiger shortstop Mickey Stanley led off the ninth with a single. Up next was the heart of the order: Al Kaline, Norm Cash, and Willie Horton. Gibson went to work on Kaline, striking him out for the third time. The crowd roared—and then did so again, although Gibson had no idea why.

Tim McCarver got out of his crouch and pointed with his mitt toward the scoreboard behind Gibson's head.

Gibson yelled at his catcher. "Throw the goddamn ball back, will you! C'mon, c'mon, let's go!"

McCarver pointed again, and this time Gibson turned around and saw the flashing message: *Gibson's fifteenth strikeout in one game ties the World Series record held by Sandy Koufax.*

Gibson turned back toward the plate, uneasily raised his cap, and yelled at McCarver to get back to work. The next batter, Norm Cash, went down for strikeout number sixteen.

The crowd got to its feet again.

Gibson, his face shiny with sweat, took a deep breath and waited impatiently for the cheers to die down.

Then he struck out Willie Horton on four pitches and walked off the mound with a complete-game, five-hit shutout—and a record-shattering seventeen strikeouts.

On October 6, with the Cardinals leading the Series two games to one, Gibson and McLain faced each other again, this time in Tiger Stadium. Again McLain was off his game. A steady rain had disrupted his warmups, and he gave up four runs in the first three innings. After a second rain delay, lasting for more than an hour, McLain was gone. Gibson, on the other hand, was overpowering. He struck out ten, held the Tigers to one run, went the distance, hit a homer, and collected his seventh straight World Series victory.

The Cardinals were within one victory of a world championship.

Fifty-three thousand fans jammed into Tiger Stadium for game five. As they settled into their seats, guitarist and singer José Feliciano made his way to centerfield to perform the national anthem. Feliciano, a lifelong Tigers fan, had just hit number three on the Billboard charts with his interpretation of the Doors' *Light My Fire* and had been invited at the suggestion of Tigers announcer Ernie Harwell.

"Ladies and gentlemen, your attention please," came the disembodied voice from the PA. "Please rise and join the singing of our national anthem, which will be played by Merle Alvey's band, and will be sung by José Feliciano."

Feliciano took his seat on a stool in front of Alvey's musicians. Dressed in a maroon suit with dark sunglasses hiding his eyes, he crooned the anthem in a style that was quickly becoming his trademark: stirring, soulful, and infused with a Latin-jazz feel. It was pure Feliciano. It was also unlike any version heard before. For the blind singer, who was born in Puerto Rico and raised in New York City, his rendition was a love letter to America, a thank-you to the country that had given him so much. For many onlookers, it was blasphemy, a gesture of disrespect for the country, and by extension, an antiwar statement being made on the most inappropriate stage.

While Feliciano sang, the crowd offered up a smattering of boos and cheers. The five band members stood at attention behind the singer, apparently unsure of what to do. No one lifted an instrument.

In no time, NBC's switchboard lit up with calls from enraged viewers. Veterans were said to throw their shoes at their TV sets. Conservatives ripped into Feliciano for sitting on a stool and wearing sunglasses, apparently unaware that he was blind.

NBC quickly cut away from the singer. After the third line of the song, "*what so proudly we hailed*," Feliciano wasn't seen again on screen. Instead, viewers were shown the flag, the color guard, the ballplayers—anybody or anything but Feliciano.

Tim McCarver spoke about Feliciano's performance years later. "The social unrest and the political situation was the backdrop for that Series and that season," he told the *New York Times*. "[Feliciano's anthem] was longer than most versions but it didn't bother me at all. It bothered some people. . . . But, back then, even our sideburns bothered people."

After the performance, Harwell escorted Feliciano to a box behind first base, where the singer sat with his guide dog, Trudy, and his wife, Hilda. They stayed for a few innings before leaving for the airport.

When questioned, Feliciano told reporters, "I love America. The only reason I sang it that way was to express my love for my country. I am very happy that I did it that way."

Once the commotion died down, Tigers starter Mickey Lolich got going. He had a shaky first inning—giving up three quick runs—but soon settled down.

In the fifth inning, with St. Louis leading 3–2, Cardinals speed demon Lou Brock doubled to left-center. The next batter, second baseman Julian Javier, singled to left. Willie Horton charged the ball and threw to the plate as Brock raced home for the insurance run. Horton's throw, a bullet that hit Detroit catcher Bill Freehan's mitt on a single bounce, beat Brock by a step. The play seemed to rejuvenate the Tigers, who went on to win 5–3. They were still alive but, to take the championship, would need to win two straight games in St. Louis.

Detroit manager Mayo Smith, facing a do-or-die situation, had little choice but to go with his ace for game six. Pitching on two days' rest—and with his right arm shot full of Xylocaine and cortisone—McLain returned to form. The Tigers exploded for ten runs in the third inning, and McLain sailed to a 13–1 victory.

The Series came down to game seven. Winner-take-all. Bob Gibson was going for the Cards on three days' rest; Mickey Lolich for the Tigers on two.

Neither team scored in the first six innings. Then, in the top of the seventh, with two out and two on, Jim Northrup drove a Gibson fastball to deep left center. Curt Flood, who two months earlier had been declared "Baseball's Best Center Fielder" by *Sports Illustrated*, lost sight of the ball and took a couple of steps in toward home plate. When he reversed direction, he slipped on wet grass and the ball skidded by him. Two runs scored, and when Bill Freehan doubled in Northrup, the Tigers led 3–0.

That was all Lolich needed. He won 4–1 and went the distance for his third complete-game victory of the Series. The Tigers were world champions and the unheralded Lolich was their hero, leaving McLain to celebrate in his shadow.

Six days later, on October 16, with the World Series fading from the spotlight, the sports world was focused on Mexico City. Having just won the gold and the bronze in the two hundred meters, Olympians Tommie Smith and John Carlos stood on the victory podium about to accept their medals. Harry Edwards had called off his Olympic boycott, but Carlos, who was born and raised in Harlem, and Smith, the son of Texas sharecroppers, hadn't let go of the cause. Each wore the badge of the Olympic Project for Human Rights, and as the national anthem was being played, both men turned away from the American flag, bowed their heads, and raised their black-gloved fists in a salute to black power.

The crowd seemed to make little of the gesture, but the press jumped on it as a subversive act, a fuck-you to America.

To Smith and Carlos, the statement was not one of hate but of frustration.

Kenny Moore, writing in *Sports Illustrated*, supported the athletes. "Any resemblance to Lady Liberty lifting her torch was ironic," Moore wrote. "Smith and Carlos were taking U.S. society to task for having failed to extend liberty and justice to all."

The U.S. Olympic Committee didn't share Moore's opinion. Two days after the incident, it suspended both athletes from the U.S. track team and expelled them from the Olympic Village. Smith and Carlos, the Committee said, had "violated the basic standards of sportsmanship and good manners, which are so highly regarded in the United States."

By 1968, Richard Nixon had been out of elective office for eight years. After losing the 1960 presidential election to John F. Kennedy—and the 1962 California gubernatorial race to Democrat Pat Brown—he had opted for private practice and joined a Wall Street law firm. But somewhere along the way, he'd regained his lust for political power and was back on the campaign trail. In August, at the Republican National

Convention, he won his party's nomination for president, beating out his chief opponent, Ronald Reagan.

One person who wouldn't be campaigning for Nixon was Jackie Robinson. The one-time Nixonite had switched allegiances when the candidate courted South Carolina senator Strom Thurmond. The interaction was more than a handshake. Nixon had given the avowed segregationist veto power over his choice of running mate (Maryland governor Spiro Agnew). He also had Thurmond arrange a get-together with southern delegates, a secret meeting in which Nixon promised to appoint like-minded Supreme Court justices.

In the primary, Robinson had publicly backed New York governor Nelson Rockefeller. When Rockefeller got trounced, Robinson switched his allegiance to the Democratic nominee Hubert Humphrey. Anybody but his old friend Richard Nixon.

"He's sold out," Robinson told a reporter. "He's really prostituted himself to get the Southern vote."

Days before the general election, Humphrey gained significant ground when news broke that President Johnson had made an offer to the North Vietnamese: Let's talk peace and halt bombing while we do so.

But Nixon, seeing the election slip away, sabotaged the talks. In public, he trumpeted Johnson's success, but in private he urged the South Vietnamese not to meet with the North, thus extending the war to Election Day—and keeping America hungry for a new administration.

Nixon's plan worked; he squeaked by Humphrey, taking the election by less than 1 percent of the popular vote—31,783,783 to 31,271,839.

America had a new president.

And once again, Jackie Robinson was on the losing side of electoral politics.

17

The 1968 baseball season was barely over when the press began referring to it as "the year of the pitcher." Of course, that also meant it had been a year of weak hitting. In the American League, Boston's Carl Yastrzemski won the batting title with a .301 average. In the National League, only five players hit above .300.

The lopsided numbers didn't go unnoticed.

Baseball's higher-ups had spent the off-season tweaking the game, trying to restore power into big-league bats. They shrunk the strike zone, lowered the pitcher's mound, and in several ballparks, brought in the fences. Some owners sped up their infields with artificial turf.

There were other changes in 1969, too.

Baseball had a new commissioner, Bowie Kuhn, the forty-two-year-old insider who'd served as assistant counsel to the National League. The game also expanded to twenty-four teams: The Seattle Pilots and the Kansas City Royals were added in the AL, and the San Diego Padres and the Montreal Expos in the NL. Each league was split into two divisions, the East and the West, and come October the winners of each division would play a best-of-five playoff series to decide the pennant.

In New York, the most dramatic change was taking place at Shea Stadium. The Mets were no longer the worst team on the planet or, for that matter, the city. Under new manager Gil Hodges, the team had started out in typical losing fashion, going 18-23, but then reversed direction and reeled off eleven wins in a row. In the Bronx, the Yankees were trending in the opposite direction, and CBS, their absentee owner, didn't seem to care. On June 17, as the Yankees dropped five games below .500, the Mets raised their record to 31-27.

One major reason for the Mets' surprising turnaround was fresh-faced pitching phenom Tom Seaver. A graduate of USC, Seaver was all of twenty-one when the Mets signed him in 1966—and twenty-two when he joined the big-league club. Right out of the gate, he'd shown a blazing fastball, hard slider, and a burning desire to win.

One of Seaver's teammates, Ron Swoboda, remembers his early years on the Mets.

"What's interesting about Seaver was there was no sort of learning curve," Swoboda says. "He was a great pitcher from the first game. . . . It was hard to tell Tom Seaver in '67 from Tom Seaver in '68 and '69 in terms of stuff and how he pitched, and how tough he was. He had Hall of Fame stuff from the get go, all he needed was the numbers."

Equally important to Seaver's stuff—and in direct contrast to his boyish good looks—was his maturity on the pitching mound. In his second Major League start, Seaver threw seven and a third strong innings against the Cubs. In the eighth, manager Wes Westrum (who'd taken the reins from Casey Stengel in 1965) strolled to the mound. Seaver had the confidence to admit he was running out of steam, effectively taking himself out of a game that he was winning 3–1 and exhibiting a self-awareness rarely seen in wide-eyed rookies.

It was pure luck that had brought Seaver to Queens in the first place. In 1965 the Dodgers had drafted him out of college but never made an offer, thus landing him back in the draft pool. The following June, the Braves selected him and agreed to a fifty-thousand-dollar bonus, but there was a hitch. The USC Trojans had already played two exhibition games, and since college players couldn't sign pro contracts once their season had begun, the deal was dead. Worse yet, by signing with the Braves, Seaver had lost his amateur status. He was left without a team, college or pro.

"I wrote to the commissioner [William Eckert]," Seaver later told the *New York Times*. "I told him that it wasn't fair to me and that I was being victimized by circumstances. So he notified the other clubs that any team willing to match the Braves' price could enter a special drawing for my services. The Mets, Phillies, and Indians responded and the Mets drew my name out of a hat. So here I am."

Seaver was named Rookie of the Year, and in his first two big-league seasons collected thirty-two wins. He'd also shown little patience for his older teammates' losing mentality, the sad-sack attitude that had permeated all of Queens.

As George Vecsey wrote in the *New York Times*, "the Youth of America arrived in the spring of 1967 with thick thighs and a stocky butt and a wise head and excellent pitching mechanics and a cackling laugh about clubhouse pranks, but no sense of humor about losing. . . . Seaver fixed us with a cold stare and did not allow himself to be incorporated into the shtick of the Mets."

Seaver told *Sports Illustrated*, "When I came to the Mets, there was an aura of defeatism on the team, and I refused to accept it. That lovable loser stuff was not funny to me."

What Seaver wanted was a team of strivers, a lineup filled with Henry Aarons. He had idolized Aaron growing up in Fresno, California, and continued to look up to him when he got to the Majors. In his rookie year, when the Mets were playing the Braves in Atlanta, Seaver sheepishly asked Aaron for a signed copy of the slugger's new autobiography and then ever so politely suggested that Aaron might bring it on his next trip to Shea. Seaver figured Aaron had more important things on his mind, but the day the Braves arrived in New York, Seaver found sitting on the stool in front of his locker an inscribed copy of *Aaron, r.f.*

"Henry was always first with me," Seaver told SI. "I don't find it strange at all that a white boy who wanted to become a Major League pitcher identified with a black hitter. I thought of Aaron as excellence. He was so much fun to sit and watch because he was consistent, dedicated and yet capable of making the game look so easy to play. Confidence flowed out of him, and I memorized his every move."

At the end of June, the Mets were seven and a half games behind the Cubs, but they were playing well above .500, and their young ace was 12-3 with a 2.57 ERA.

More important than Seaver's record, though, was the energy he'd injected into the Mets' dugout—and the city. For the first time since they came into being, the Mets were being taken seriously.

In 1969 John Lindsay was in his fourth year as mayor of New York. He was blond, six-four, and movie-star-handsome. Lindsay, forty-seven years old, was born into an upper-middle-class family in Manhattan. He'd gone to Yale and Yale Law School and then spent seven years representing the city's 17th Congressional District, a wealthy enclave popularly known as the Silk Stocking District.

Lindsay was a Republican in name only. He'd voted for the Civil Rights Act of 1964, opposed the Vietnam War, and refused to back his party's nominee, Barry Goldwater, against LBJ in the '64 presidential race.

So it stood to reason that the city's middle-class voters saw the dapper, liberal Lindsay as the second coming of JFK and in November 1965, in a surge of late-night votes, elected him mayor over the diminutive comptroller Abe Beame.

Lindsay was crowned king of New York on January 1, 1966—and from day one, his kingdom was in turmoil.

Just as he was being inaugurated, thirty-six thousand transit workers walked off their jobs, leaving six million commuters without bus or subway service and crippling the city. Michael J. Quill, the head of the Transport Workers Union, set the tone for the contract negotiations when he called the new mayor a "pipsqueak." The strike was settled three months later, but Lindsay's troubles—and his reputation as a political lightweight—were just beginning.

In February 1968, eleven thousand sanitation workers hit the picket lines demanding a $600-per-year raise. Lindsay refused to go higher than $400—and the mounds of stinking garbage grew to more than a hundred thousand tons. The governor, Nelson Rockefeller, eventually stepped in and settled the issue by offering $425, but the strike had lasted nine long, smelly days—and city dwellers placed the blame squarely on Lindsay's shoulders.

It's possible the mayor's greatest achievement can be seen in what *didn't* happen on his watch. The night of Martin Luther King's assassination, Lindsay, with only a detective at his side, had walked the streets of Harlem talking to the neighborhood's mostly black residents. He was calming and consoling, and his gesture may have been the reason New York escaped the riots that ravaged so many other cities.

But nobody was handing out credit for problems that didn't happen—especially when there were so many more that did.

Most notably, at the start of the 1968 school year, fifty-four thousand public school teachers had walked off the job—and stayed off for nearly two months.

Then, in February 1969, a nor'easter dumped a foot and a half of snow on the city, handing Lindsay a made-to-order shot at redemption. But he still came up short. Many neighborhoods went unplowed for days, and the borough of Queens was ignored for more than a week. Schools closed. Postal services, sanitation pickups, and other services were erratic at best. Queens residents, barricaded in their homes, accounted for nearly half of the forty-two deaths attributed to the storm.

Perhaps to salvage his plummeting poll numbers, Lindsay visited the borough to survey the damage. When his limousine got stuck in the snow, he got out and walked the blanketed streets alone. Residents booed him. In Kew Garden Hills, one woman shouted, "You should be ashamed of yourself." In Fresh Meadows, another yelled, "Get away, you bum."

It was all front-page news.

So when the time came for the Republican primary, voters passed over Lindsay in favor of the little-known John Marchi, a state senator from Staten Island. The Democrats didn't want Lindsay, either. They'd nominated the conservative comptroller, Mario Procaccino, who established an anticrime platform by warning voters, "It's safer to be in Vietnam than to be in New York at three o'clock in the morning."

So in July 1969, Lindsay was running for reelection as an independent.

He didn't stand a prayer.

On Sunday, July 20, at 4:18 p.m. Eastern daylight time, the Apollo 11 lunar module, the Eagle, became the first manned spacecraft in history to land on the moon. One hundred two hours, forty-five minutes, and forty seconds after launch, Commander Neil Armstrong radioed to NASA, "Houston, Tranquility Base here. The Eagle has landed."

The historic mission fulfilled the pledge President Kennedy had made eight years earlier. On that day, in 1961, he told Congress: "I believe that this nation should commit itself to achieving the goal, before this decade is out, of landing a man on the moon and returning him safely to the earth. No single space project in this period will be more impressive to mankind, or more important for the long-range exploration of space."

The moon landing was broadcast live on national television and reached an estimated six hundred million people around the world. In baseball parks across the United States, games were interrupted in honor of the event.

At Connie Mack Stadium, where the Phillies were hosting the Cubs, players and coaches left the field and stood along the baselines, bowing their heads and joining the crowd in a silent prayer for the three astronauts—Commander Armstrong, Command Module Pilot Michael Collins, and Lunar Module Pilot Edwin "Buzz" Aldrin—to return safely. The game resumed after the 12,393 fans sang along to *God Bless America*.

Similar scenes played out in other Major League parks. Games were stopped; crowds cheered, prayed, and erupted in patriotic fervor.

In the Bronx, where the Yankees were hosting Bat Day, public address announcer Bob Sheppard's voice came through the stadium speakers.

"Ladies and gentlemen, your attention please."

The Yankees and the visiting Washington Senators looked confused as the umpires waved their hands in the air to stop play.

"You will be happy to know," Sheppard said, "that Apollo 11 has landed safely . . ."

The crowd cheered so wildly that no one heard Sheppard's last three words: "on the moon." The din continued for forty-five seconds before *America the Beautiful* rang out through the loudspeakers. When the song was over, the fans let out another mighty cheer, the kind reserved for a home team taking the field on opening day—or leaving it after winning the World Series.

In Montreal, where the Mets had dropped the first game of a doubleheader, the Expos delayed the start of the second game so fans could listen to the broadcast of the landing without interruption.

Later that evening, after taking the second game of the twinbill, the Mets arrived at the Montreal airport only to be delayed by a mechanical problem that grounded their plane. It was almost eleven o'clock when they finally made their way through customs—and spotted a crowd of people gathered in front of a TV in the airport lounge. On the screen, Neil Armstrong could be seen making his slow-motion descent from the lunar module and then setting foot on the surface of the moon.

Tom Seaver shared his memories of the moment with the *New York Times*: "The thing I remember is Tug McGraw, God bless him, watching Neil Armstrong and saying, 'If we can get a man on the moon, we can win the World Series.'"

Actually, the Mets were already doing the unimaginable. At the All-Star break they were in second place, five games behind the Cubs. Their vaunted pitching staff, the backbone of the team, was as impressive as any in the big leagues. Seaver was 14-5 with a 2.59 ERA; Jerry Koosman was 8-5 with a 1.88 ERA; and rookie Gary Gentry was 9-8 with a 3.36 ERA.

In mid-August, things began to seem even more fated. The Mets had slipped into third place—one game back from the Cardinals and ten behind the Cubs—but when they returned to Shea after a lengthy road trip, they rallied. On August 16, Seaver kicked off a doubleheader with a sparkling 2–0 win against the Padres, and spot-starter Jim McAndrew followed with a gem of his own. The Mets won their next four and, after dropping an extra-inning heartbreaker to the Giants, took another six in a row. On September 10, they snatched first place from the Cubs, and never gave it back—winning thirty-eight of their last fifty games.

Ron Swoboda remembers the invincible feeling the team had during that incredible run.

> It was the first time in my career where I had this sense that you know, hell, we can play with all these people. We already have. And we got on these rolls . . . and we got to a point where we felt like we could go out there every day and win. There isn't anybody we can't play with. We were so much in the moment because we didn't have responsibility; we weren't defending a title. The easiest baseball I ever played in my career was 1969. We just felt like we were sitting up on the waves surfing. Just riding it. It was exciting. We were young enough that there wasn't any sense of fatigue. It was all coming to us, you know. It was pretty cool. Never felt that before. Never felt that after.

The Mets ended the season in first place with a record of 100-62. It was a spectacular turnabout from their inaugural season seven years earlier, when they won all of forty games.

They also rolled through the National League Championship Series, sweeping the Atlanta Braves in a best-of-five playoff. Even Henry Aaron's three home runs, seven RBIs, and .357 batting average weren't enough to stop the Mets.

After the last out—a Tony Gonzalez groundout to third baseman Wayne Garrett—the fifty-four thousand Shea Stadium faithful rushed onto the field in a spontaneous burst of celebration. Fans ran in circles, shouted, and sang. They dug up chunks of sod, made off with home plate and second base, and pulled up sections of the outfield fence.

As they rejoiced, Mayor Lindsay walked into the Mets' locker room to congratulate the city's miracle team. Catcher Jerry Grote and outfielder Rod Gaspar, in full celebration mode, spotted the stiff, buttoned-up politician and doused him in champagne, pouring the bubbly over his neatly coiffed hair as newspaper photographers clicked away.

The Mets had done the unfathomable. The team, which had been a hundred-to-one shot to win the pennant, was on its way to the World Series.

18

The day after the National League Championship Series ended, the Phillies traded Dick Allen to the Cardinals for Curt Flood. It was a seven-player swap: Jerry Johnson and Cookie Rojas also went to the Cardinals while Tim McCarver, Byron Browne, and Joe Hoerner went to the Phillies.

Allen packed his bags without a moment's hesitation. Since the day he and Frank Thomas had come to blows, his relationship with Philadelphia—the team, the writers, and the fans—had been contentious. To his detractors, he was a malcontent. To his supporters, he was unfairly maligned.

Two years earlier, in 1967, he'd cut a pair of tendons and a nerve in his right hand and missed the last five weeks of the season. (He claimed he'd accidentally pushed his palm through the headlight of his car; the press suspected he'd been in a bar fight.)

In 1968 he'd begun showing up late for batting practice, a habit that he apparently found hard to break. In May of '69, he'd arrived late for a game and was hit with a thousand-dollar fine. A month later, he did it again. This time, he was suspended indefinitely—and the terms were left up to him. In July, Allen was still mulling it over.

When the '69 All-Star game at RFK Stadium was rained out, President Nixon invited the players to the White House. Nixon made his way over to lefty pitcher Grant Jackson, the sole Phillies player on the All-Star team (Allen hadn't been elected). The president spoke directly into the pitcher's ear. Naturally, his topic was Jackson's teammate.

"You tell Richie Allen to get back on the job," Nixon said, alluding to Allen's recent suspension. "You tell Richie it's not for the good of the Phillies, or the good of the fans, but for the good of Richie Allen that he get back."

In fact, Allen *had* come out of seclusion the previous Sunday—the day of the moon landing—prompting teammate Cookie Rojas to remark, "This must be the greatest day in history. The astronauts come down on the moon and Richie Allen comes down to Earth."

As for Allen, his way of handling the increased scrutiny had been to sink deeper into the bottle, grow angrier, and double down on his requests to be traded.

In August, he'd come up with a new way to piss off Philly fans—by scratching messages in the infield dirt with his cleats. When Phillies fans harassed him with catcalls and insults, he wrote "Boo." When they continued, he wrote, "Coke," later explaining that he planned on shutting up the hecklers by hitting a homer over the Coca-Cola sign in Connie Mack's outfield.

Baseball Commissioner Bowie Kuhn had attended a doubleheader in Philly, and when he saw Allen cleating the dirt, he'd ordered the Phillies to make him stop. After receiving Kuhn's dictum, Allen had scratched out a couple of messages to the commissioner: "Why?" and "No." When the home plate umpire obliterated the words, Allen wrote "Mom," which he later said was his way of showing that his mother "was the only one who could tell him what to do."

Years later, Bill Conlin of the *Philadelphia Daily News* would look back on Allen's tenure in Philly. "I kept veering from one viewpoint to another; awe, empathy and finally disgust. The awe was for his huge talent, the empathy was for his rebellious streak and his endurance for needless racial hassles—many inflicted by his own ball club. The disgust was for his self-regard and indifference to the team, which became total by 1969. That year I called him the 'Maharishi of Mope.'"

Columnist Jim Murray penned the following in the *Los Angeles Times*:

> The case of the city of Philadelphia vs. Richard Anthony Allen together with the cross-complaint of the defendant might go as follows:
>
> "He drinks." (Does he now? Well, that makes him unique in baseball. Think what it might have done to Babe Ruth's career. Or General Grant's.)

"He forced the trade of Frank Thomas after they got in a fight." (Frank Who?! Oh, you mean the guy who's playing slow-pitch softball now? Is that Richie Allen's fault, too?)

"He feuds with the fans." (You mean those lovely people who call his wife at all hours of the night, throw bricks through his windows, insult his kids? This time, Richie Allen, you've gone too far! I mean, those people *pay* for the privilege. Always remember who pays your salary, boy!)

The point became moot after the 1969 playoffs, when Allen was finally traded. Most involved felt he would be more at home on the Cardinals, a team known for its large contingency of minority players. Some insiders disagreed, feeling that Allen's issues went beyond race, that he often waged war on himself.

Many in the black press had yet another view.

Shortly after the trade, *Ebony* magazine came out with the following about Allen (again using the name Richie instead of Dick): "Richie says he's his own man and he's going to live his own life no matter what, and that should cause little commotion. But Richie Allen is black and he's proud and he has the gumption to be a proud, black man in one of America's most conservative sports. He sprouts a lush Afro that's anchored with long and wide sideburns."

To *Ebony* Allen responded, "In Philly, white barbers won't even let you in their shops, and whites were hollering from the stands, 'Get your hair cut!' My hair is my business. It's neat and clean, and that's what matters to me. I wouldn't say that I hate Whitey, but deep down in my heart, I just can't stand Whitey's ways, man. . . . Philly taught me that people can be the cruelest things in the world."

And so, with Philadelphia fading in his rearview mirror, Dick Allen happily headed off to St. Louis.

On October 11, the 1969 World Series opened in seventy-five-degree weather in Baltimore's Memorial Stadium. Despite their magical season, the Mets were underdogs against the Orioles, who had won 109 games and run away with the AL pennant.

The Series opener did nothing to prove the oddsmakers wrong.

Tom Seaver, who'd won the Cy Young award with a 25-7 record and had beaten the Braves in the first game of the playoff series, left after five innings, down 4–0. The Mets eked out a run against Mike Cuellar, but that was all they'd get. It was Seaver's first loss in twelve starts.

But in game two, the Mets rode the left arm of Jerry Koosman to a 2–1 victory. Then, in New York for game three, they shut out the Orioles, 5–0. The box score gave the victory to Gary Gentry, but the day belonged to center fielder Tommie Agee, whose two spectacular catches prevented as many as five Orioles from crossing the plate.

Going into game four, the Mets were up two games to one and had their ace, Seaver, on the mound seeking redemption. They also had a throng of fans outside the stadium seeking justice.

This was October 15, Moratorium Day, a national day of protest against the Vietnam War—and a time of mourning for the thirty-eight thousand Americans who'd lost their lives in it. Rallies were being held across the country. Ninety thousand protesters gathered on the Boston Common, twenty-two thousand congregated at the Washington Monument, eleven thousand rallied in Iowa, and twenty thousand assembled in Washington State. It was the largest antiwar demonstration America had ever experienced.

In New York, protesters marched on Wall Street, in Central Park, at St. Patrick's Cathedral, and in front of the United Nations. They lit candles, wore black armbands, and pinned peace buttons onto their clothing.

Mayor Lindsay, who supported the antiwar movement—and perhaps sought political gain by backing the moratorium—directed the American flag to be flown at half-mast at all city properties. The move only brought the mayor more headaches. The police refused to lower the flag, as did the fire department.

At Shea Stadium, a military color guard consisting of wounded Vietnam veterans refused to participate in the pregame ceremony unless the stadium flag was fully raised. The Maritime Academy marching band, scheduled to play the national anthem behind singer-actor Gordon MacRae, bowed out altogether.

Bowie Kuhn, baseball's new commissioner and the owners' new mouthpiece, called Lindsay, pleading with him to soften his stance regarding the flag. The mayor relented, and the pregame festivities went ahead as planned—although MacRae sang the *Star-Spangled Banner* with no musical accompaniment.

Once the game started, the nearly fifty-eight thousand fans at Shea had their eyes on the field, not the flag. They cheered, chanted, and rolled out their trademark banners. (One such banner was directed at the Mets' center fielder: "Go, Tommy Agee, Go. Black is beautiful.")

But outside Shea, dozens of fans were still focused on the moratorium. They carried placards and handed out leaflets sponsored by "Met Fans for Peace." On the front of the flyer was a photo of Seaver; on the back were his words pulled from a recent *New York Times* article. "If the Mets can win the World Series," he'd said, "we can get out of Vietnam."

It was common knowledge that Seaver opposed the war. In the same *Times* article, he'd also been quoted as saying, "I think it's perfectly ridiculous what we're doing about the Vietnam situation. It's absurd. When the Series is over, I'm going to have a talk with Ted Kennedy, convey some of my ideas to him and then take an ad in the paper. I feel strongly about it."

When game four started, Seaver was supremely focused. The Mets got him a run in the second, and despite several Baltimore threats, he pitched shutout ball through eight innings. In the ninth, the Orioles threatened again, putting runners on first and third with one out—which is when right fielder Ron Swoboda raced in to make an acrobatic sliding catch of a Brooks Robinson sinking liner. One run scored, but the damage could have been much worse. Instead, the Mets lived to see extra innings.

In the bottom of the tenth, with the game still tied, they got the kind of luck that makes one wonder whether miracles really do happen.

J.C. Martin, pinch-hitting for Seaver, bunted a ball back to Orioles reliever Pete Richert, who scooped it up and threw to first. The ball hit Martin, who was out of the baseline, but the umpire didn't make the interference call. As the ball rolled along the infield dirt, pinch-runner Rod Gaspar raced home from second with the winning run.

After the game, Seaver spoke to the press about the protesters. He made it clear that he hadn't given anyone permission to use his photo, nor had he endorsed a group called "Met Fans for Peace." He said he'd share his views of Vietnam after the Series and that whatever he said or did at that point, he would be doing so on his own, not as part of a group.

The Mets, meanwhile, had a three-games-to-one lead in the Series. One more victory and they could erase seven years of second-class citizenship, replace the Yankees as the baseball kings of New York, and bring victory to the neglected borough of Queens.

In game five, the Mets sent Koosman to the mound. The left-hander, who'd been dependable all season and nearly unhittable so far in the Series, unraveled in the third inning. He gave up a two-run homer to the Orioles' pitcher Dave McNally, then a solo shot to Frank Robinson. But he settled down again and the Mets scratched back with two runs in the sixth and another in the seventh. In the eighth, they went up, 5–3.

Koosman took the mound in the ninth holding a two-run lead. The crowd was buzzing. The Mets were three outs away from a championship; strips of newspaper, napkins, and torn scorecards sailed onto the field like confetti.

The first two pitches to Frank Robinson were balls, and the crowd groaned after each one. Koosman lost Robinson—he walked him on five pitches—but got Boog Powell to ground out to second, and Brooks Robinson to fly out to right.

When Davey Johnson lofted a soft fly to Cleon Jones in left and the Series was officially over, all hell broke loose. Fans vaulted over the stadium walls, spilling onto the field with their fists raised over their heads in triumph. They mobbed Koosman and the other Mets players as they ran toward the safety of the clubhouse, congratulating them, shaking their hands, patting their backs. Shea Stadium ushers, dressed in red jackets and hats, tried their best to protect the players but were outnumbered.

Swoboda remembers the moment vividly, as well as the team's journey from punch line to finish line.

"You feel like you've closed the circle of being on those horrible Met teams in the beginning, and here you won it all," he says. "That was the thing that felt the best. I don't think I had a reprise after that. I really don't. I just felt like, 'I don't know what else is going to happen to me in my baseball career, but it ain't ever gonna be like this.'"

As he'd later tell American soldiers on a USO tour in Southeast Asia, it was "like driving a Volkswagen then suddenly falling heir to a Cadillac."

On October 20, four days after winning the Series, the Mets rode in open cars from Battery Park to Bryant Park, as 578 tons of ticker tape and confetti rained down from the open-windowed skyscrapers around them. It was New York's third victory parade of the year: the first had been in January when Joe Namath and the Jets upset the Colts to win the Super Bowl; the second had been in August when the Apollo 11 astronauts returned home. Make no mistake, though, to New Yorkers, the Mets winning the World Series was the most miraculous feat of all.

Sports Illustrated summed up the celebration as follows: "From the Hudson to the hinterlands people turned the Mets' victory into a national cliché of hope. 'If the Mets can win, anything can happen.' Thus the Mets, the decade's symbol of ineptitude, ended the '60s as the darlings of baseball—and more."

Shortly after the parade, New York's public radio station, WNYC, interrupted its broadcast of the UN Special Session on nuclear disarmament to join the Mets' reception at city hall. (Even the sign man, Karl Ehrhardt, was on hand to receive accolades from the city's dignitaries.)

Mayor Lindsay, who'd never been one to follow baseball or any other sport, stood front and center as he bestowed the key to the city onto the players.

"We are here today to honor the world champions of baseball, the New York Mets," he told the crowd. "For eight years, New York has loved this team and today they're number one. The Cardinals and the Cubs know it, the Braves know it, and the Baltimore Orioles know it. And they're number one not because of a miracle but because they were a team that never gave up."

Lindsay then declared that the street where Mets manager Gil Hodges lived—the 3400 block on Bedford Avenue in Brooklyn—would be renamed "Gil Hodges Place" for the day.

Francis X. Smith, president of the city council, followed the mayor with remarks of his own.

Holding up the pitching rubber from the mound at Shea Stadium, Smith declared, in his inimitable Queens accent: "Hear ye! Hear ye! That forever there will be a piece of Metland in City Hall. And the members of the council will let mayors, governors, and presidents eat their hearts out looking at it."

It was true: the Mets—and their fans—had reached the summit.

Lindsay, though, still had one more hurdle in front of him: The mayoral election was only two weeks away.

He had done everything in his power to get reelected—he'd beefed up city services, campaigned in remote neighborhoods, and secured the endorsement of the city's liberal Jewish Democrats. But it turned out that his smartest move had been complete happenstance. The photo of him in the Mets' clubhouse—the one of Jerry Grote and Rod Gaspar dousing him in champagne, the one that made the front page of so many papers—had transformed his image. It had turned the debonair politician into an everyday New Yorker, woven him into the fabric of the city. Simply by standing in the center of the team's festivities, by letting the champagne run down over his gleeful face and drench his starched white collar, he'd aligned himself with the city's favorite sons, the New York Mets.

As Lindsay's campaign manager, Robert Aurelio, told author William J. Ryczek, "we spent the whole campaign trying to cut Lindsay down to size, humble him. We never could have planned anything that effective."

On November 4, 1969, Lindsay won reelection by 180,000 votes over Democrat Mario Procaccino, and by 470,000 votes over Republican John Marchi. He took 42 percent of the vote, scoring highest with blacks, Puerto Ricans, and liberal Manhattanites.

The Lindsay years coincided with a period of upheaval, and in 1969, perhaps no issue was more divisive than America's role in Vietnam.

On December 21, the Beatles' John Lennon put the issue in his crosshairs by running an ad for peace in the *New York Times*—and another on a giant billboard in Times Square (next to an armed forces recruiting office).

Lennon, who'd married Yoko Ono in March and announced privately in September that he was leaving the group, had been distributing peace and goodwill messages to his fans at Christmas for years. But he'd been growing increasingly more vocal, and upon getting married, spent a not-so-private week with Ono in the presidential suite of the Hilton Amsterdam—in bed. It was, in their words, a "bed-in" for peace.

In this excerpt from the *Beatles Anthology*, Lennon explained:

> We sent out a card: "Come to John and Yoko's honeymoon: a bed-in, Amsterdam Hotel." You should have seen the faces on the reporters and the cameramen fighting their way through the door! Because whatever it is, is in people's minds—their minds were full of what they thought was going to happen. They fought their way in, and their faces dropped. There we were, like two angels in bed, with flowers all around us, and peace and love in our heads.

Lennon had considered staging a second demonstration in New York but was denied entry into the United States because of visa complications. So, two months later, he and Ono staged another bed-in at the Queen Elizabeth Hotel in Montreal. On June 1, dressed in white pajamas, the newlyweds recorded *Give Peace a Chance* with a roomful of guests that included comedian Tommy Smothers, civil rights activist Dick Gregory, Harvard psychologist Timothy Leary, and members of the Canadian Radha Krishna Temple.

The ad campaign in New York was part of an eleven-city, three-continent media blitz that featured newspaper ads, outdoor billboards, television interviews, performance art, and rock concerts. Funded by Lennon, the ads read, "War is Over! If You Want It. Happy Christmas from John & Yoko."

Tom Seaver, having promised to express his views on the war after the World Series, ran a similar ad ten days later. Perhaps taking his lead from Lennon, Seaver and his wife, Nancy, placed theirs in the sports section of the *Times*, on December 31, 1969.

The ad read, simply, "On the eve of 1970, please join us in a prayer for peace."

When the ball dropped to ring in the new year—and the new decade—the Mets were the champions of baseball, John Lindsay was again the mayor of New York, and Richard Nixon was president of the United States.

John Lennon was speaking out for peace.

Tom Seaver was doing the same.

And the Vietnam War was still raging.

Fig. 17. (*top*) Sandy Koufax (*second from right*) and Don Drysdale (*left*) announce the end of their joint holdout, 1966. With them are Dodgers GM Buzzie Bavasi (*holding paper*) and actor Chuck Connors. (Joe Rustan, *Herald-Examiner* Collection/Los Angeles Public Library.)

Fig. 18. (*bottom*) Marvin Miller, executive director of the Major League Baseball Players Association, at his office in New York City. Miller revolutionized the economics of the game. (Courtesy of the Tamiment Library, New York University.)

BOND
ZACHRY
HIRSCH
FLORSHEIM
SHOES
2
PANTS
SUITS
BOOST
YOUR
BRAVES
HARDY
NO
LEFT
TURN
POLICE

Fig. 19. (*opposite*) Thousands of Atlantans welcome their new baseball team, the Braves, with a parade along Peachtree Street, 1966. (Photo by Art Rickerby/The LIFE Picture Collection/Getty Images.)

Fig. 20. (*above*) *From left*: Joe Torre, Henry Aaron, Harmon Killebrew, Brooks Robinson, and Stan Musial on a USO tour in South Vietnam, 1966. (Ray Bedford, © 1966, 2016 *Stars and Stripes*, All Rights Reserved.)

JEFFERSON
GROCERIES
MEATS
RESTAURANT
JACK'S
JACK'S
I AM
A MAN

WALK
BEALE ST.
END
WORKING
CONDITIONS
NOW
MACE
WON'T
STOP
TRUTH!

Fig. 21. (*opposite top*) Memphis sanitation workers strike for higher pay and safer working conditions, 1968. Mayor Henry Loeb called for martial law and brought in four thousand National Guard troops. (Preservation and Special Collections Department, University Libraries, University of Memphis, *Commercial Appeal* Collection.)

Fig. 22. (*opposite bottom*) Armed soldiers seal off Beale Street as striking workers march along Main Street in Memphis, 1968. (Preservation and Special Collections Department, University Libraries, University of Memphis, *Press-Scimitar* Collection.)

Fig. 23. (*above*) Martin Luther King visits Memphis in support of the city's striking workers, 1968. (Preservation and Special Collections Department, University Libraries, University of Memphis, *Press-Scimitar* Collection.)

Fig. 24. (*above*) The body of slain civil rights leader Martin Luther King lies in state as mourners pay their respects. Memphis 1968. (Preservation and Special Collections Department, University Libraries, University of Memphis, *Press-Scimitar* Collection.)

Fig. 25. (*opposite top*) Denny McLain, a self-described media hound, signs autographs for youngsters during his historic season of 1968. (LOOK Magazine Photograph Collection, Library of Congress, Prints & Photographs Division.)

Fig. 26. (*opposite bottom*) Bob Gibson, winner of the 1968 National League MVP and Cy Young awards, with (*from left*) Curt Flood, Lou Brock, and Vada Pinson. (The State Historical Society of Missouri Research Center, St. Louis.)

GIBSON
45
Cardinals
20
Cardinals
28

LENSES
Pearle
Optical

Fig. 27. (*opposite top*) Richard Nixon campaigns for president in Atlanta, 1968. Jackie Robinson (*not shown*), a one-time Nixon supporter, backed Democratic nominee Hubert Humphrey. (LOOK Magazine Photograph Collection, Library of Congress, Prints & Photographs Division.)

Fig. 28. (*opposite bottom*) The 1968 Democratic National Convention brought antiwar protesters to Chicago. For five days, demonstrators clashed with police and National Guard troops. (Library of Congress, Prints & Photographs Division, *U.S. News & World Report* Magazine Collection [LC-U9-19759].)

Fig. 29. (*above*) The Phillies and the Cubs interrupt play to honor the *Apollo 11* astronauts, July 20, 1969. Moments earlier Neil Armstrong had radioed to NASA, "The Eagle has landed." (Special Collections Research Center, Temple University Libraries, Philadelphia PA.)

NEW YORK
Mets
WORLD CHAMPIONS

Fig. 30. (*opposite*) The 1969 victory parade for the world champion New York Mets left behind 578 tons of confetti. (George Eastman Museum.)

Fig. 31. (*above*) Curt Flood (*right*), with Missouri secretary of state James C. Kirkpatrick, cuts the ribbon on his new photography studio in St. Louis, June 1969. Flood was traded to the Phillies four months later. (From the collections of the St. Louis Mercantile Library at the University of Missouri–St. Louis.)

Fig. 32. In 1970 ex-Yankee Jim Bouton became the most famous sportswriter in America when he released his controversial tell-all, *Ball Four*. (Associated Press.)

19

Curt Flood waited for Marvin Miller to pick up the phone. The veteran center fielder had been sent to the Phillies in the Dick Allen deal, and he was furious.

Flood felt he'd been screwed on two counts. First, he'd have to leave St. Louis, the city in which he'd blossomed as a ballplayer, made his home, and opened a photography business. Second, the news had been delivered by a front-office lackey. Bing Devine, the GM who engineered the trade, hadn't even had the decency to tell Flood to his face that he'd been traded.

To make matters worse, Flood was being shipped to Philadelphia: the city that had run Allen out of town, the place known as the country's "northernmost southern city," the town where Jackie Robinson had been so mercilessly taunted.

Flood was a sensitive man who still felt wounded by the racism he'd encountered playing in the South during the minors. The last place he wanted to land was the City of Brotherly Love.

Besides, St. Louis had been good to him. He'd arrived in 1958, traded to the Cardinals by the Reds, who'd been too apprehensive to field an all-black outfield. Over the next twelve years in St. Louis, Flood had stumbled into manhood by marrying his girlfriend, Beverly Collins, adopting her two children, having three more, getting divorced, and marrying again, this time to actress Judy Pace. As a Major Leaguer, Flood was outstanding—a swift, graceful center fielder and steady hitter who won seven straight Gold Gloves, played in three All-Star games, and hit over .300 six times. It was no coincidence that with Flood in the lineup, the Cards had won three pennants and two world championships.

But by 1969, Flood's relationship with the Cardinals had begun to fray. Before the season, he'd rejected the team's salary offer of $77,500, which represented a $5,000 raise, choosing instead to hold out. Bing Devine eventually offered $90,000, making Flood one of the highest-paid players in the game, but the GM hadn't appreciated being pushed to the wall. In May, when Flood missed a public event, claiming to be injured, the team fined him $250. In September, when the Cards faded from the pennant race—and veteran players were quoted anonymously in the papers as saying that management had given up on the team—the front office zeroed in on the increasingly ornery center fielder.

Despite Flood's twelve years of service, his trade notice offered little in the way of empathy. "Enclosed herewith is Player Report notice No. 614 covering the OUTRIGHT assignment of your contract to the Philadelphia Club of the National League, October 8, 1969. Best of luck."

The terse note had Flood seething. His first move had been to call Missouri lawyer Allan H. Zerman, who suggested that Flood might be able to void the trade by challenging baseball's antitrust exemption. In Zerman's view, Flood could make a case that since he was no longer contractually tied to the Cardinals, he was free to sell his services to any club of his choosing.

That's when Flood picked up the phone and called the Players Association. He wasn't going to report to the Phillies, he told Miller. Instead, he wanted to go after baseball's business model, the hook on which owners hung their players' souls.

He wanted to challenge the reserve clause.

Miller met with Flood and spoke frankly. The Supreme Court had already ruled, twice, that Major League Baseball was not covered by federal antitrust law, which meant that the reserve clause was unimpeachable. Miller told Flood he had a million-to-one shot of winning—and even if he did, he'd probably never again wear a pro uniform.

"I don't know what your ambitions are after playing, but you can forget them," Miller told Flood. "Forget about being a manager, a coach, or anything else. This is the most vindictive group of people you'll ever meet."

Flood, aware that his only other option was reporting for duty in Philadelphia, told Miller he didn't care about retribution, he was determined to go ahead with the lawsuit.

He would later explain his decision to his close friend and former Cardinals roommate Bob Gibson. The following are Flood's words, taken from Gibson's *Stranger to the Game*:

> Players would come into the owners after the season had ended and need money. The owner would say, "Okay," and begin advancing the player money from next season's salary. By the time the following season began, that player would be indebted, literally, to that owner. I always likened it to a plantation owner, allowing his players to play for him in the same way the plantation owner allowed the sharecropper to work his land while at the same time keeping him deep in debt and constantly beholden. I couldn't stand to be treated that way. When I was traded, it drove me up a wall.

Flood's case boiled down to the reserve clause, which the owners had interpreted as giving each club the right to renew a player's contract, year after year. Miller read it differently. To him, the language clearly stated that each club had the right to renew a player's contract for one year, period.

The clause in question read as follows:

> On or before December 20 (or if a Sunday, then the next preceding business day) in the year of the last playing season covered by the contract, the Club may tender to the Player a contract for the term of that year by mailing the same to the Player at his address following his signature hereto, or if none be given, then at his last address of record with the Club. If prior to the March 1 next succeeding said December 20, the Player and the Club have not agreed upon the terms of such contract, then on or before 10 days after said March 1st, the Club shall have the right by written notice to the Player at said address to renew this contract for the period of one year on the same terms.

Miller studied the passage again and again, and kept coming up with the same interpretation.

"I knew that if we had impartial arbitration to interpret the contract—not the commissioner of baseball, who was paid by the owners—no professional arbitrator could rule any other way except that 10a means one additional year," Miller said in an interview with MLB. "And that any player who has his contract renewed without his signature after a year is a free man."

Convinced that Flood was ready to go the distance, Miller invited the center fielder to the Players Association's executive board meeting in Puerto Rico. There, Flood met with more than two dozen representatives, including his former Cardinals teammates Tim McCarver, Joe Torre, and Dal Maxville.

Miller was hoping the association would throw its financial support behind Flood. But in evaluating the case, the board members asked Flood a battery of questions—one of which surprised even Miller.

"Why are you doing this?" a board member asked. "Is it to stop the owners from trading players to places they don't want to go? [Or] is it a sign of 'black power'?"

Undaunted, Flood responded, "I'd be lying if I told you that as a black man in baseball I hadn't gone through worse times than my white teammates. I'll also say that, yes, I think the change in black consciousness in recent years has made me more sensitive to injustice in every area of my life. But I want you to know that what I'm doing here I'm doing as a ballplayer, a major league ballplayer, and I think it's absolutely terrible that we have stood by and watched this situation go on for so many years and never pulled together to do anything about it."

After an hour, Flood was excused from the room to await the vote. Satisfied that Flood's intentions were honorable and that he was prepared to take his fight to the finish, the board agreed to support the action. Miller, always one move ahead, already knew the lawyer he'd call to handle the case. Arthur Goldberg had worked with Miller on behalf of the Steelworkers; he'd also served as secretary of labor under Kennedy and sat on the U.S. Supreme Court as an associate justice.

Miller also realized Flood's would be a groundbreaking lawsuit—and that Flood was the person to bring it.

"To me, Flood epitomized the modern player who began to think in terms of union," Miller would later say in an interview with *Counterpunch*. "[He'd ask] questions like, 'Why is baseball an exception to how labor is treated in other industries? Why should we be treated like property? Why should we agree to have a reserve clause?'"

Flood's wife, Judy Pace, would later tell author Cal Fussman, "It's not surprising that a black man did this. A white man wasn't going to have that consciousness. A white man was not walking around thinking, 'My rights are always being penalized.'"

On Christmas Eve, December 24, 1969, Flood sent the following letter to baseball commissioner Bowie Kuhn:

> Dear Mr. Kuhn:
>
> After twelve years in the major leagues, I do not feel that I am a piece of property to be bought and sold irrespective of my wishes. I believe that any system which produces that result violates my basic rights as a citizen and is inconsistent with the laws of the United States and of the several states.
>
> It is my desire to play baseball in 1970 and I am capable of playing. I have received a contract from the Philadelphia club, but I believe I have the right to consider offers from other clubs before making any decisions. I, therefore, request that you make known to all the major league clubs my feelings in this matter, and advise them of my availability for the 1970 season.
>
> Sincerely Yours,
> Curt Flood

Flood was merely documenting his stance with the commissioner's office. He and Miller surely realized no commissioner would eliminate the reserve clause simply because a player had sent him a letter requesting he do so.

Especially the conservative, imperious Bowie Kuhn.

In the words of *New York Times* writer Robert Lipsyte, Kuhn "exuded the moral righteousness of a Princeton-Wall Street-WASP whose ancestors had arrived before there was even a nation for the pastime."

To Dick Moss, general counsel to the players, the commissioner was more than old school; he was pompous and full of himself. "[Bowie

Kuhn] always said he was the commissioner of the players, too," Moss says now. "It was a fairytale."

Kuhn was born into his stature, the descendant of a long line of politicians. Five of his ancestors were governors and two were senators—and Kuhn brought that same politician's mentality to baseball. After graduating from Princeton in 1947, he'd earned a law degree at University of Virginia. From there he went to the white-shoe law firm, Willkie Farr & Gallagher, where he became counsel to the National League. By 1966, he'd won the trust of management after successfully representing the NL when the state of Wisconsin sued the league over keeping the Braves in Milwaukee.

In 1969 he'd become commissioner.

Despite Kuhn's pedigree, baseball insiders viewed him as having an average intellect at best. When speaking frankly, most referred to him as the owners' puppet. Columnist Red Smith summed up the general attitude toward Kuhn with one of sports' sharpest zingers. In recalling Kuhn's appearance at a labor summit, Smith wrote, "An empty car pulled up and Bowie Kuhn got out."

Kuhn answered Flood's letter with one of his own, the gist of which appears below:

> I certainly agree with you, that you, as a human being, are not a piece of property to be bought and sold. That is fundamental in our society and I think obvious. However, I cannot see its applicability to the situation at hand.
>
> You have entered into a contract with the St. Louis club which has the same assignment provision as those in your annual Major League contracts since 1956. Your present contract has been assigned in accordance with its provisions by the St. Louis club to the Philadelphia club. The provisions of the playing contract have been negotiated over the years between the clubs and the players, most recently when the present Basic Agreement was negotiated two years ago between the clubs and the Players Association.

Flood and Miller proceeded as planned. When word of the upcoming lawsuit leaked to the press, it made headlines across the country.

To address the media, Flood appeared on ABC's *Wide World of Sports*, accompanied by Marvin Miller. Dressed in a light blue suit, and looking more like an accountant than a baseball player, Flood made his case to sportscaster Howard Cosell. Being traded or bought or sold like a piece of property, he said, was damaging to a person's ego.

Cosell, reflecting the attitude of millions of working Americans, was baffled.

"It's been written, Curt, that you're a man who makes $90,000 a year, which isn't exactly slave wages," he said. "What is your retort to that?"

"A well-paid slave," Flood said without a moment's hesitation, "is nonetheless a slave."

In January 1970, the case of *Flood v. Kuhn* was filed in federal court in New York.

And, once again, the issue of slavery haunted America.

20

Two months into the 1970 season, Jim Bouton warmed up in the visitors bullpen at Shea Stadium. His fastball long gone, he was now officially a journeyman pitcher; the one-time ace had bounced from the New York Yankees to the expansion Seattle Pilots to the Houston Astros. At this point, he was doing whatever he could to stick around the Majors, including resurrecting the knuckleball he'd learned how to throw by reading the back of a cereal box when he was ten.

But this weekend, Bouton's problems had nothing to do with his pitching arm.

Look magazine had just released its first excerpt of Bouton's soon-to-be-published diary of the 1969 season. To say *Ball Four* was juicy didn't quite cover it. Judging from the ten-page excerpt "My Love/Hate Affair with Baseball," Bouton's memoir did what no other baseball book had ever done—it blew the cover off the sport. It invited readers to become proverbial flies on the wall as the pitcher navigated his way through locker rooms brimming with oversexed, liquor-swigging, pill-popping man-children. And Bouton didn't tattle only on the Pilots; he also blew the façade off the Yankees. If baseball had ever had a smoking gun, this was it.

It turned out that Bouton (with guidance from original Chipmunk Leonard Shecter, who served as *Ball Four*'s editor) had a sharp, witty writing style that made the book impossible to put down. After reading the excerpt, most baseball fans couldn't wait to get their hands on the other four hundred pages. But in the eyes of some, the pitcher-cum-author had turned on his teammates—and that catapulted him up the charts to public enemy number one.

"How fabulous are greenies?" Bouton wrote. "The answer is 'very.' Greenies are pep pills—dextroamphetamine sulfate—and a lot of ballplayers couldn't function without them. They need one just to get their hearts to start beating."

If that wasn't revelatory enough, Bouton also took on the media's golden boy Mickey Mantle. Bouton came clean about the Mick's drinking and suggested that Mantle might have had a more illustrious career if he'd spent more time at the gym and less at the bar. Even worse (or better, depending on one's point of view), the *Look* excerpt showed Mickey and the boys stealing off to hotel rooftops to catch glimpses of women undressing—a rollickin' good time referred to by the players as "beaver shooting" and by the law as voyeurism.

In Bouton's words, "beaver shooting" was "anything from peering over the top of the dugout to look up dresses to hanging from the fire escape on the 20th floor of some hotel to look through a window." As Bouton told it, "I've seen guys chin themselves on transoms, drill holes in doors, even shove mirrors under a door."

The excerpt didn't only name names—it listed dates and locations. In one passage, Mantle brings the boys "beaver-shooting" at a Washington DC hotel.

"One of the first big thrills I had with the Yankees," Bouton wrote, "was joining about half the club on the roof of the Shoreham at 2:30 in the morning. I remember saying to myself: 'So this is the big leagues.'"

Word of the book had blown through baseball like a tornado even before *Look* released its first excerpt, wreaking the most havoc in the commissioner's office. Bouton had done nothing to calm the rumors of its impending publication. If anything, he'd been talking up the book since spring training, perhaps to prepare players for what was coming, and surely to steal a few extra inches of real estate in the major dailies.

"Bill Freehan's diary will be pablum next to *Ball Four*," he'd said, referring to the Detroit catcher's *Behind the Mask*, another baseball memoir being released that same season.

The writers, knowing Bouton had the smarts to put together a far-better-than-average sports book, wrote openly of the baseball world's jitters. The *San Diego Tribune* gave the memoir a day in the spotlight under the headline "All Baseball Trembling."

The promotional staff at World Publishing had also done its part by sending advance copies to reviewers. Once the copies landed on the desks of critics, the rumors flew: Bouton wasn't overhyping his diary, Freehan's book *was* pablum compared to *Ball Four*.

Hundreds of thousands of fans across the country were itching to get their hands on the book. But at Shea Stadium in late May, a sizable faction of Mets fans wanted blood. Credit Dick Young. The *Daily News* columnist had hammered out three successive anti-Bouton broadsides, one of which portrayed the pitcher as a commie in baseball stirrups. Young warned his two-million-plus readers that the bigmouth knuckleballer had committed the cardinal sin of spilling inside dope about his teammates—the Yankees, no less.

Young saw the book—not the rooftop hijinks, the greenies, or the sleeping around—as a symbol of a deteriorating American culture. Rather, he vilified Bouton for breaking the game's code of silence and for selling out his teammates to advance his own agenda. The columns were typical Young diatribes: from-the-gut rants that, according to the *New York Times*, had "all the subtlety of a knee in the groin."

The following is from Dick Young's column on May 28, the day before the Astros arrived at Shea Stadium:

> I feel sorry for Jim Bouton. He is a social leper. He didn't catch it, he developed it. His collaborator on the book, Leonard Shecter, is a social leper. People like this, embittered people, sit down in their time of deepest rejection and write. They write, oh hell, everybody stinks, everybody but me, and it makes them feel better. . . . He will receive fewer invitations to dinner than Phyllis Diller. He will be summoned by the commissioner of baseball, and reprimanded, perhaps fined. His big-league career will be shortened considerably. He may not finish the season. . . . [His] writings could tear apart team morale on the Astros.

Young used a bit of twisted logic to re-shine Mantle's halo by explaining that "Mantle drank liquor instead of going to bed to kill the ache in his knee. . . . I don't recommend it, but perhaps [Bouton] should take an unwinding drink or two. It probably never occurred to Jim Bouton that a tee-totaling Mickey Mantle might have batted .220 lifetime, beating out ground balls."

Bouton still remembers how Young's vitriol brought to light the political strife going on around him.

"As far as Dick Young was concerned," Bouton says, "the book was a reinforcement of society falling apart. I was part of the failure of young people to understand what's important in the world. Hippies and the war and all of that stuff going on were part of it. There was definitely a left-right thing about the war and everybody was taking sides. [To Young], I was among the communists—an example of the deterioration. And the funny thing was, I grew up as a conservative kid. All this stuff opened my eyes to a lot of things."

Bouton never came out of the bullpen at Shea Stadium on Friday and Saturday, but he couldn't hide forever. In the first game of Sunday's doubleheader, he was called on to pitch the bottom of the seventh. It was mop-up duty—the Astros were losing 9–2—but the forty-seven thousand newspaper-reading fans reacted to Bouton the way a pack of pit bulls might respond to a lobbed porterhouse. As soon as the PA announcer intoned, "Now pitching . . ." the crowd erupted with a chaotic outpouring of boos, curses, and obscene gestures.

Bouton figured he could quiet the place simply by shutting down the Mets' lineup, but he fell behind on nearly every batter. Buckling under the incessant catcalling—or, perhaps, a knuckleball that wouldn't knuckle—Bouton gave up three runs.

When Houston manager Harry Walker came out to get him, Bouton had to take the walk of shame from the mound to the dugout, an agonizing journey serenaded by another round of boos.

"My parents were there," Bouton recalls. "My mom and dad, who lived in New Jersey, came out with some friends and were sitting in the stands. When I met up with them after the [second game] my mom was crying. 'This is a terrible thing,' [she said]. 'You shouldn't have written that book. These people are saying such awful things about you.'"

Bouton did his best to ease her mind. All he'd done, he insisted, was write a book that shared the fun of baseball. His mother wasn't buying it. How could she? Not only was the public vilifying him, but Bowie Kuhn had summoned him to his office.

He was due there at nine o'clock the next morning.

Bowie Kuhn had been steaming over *Ball Four* since the excerpt hit the newsstands. It didn't help that AL president Joe Cronin called Kuhn in a fury, denouncing Bouton's diary as "unforgivable." Most vexing to Cronin—and by no coincidence Kuhn—was the opening section that recounted, word for word, Bouton's 1963 and '64 contract squabbles with the Yankees. Told first-hand, the story laid bare the club's manipulative strategies, including the threat of a hundred-dollar-a-day fine for every day Bouton refused to sign his contract.

The commissioner wasn't about to let some has-been pitcher jeopardize the lavish lifestyles of the owners, not to mention his own cushy position. Leaving nothing to chance, he'd switched into crisis mode and launched a campaign to discredit Bouton's diary. His approach was simple: ignore the damaging stuff about front-office shenanigans and focus on Bouton's betrayal of his teammates, particularly that of Mantle. If Kuhn had his way, the name Jim Bouton would get the same response in Major League stadiums as Benedict Arnold got in grammar school classrooms. His first move was to issue an edict to every Major League team, one that Astros skipper Harry Walker passed on to Bouton and his teammates before the Mets series: the commissioner's office would come down hard on any player that knocked his teammates, or criticized anyone in the upper echelons of the game.

Unfortunately for Bouton, most sportswriters had bought Kuhn's spin. Before *Ball Four* hit the bookshelves—and before a single player had read it—the papers were printing what Bouton, that turncoat, had said about Mantle. There was no mention of the way the Yankees' front office had handled the pitcher's contract negotiations.

John Hall of the *Los Angeles Times* suggested that Bouton had "gone beyond the foul line in the matter of good taste a few times. For instance, it probably wasn't necessary . . . to give all the intimate details of his former mates in action on the roof of the Shoreham Hotel in Washington DC—leaving us with the inescapable conclusion that the mighty Yankees were nothing more than slobbering peeping Toms."

Harold Kaese of the *Boston Globe* called the book "tawdry" and "sordid" and a "verbal cesspool." He quoted Red Sox left fielder Carl Yastrzemski as saying, "Bouton's got a nerve writing stuff like that with his ability. He should have written it when he was in the league. He'd have been knocked out in an inning or two, maybe."

Jerry Nason, also of the *Globe*, was convinced that once the book went on sale, Bouton's seven-year career would last another seven minutes.

Suddenly, the faces Bouton saw every day at the ballpark—the cops, the ushers, the vendors, and the autograph-seekers—were ignoring him. Even his Houston teammates did little more than nod when he walked into the locker room. Some acted as though he were contagious. Bouton considered posting a letter to his teammates on the clubhouse bulletin board but changed his mind, figuring the whole mess would blow over.

But, according to Bouton's roommate Norm Miller, Kuhn had wielded the mightiest of weapons—Mickey Mantle—and the damage was irreversible.

"Mickey Mantle was everybody's hero," Miller says now, looking back. "It's like writing that John Wayne was gay or something. Back then we didn't know anything about the players once they left the field. We didn't build up our heroes to knock them down."

It's worth noting, though, that through it all—the scalding reviews, the locker-room speeches, the name-calling—nobody ever suggested that anything in the book was a lie.

Except for Bowie Kuhn.

On May 31, the night before his meeting with the commissioner, Bouton had dinner with Leonard Shecter at the Lion's Head, a Greenwich Village tavern popular with leftist writers, musicians, and artists.

"I was more comfortable at the Lion's Head than I was in the clubhouse," Bouton says. "This was a very sympathetic location. You had writers there! There was lots of support among sportswriters and casual guys: 'Nice going. Hang in there.' Mostly they were guys with beards and long hair. At that point, I was feeling more like a writer than a baseball player. The clubhouse was not a comfortable place."

On the way to the Lion's Head, Bouton had picked up a copy of the *New York Times* at a newsstand on Seventh Avenue. When he spotted Robert Lipsyte's review of *Ball Four* inside the paper, he stopped dead and read it on the street. Then he raced to the bar to show it to Shecter. They now had a reason to keep their chins up. Lipsyte had called *Ball Four* baseball's "most honest diary to date."

"Bouton should be given baseball's most valuable salesman of the year award," Lipsyte wrote. "His anecdotes and insights are enlightening, hilarious, and most important, unavailable elsewhere. They breathe a new life into a game choked by pontificating statisticians, image-conscious officials and scared ballplayers."

It was just what Bouton needed as he prepared to meet with Kuhn.

"Once I read Bob Lipsyte," Bouton says, "I was feeling pretty good about things. I was not going to roll over; I was going to stand up to Bowie. I wasn't afraid of him. . . . I wasn't going to be pushed around by the baseball commissioner."

And so, the next morning, Bouton woke up with a little extra verve. He shaved, palmed his blonde hair off his forehead, and donned a starched white shirt, black necktie, and conservative grey suit. He left his parents' house in New Jersey and drove into the city. There he hooked up with Shecter and his security detail, Marvin Miller and Richard Moss. (According to Moss, he and Miller had no agenda going into the meeting; they were there simply to make sure Kuhn wasn't "up to no good.")

Bouton, Shecter, Miller, and Moss made their way to the twentieth floor of 680 Park Avenue. After waiting more than half an hour, they were led into Kuhn's inner sanctum, which, as Bouton puts it, was decorated with "lots of mahogany" and "old authority." The commissioner wore his usual suit, tie, and trademark wireframe glasses. His demeanor, as always, was stiff and uptight.

Had he looked out his window, Kuhn would have seen the small crush of reporters gathered in front of the building, hoping for a scoop. He never realized it, but simply by calling the meeting, he'd ignited a national debate between his fellow conservatives and Bouton's fellow liberals.

Waiting outside the glass doors of his office were two such liberals. Steve Bergen and Richard Feuer, both college freshmen, had driven the thirty-plus miles from their parents' homes in Rockland County to protest the commissioner's actions against Bouton. Their friend, Lynne Schalman, couldn't get the day off from her summer job at the local dry cleaner. But she helped make the cardboard picket signs the two demonstrators now held: "Jim Bouton is a Real Hero. No Punishment for Exposing the Truth. Kuhn: Stop Repression and Harassment."

Bergen and Feuer represented a small sampling of young, antiwar students gathering steam across America. In their view, the meeting was the latest example of the establishment's clamping the mouths of their generation. They were tired of the lies and sick of the cover-ups. Bouton's was a voice against authority, and they instinctively aligned with his politics.

"It was absolutely establishment vs. anti-establishment," Bergen says. "Dick Young's comments smacked of the same authoritarian putdown of kids growing up in the '60s. Bouton was a hero for being willing to tell the truth about an aspect of society. . . . The whole '60s movement was about questioning authority, whether it was the high school principal or the president of the United States, and Bouton represented one more instance of hearing firsthand that it's not the way you thought it was. There's a public side and then there's what's really going on."

Feuer remembers meeting Bouton outside Yankee Stadium in the early '60s. Bouton had been sitting on the trunk of his light-green 1954 Mercury before a game, talking with the eleven-year-old Feuer and a group of other fans, and signing autographs. Feuer had left with a good feeling about the guy.

"[Bouton] was my guy," he says, looking back. "And you know what? He was funny, he was honest, and he was decent. . . . [Kuhn's] was a kneejerk reaction: 'This is not good. This is not wholesome.' Kuhn didn't get it, just didn't get the changing times. And he didn't realize that maybe these players should have civil liberties."

Schalman remembers how she and her friends felt about the situation. "With all the stuff that was going on in the world, Bowie Kuhn was upset about the fact that Bouton had written that Mickey Mantle was a drunk? Mickey Mantle, in some ways, became a more attractive figure because he was someone who wasn't obeying rules that we thought were stupid."

But Kuhn didn't pop his head out of his office and ask Bergen or Feuer for their opinions. Instead, after a few courteous comments, he demanded Bouton tell him how the hell their meeting had become public. Bouton suggested that Kuhn ask his buddy Dick Young, since the writer had mentioned it in his column nearly a week earlier.

Bouton was onto something. Marvin Miller, in his autobiography, claimed that by the mid-'60s Young was no longer a rebel but a management lackey, "as reactionary and virulently antiunion as any owner in baseball." Miller went on from there. "There was a stable of sportswriters around the country spoon-fed inside information as long as they spouted the company line," he wrote. "Young used to brag to other sportswriters: 'You'd kill for my access.' But he never told them what he gave up in return."

Kuhn ignored Bouton's comment and ripped into him, telling him that the *Look* excerpt stretched the limits of believability—and those of propriety. He was so disgusted by the stories, he said, that he'd removed the magazine from his house before his son could see it.

Bouton wasn't sure how to respond. He wanted to stand up to Kuhn, but he'd also been instructed by Miller to say as little as possible, that if they gave the commissioner enough time, he'd hang himself.

But Bouton couldn't stay quiet.

"I think you're wrong," he told Kuhn, "There aren't any words in the book that don't appear in a lot of writing and magazines. I think it gives an accurate view of what baseball and baseball players are like. As a result, I think people will be more interested in baseball, not less. I think people are turned off by the phony goody-goody image. So I think you're wrong about what's good and bad for baseball."

Kuhn bristled. "I'll decide what's good and bad for baseball," he said. "That's my job, not your job."

"I suppose so," Bouton said. "But I'm not obligated to write a book about baseball that only has good things about baseball in it."

"Well, you make your living in baseball and you should support it. You owe it to the game because it gave you what you have."

"I always gave baseball everything I had," Bouton said. "Besides, baseball didn't give me anything. I earned it."

Stymied, Kuhn moved on to the next item on his list.

"Now you've got a part in there that is going to be very bad for players' relationships with their wives and their marriages. You have Gary Bell telling Ray Oyler to bring home his socks because he'd left them under Oyler's bed. People are going to read that and they're going to think that ballplayers are sleeping with each other's wives."

Bouton explained he'd been repeating a joke that was common in locker rooms, schoolyards, and, well, just about everywhere.

Kuhn didn't get it.

After a few more rounds of pin-the-tail-on-the-author, Kuhn suggested that Bouton release a statement saying that he'd exaggerated the stories in the book. Bouton refused.

Frustrated, Kuhn told Bouton to consider the meeting a warning. That's when Marvin Miller piped in.

"A warning against what, Bowie? Is this a warning against writing? Is it a warning against writing about baseball? Is it a warning against using four-letter words?"

Kuhn stammered and said he couldn't get into specifics, but that Miller and Bouton damned well knew what he meant.

"I don't understand what you're talking about," Miller pressed. "You can't subject someone to future penalties on such vague criteria. Why, that's like a policeman walking up to someone in a crowd and saying, 'I'm warning you.' Against what? The expression on my face?"

Kuhn moved on—but when he told Bouton how to deal with the press, he stepped on another legal landmine. He said he'd issue a statement about the book and that Bouton should remain silent. Miller scoffed at the plan. Kuhn was going to make a statement, but Bouton couldn't? Bouton had every right to respond to anything Kuhn said about him, or about *Ball Four*.

At that point, Kuhn sent Bouton and Shecter out of the room. Behind closed doors, Miller, Moss, and Kuhn drafted a statement that would be released by the commissioner. It would say: "I advised Mr. Bouton of my displeasure with these writings and have warned him against future writings of this character. Under all the circumstances, I have concluded that no other action was necessary."

Two and a half hours after it began, the meeting came to a close.

On the elevator ride to the lobby, Shecter was in the same car as the young protesters. When he saw their picket signs, he jotted down their names and numbers.

"We'll be writing a sequel," he told them. "We'll send you free copies."

Bouton left shortly after. When he stepped out of the building and into the warm, fresh air, he walked smack into the waiting reporters. It was suddenly clear just how badly Kuhn had misfired.

"I thought to myself, boy that wasn't a very smart idea for Bowie Kuhn," Bouton says now. "All it did was draw people's attention to the book, and it showed Bowie's lack of understanding about how the world works."

Sure enough, by branding Bouton a turncoat, Kuhn had made *Ball Four* an instant bestseller—and the more the media spoke about it, whatever their opinion, the higher on the charts it climbed.

And the media spoke plenty.

In Houston, where Bouton was still on the roster, the Astros were so stymied by how to stop the book's rise, they went as far as forbidding their radio announcers from mentioning *Ball Four*.

"One wonders what the announcers will do when Bouton goes 3-2 on a batter and then throws a bad pitch," wrote Chipmunk Stan Isaacs in *Newsday*. "Will they refuse to say 'Ball Four'?"

Rep. Richard Ottinger of New York, who was campaigning for the senate in 1970, wrote to Kuhn, saying he was "deeply disturbed" by the way that Kuhn had pressured Bouton. He went on to say that Kuhn's actions were part of a "growing mood of repression in the country" and that it was "indicative of an intolerable arrogance on the part of the official baseball establishment." Ottinger said he planned to ask House Judiciary Committee chairman Emanuel Celler "to look particularly hard at the question of individual rights: Are baseball players chattels or free human beings?"

In his 1987 autobiography, *Hardball*, Kuhn acknowledged that he should have ignored the whole affair. But many baseball insiders don't buy his regret.

Murray Chass was covering baseball for the *New York Times* when *Ball Four* was released. "If [Kuhn] could have, he would've banned the book," he says. "I'm sure he either knew, or was told, that if he tried to do anything like that there'd be an outcry to make him and baseball look bad. If Kuhn had gotten his way, there wouldn't be free agency, there wouldn't have been *Ball Four*."

Fay Vincent, who would serve as commissioner from 1989 to 1992, agrees. "It was in keeping with Bowie's effort to protect the romanticism of baseball. He wouldn't want the vulgar underbelly of baseball to come out. It was silly; it was like trying to suppress a movie. All you're doing is making it more popular. I think that was one of the dumbest things he did. Once the book came out, the idea of trying to get [Bouton and Shecter] to do something to undercut it was ridiculous. We know from following Bowie's career that good judgment was not his strong suit. Unlike the rest of the world, Bowie just didn't get it."

Kuhn may or may not have regretted his handling of *Ball Four*. But there's little doubt that after meeting with Bouton, he sat in his office, ruing the day the pitcher first picked up his pen.

And he surely knew that his phone would be soon ringing, that on the other end would be a club owner asking how the meeting had gone, and that he'd have only one truthful answer: he'd just made Jim Bouton the most popular sportswriter in the country.

21

On May 19, 1970, Curt Flood walked into room 1505 of the federal courthouse in Manhattan's Foley Square. He and his legal team—Marvin Miller, Dick Moss, Arthur Goldberg, and Jay Topkis—were presenting their case before Irving Ben Cooper, a veteran district court judge who'd been appointed to the federal bench by President Kennedy.

Flood's case was built on a single argument: The reserve clause violated federal antitrust laws, and teams were exerting a monopolistic hold over their players.

The owners' response was the same as it had always been: their business model was necessary to the league's survival, and it benefitted the "totality of players." Any change, they said, would send smaller-market teams into bankruptcy court.

If Flood's lawyers were to win on this point, they could move to abolish the reserve clause.

Across from Flood sat Kuhn's team: nine lawyers, plus American League president Joe Cronin and National League president Chub Feeney. Behind them was Kuhn himself. It was a non-jury trial, so reporters covering the case filled the twelve leather chairs in the jury box.

For baseball fans, the trial was a legal All-Star game, one that included some of the biggest personalities in all of sports.

Flood's lawyers called upon Bill Veeck, the former owner of the White Sox, and player-turned-executive Hank Greenberg. They also brought in officials from the National Basketball Association and the National Hockey League, two leagues that gave more leeway to their players when it came to negotiating contracts. Most surprising was that Flood's lawyers *didn't* call Flood's former teammates—most notably, Bill White and Bob Gibson—raising questions as to whether players were afraid to speak openly, fearing retribution from the owners.

In his book, *Uppity*, Bill White, who'd retired as a player after the '69 season, said that he publicly backed his former teammate; he even reported on his trial as a sportscaster for a Philadelphia TV station. "But," White wrote, "privately I thought Curt was nuts. I didn't think he could win, and I was sure it would destroy what was left of his baseball career."

Bob Gibson also supported his friend, but wasn't about to walk into the crossfire. "Was I behind Curt?" he asked in the HBO film, *The Curious Case of Curt Flood*. "Absolutely. But I was about ten steps back just in case there was some fallout."

The league had its own list of witnesses, including player-turned-broadcaster Joe Garagiola. All of them supported the owners even though some did admit that the current system was flawed.

During the trial, courtroom spectators were treated to several dramatic exchanges and humorous moments. (Judge Cooper often referred to recesses as "seventh-inning stretches.")

When Flood took the stand as the first witness, Cooper had to remind him to speak up, and he repeatedly lectured Flood on the proper way to respond to questioning.

Cooper: Now, Mr. Flood, I presume you are not finding this as easy as getting up to bat, is that right?
Flood: No, sir, it is not.

When one of Flood's attorneys, Arthur Goldberg, asked about his batting averages between 1959 and 1961, Flood couldn't remember and was handed one of his trading cards.

Goldberg: What are you looking at?
Flood: This is a baseball card.
Goldberg: Published by whom?
Flood: I think it is by either Topps or MLB.
Goldberg: And with the use of that card, can you refresh your recollection as to your batting averages during those years?
Flood: Yes, sir, I can.

At another point, a defense lawyer asked Flood, "What do you think would happen if every player were a free agent after each playing season?"

Goldberg objected to the question, but Cooper allowed Flood to respond.

"I think every ballplayer would have a chance to really negotiate a contract just like in another business," Flood said, bolstering his argument.

Cooper looked at Goldberg with a knowing grin. "Do you want that stricken, Mr. Goldberg?"

"No," he said. "I like that answer."

Jackie Robinson, diabetic and nearly blind at the age of fifty-one, testified on Flood's behalf. Perhaps more than anybody else in the room, Robinson understood the sacrifices Flood was making for the benefit of other players.

"It takes a tremendous amount of courage for any individual—and that's why I admire Mr. Flood so much for what he is doing—to stand up against something that is appalling to him," Robinson said on the witness stand. "And I think that they ought to give a player the chance to be able to be a man in situations like this, and I don't believe this is what has happened. Give the players the opportunities to be able to say to themselves, 'I have a certain value and I can place it myself.'"

It was hard not to see Robinson's point, even for those who took issue with it.

In the *Los Angeles Times*, Jim Murray speculated that eliminating the reserve clause would send talented players to rich teams—leaving the poorer teams to flounder in the cellar. Yet Murray had to admit that the clause did represent the last vestige of slavery in America.

"The reserve clause, to be sure, is just a fancy name for slavery," he wrote. "The only thing it doesn't let the owners do is flog the help. You can't flee over the ice, there's no underground railway. All you can do is pack your glove and hum spirituals. You can wrap an old bandana around your head and call the boss, 'Marse,' if you like. Lift that bat, chop that ball, git a little drunk and you land in sale."

After three weeks, more than two thousand pages of transcripts, and fifty-six exhibits, the trial ended. Two months after that, Judge Cooper rendered his decision: there was insufficient evidence to warrant abolishing baseball's current system, especially since doing so would involve overturning a prior Supreme Court ruling.

Flood had lost. He would appeal, but anybody could see his case was on life support.

The same could be said for his career. He hadn't swung a bat in more than a year and his skills were eroding. Besides, no owner was about to offer a contract to a player who was in the midst of suing the league.

A defeated Flood hopped on a flight to Copenhagen to soothe his post-traumatic stress with a steady diet of liquor. In October, as the Orioles were beating up on the Reds in the 1970 World Series, his phone rang. The caller was Leonard Shapiro from the *Washington Post*.

"Any feelings about being traded to the Senators?" Shapiro asked.

Apparently, Bob Short, the owner of the Senators, had sent utility player Greg Goossen and two others to the Phillies in exchange for Flood.

Had Flood not been a pariah, the deal would have made sense. Short, a trucking and hotel magnate from Minneapolis, had bought the Senators two years earlier and was signing big-name players in the hopes of filling RFK Stadium. He'd already pried Hall of Famer Ted Williams out of retirement to manage the club and traded for the Tigers' Denny McLain.

Flood was caught off guard by the phone call and didn't respond until Short himself called and made an official offer: one year, $110,000.

The legal entanglements were many. Marvin Miller, afraid that a contract with the Senators would undermine Flood's legal appeal, insisted that Short remove the reserve clause from the contract. Short balked but agreed to let Flood's attorney Arthur Goldberg add a few modifications, including a no-cut clause, a no-trade clause, and automatic free agency when the contract expired.

By November, Short had his man and Flood had a uniform.

On April 7, the second day of the 1971 season, the U.S. Court of Appeals for the Second Circuit upheld Judge Cooper's ruling, leaving Flood no option other than to petition the Supreme Court.

But Flood's problems didn't stop there. He was no longer an elite athlete able to withstand the day-in, day-out demands of being a Major

Leaguer. Instead of spending his off-year staying in shape, he'd killed it in bars—and was spiraling into the throes of alcoholism.

Later that month, instead of taking batting practice at RFK Stadium, he penned a telegram to Short.

> I tried, a year and half [away from the game] is just too much. Very serious personal problems mounting. Thanks for your confidence and understanding. Flood.

Then he checked out of his hotel, drove to Kennedy Airport in New York, and caught a flight to Barcelona.

In June 1971, the Supreme Court ruled on Muhammad Ali's case.

The beltless champion had been free on appeal since his conviction four years earlier. During that time, he'd become a familiar face on college campuses throughout the country, speaking out against the war and advocating for racial equality.

In 1970 the states of Georgia and New York had finally caved, each granting him a boxing license. The rusty, twenty-eight-year-old fighter had returned to the ring, a few pounds heavier and a bit slower than sports fans remembered him. But his talent was undeniable. He stopped journeyman Jerry Quarry in Atlanta and then beat Argentina's Oscar Bonavena at Madison Square Garden in New York.

He then took on Joe Frazier, the twenty-seven-year-old slugger who'd laid claim to the title in Ali's absence. The minute it was signed, Ali-Frazier became one of the most highly anticipated bouts in boxing history. Both fighters had been Olympic gold medalists. Both were undefeated. And both felt they were the rightful owners of the title. But the bout, which took place in the Garden in March 1971, had even bigger implications. Old-school writers and fans, still viewing Ali as a draft dodger, cast Frazier as the anti-Ali—the anti-draft-dodger—even though the quiet Frazier had never taken a public stance on political issues.

"The Fight of the Century" generated live gate receipts of $1.3 million (ringside seats fetched a record $150), and that didn't factor in the three hundred million people watching on closed-circuit television in theaters around the word. Each fighter earned an unprecedented $2.5 million.

The fight was a seesaw battle until the fifteenth round, when, to the delight of Ali haters, Frazier dropped the former champ to the canvas. Ali got back on his feet, but it didn't matter. When the final bell rang, all three judges agreed: the night belonged to Frazier.

Ali lost any claim he'd had to the world heavyweight championship, but that didn't stop him from winning his biggest battle outside the ring.

In *Clay v. United States*, the Supreme Court ruled unanimously in his favor, thus overturning his conviction. In its opinion, the Court said the Department of Justice had erred in judgment and that Ali's beliefs were, in fact, religiously based.

The court, of course, couldn't give back to Ali the three prime years they'd taken from him. But the former champion could now rejoin the boxing community, having knocked out his most formidable opponent, the U.S. government.

On Wednesday evening, September 1, 1971, the Pirates hosted the Phillies at their year-old home, Three Rivers Stadium, a circular, $55 million multiuse venue cut from the same mold as Shea and Atlanta stadiums.

The Pirates were in the thick of a pennant race. With a month left to play, they were in sole possession of first place, hoping to widen their four-and-a-half-game lead over the Cardinals in the National League East. The Phillies were simply playing out the season. They were twenty two and a half games out of first and trying to scratch their way out of the cellar.

This was not a game Pirates manager Danny Murtaugh wanted to give away. He sent his winningest pitcher, Dock Ellis, to the mound. Yet, he benched righty first baseman Bob Robertson in favor of the left-handed-hitting Al Oliver—a questionable move given that the Pirates were facing a lefty pitcher, Woodie Fryman.

With Ellis starting, and Oliver at first, the Pirates' lineup read as follows: Rennie Stennett, 2B; Gene Clines, CF; Roberto Clemente, RF; Willie Stargell, LF; Manny Sanguillen, C; Dave Cash, 3B; Al Oliver, 1B; Jackie Hernandez, SS; Dock Ellis, P.

Five blacks and four black Latinos.

For the first time in 102 years of professional baseball, twenty-four years after Jackie Robinson's historic breaking of the color barrier, a Major League team was starting an all-minority lineup.

Nobody seemed to notice—not the fans and not the press.

Some Pirates players remember Dock Ellis glancing at the lineup on the dugout wall and saying, "Aw, man, what's going on here? Who made up this lineup?" Others say they didn't notice until the third or fourth inning, when some players briefly commented about it on the bench. Their minds were on winning the game—and the pennant.

The same could be said for Murtaugh, the product of a working-class Irish family in Chester, Pennsylvania. As Dock Ellis told *Sport* magazine, "Murtaugh is a beautiful dude—beautiful. Winning, that's all he cares about. Nothing else. Screw up, you hear about it, black or white."

Murtaugh claimed he hadn't realized he was fielding an all-minority lineup, though, apparently, he'd tried the same thing in 1963 during an exhibition game in North Carolina—and been stopped. That game also happened to be against Philadelphia. Dick Allen, a rookie on that Phillies team, never forgot it. The following is an excerpt of an interview Allen gave to author Cal Fussman in *After Jackie*:

> Before the game, the Pirates manager, Danny Murtaugh, gets in the middle of a big argument. Now, Danny was the kind of guy who usually just sat in the dugout chewing his tobacco. Every once in a while, he'd spit. . . . But this argument was really raging, right out where we could all see what was going on. It was between Danny and this guy from the Chamber of Commerce. I can still see tobacco juice flying out of Danny's mouth and going all over this guy's shirt. What Danny had done was, he'd penciled-in an all-minority lineup. And the guy from the Chamber of Commerce was out there to tell him he couldn't do that. At first Danny said that he didn't know it was an all-black lineup till they told him. But he didn't want to change it, and that's when the tobacco juice started flying.

On that day, maybe because the game didn't count in the standings—or, more likely, because it was 1963 and he was in North Carolina—Murtaugh had caved and replaced his black second baseman with the white Bill Mazeroski. Now, in Pittsburgh, he did no such thing.

It seems the Pirates had been building toward this day since Branch Rickey became general manager in 1950. Rickey had come to Pittsburgh on the heels of signing Jackie Robinson to the Brooklyn Dodgers, and within two years he had signed twelve black players to the Pirates.

After the 1955 season, Joe L. Brown succeeded Rickey and expanded the team's recruiting efforts even further. He'd focused on Latino players, signing, among others, Stennett, Sanguillen, and Hernandez.

Years later, Brown was quoted in the book *Baseball's Best Kept Secret*: "[I] was always proud of the fact that we never paid any attention to color in our organization. I don't think any club in the history of baseball had as many blacks on their roster at one time like we did . . . and consistently over a period of years."

In 1971, when Murtaugh fielded his lineup, nearly half the team was made up of minority players—and morale couldn't have been better. When Richie Hebner, the team's white third baseman, discusses that season he speaks of friendships, social gatherings, and "a loose group all laughing and hollering and teasing each other."

Al Oliver has similar memories. "We had no problems at all," he told George Skornickel in the *Baseball Research Journal*. "It was a great team to play on. When we got black players, and Latin players, and white players, you think over the course of 162 games that something would go wrong. You know, someone might say something to someone. But it never happened on the '71 team. We had it together. Good people. The best way to describe our team was characters with character. We had our personalities, but we got along well."

In the game, Dock Ellis struggled and was pulled in the second inning. But the Pirates won 10–7 and pulled even further away from the Cardinals—winning the NL East by seven games. They went on to beat the Giants in the playoffs and the Orioles in the World Series.

In 1973 the Pirates hosted the Cardinals in a spring training game at McKechnie Field in Bradenton, Florida.

Cardinals catcher Tim McCarver remembers sitting in the dugout and watching his teammate, Lou Brock, walk to the plate to lead off the game.

As Brock stepped into the batter's box, he looked out at the field. Staring back at him was pitcher Dock Ellis, and behind Ellis, an all-black defense—except for Brock's pal, Bill Mazeroski, who was playing second.

A grin spread across Brock's dark cheeks as he shouted to Maz.

"Hey, Jackie Robinson!"

Players in both dugouts burst out in laughter, as did the players on the field and any fans sitting close enough to hear.

"I'll never forget that line," McCarver says. "It was one of the all-encapsulating lines that really summed up the game changing like it did."

That baseball had changed was undeniable. By the time Dock Ellis had fired his first pitch that afternoon, the game looked a lot different than it had in 1960.

In the South, Jim Crow was dead. So too was the feudal hold that team owners had used to run the game. The players had formed a powerful union, baseball had stretched across the country, grown to twenty-four teams, and become thoroughly integrated; television was turning the sport into big business, and a new breed of writer was covering the game—and revealing players as mere mortals.

Over the course of a single decade, the national pastime had come of age. It now resembled a new America, one that had survived persistent upheaval.

The game wasn't perfect. It wasn't even close.

But it finally reflected the country in which it was played.

Epilogue 1975

Three years after losing *Flood v. Kuhn* in the U.S. Supreme Court, Marvin Miller and the Players Association were back at it—this time in front of independent arbitrator Peter Seitz. On behalf of pitchers Andy Messersmith and Dave McNally, neither of whom had signed contracts, the Association was again challenging the reserve clause. As part of its evidence, Jim Bouton read excerpts of *Ball Four*, specifically those that covered his salary negotiations with the Yankees.

In the end, Miller's instincts proved correct. Seitz ruled that player contracts ran for one year, no more. Messersmith and McNally were now free to negotiate with other teams. Paragraph 10a, as originally written, was dead. The days of servitude were over—and the door to free agency had been unlocked.

The ruling is generally considered the most transforming event in baseball history.

Acknowledgments

We owe a debt of gratitude to a long list of people who helped make this book possible. At the top are those who fought for justice throughout the '60s, whether they did so at a baseball stadium, lunch counter, negotiating table, or the National Mall.

Next are the interview subjects who generously shared their time and insight, often at a moment's notice, assuring us it was no inconvenience at all. We know that wasn't true.

Regarding those interviewees, Andrew Young deserves a special mention, as do Robert Lipsyte, Bill White, Jim Bouton, and Ralph Wimbish Jr.

A special thank-you goes out to Bob Costas, who has been there for us every time we've called. His words and wisdom are appreciated. We hope someday to return the favor. Okay, favors.

The list goes on.

There were friends, readers, and ad-hoc editors who provided advice and support along the way. Thank you, Frank Caputo, Willie Weinbaum, and Tony Gloeggler.

A note about publishers: They credit authors for books but never mention researchers. We do. Their names are Justin Davidson and Andrew Distler. Both are meticulous, indefatigable, and so damned smart.

Speaking of publishers, this book is in your hands thanks to our editor, Robert Taylor, at the University of Nebraska Press, and due to the hard work of those at the Jean V. Naggar Literary Agency, especially Elizabeth Evans and Jennifer Weltz. They put a bat in our hands and told us to swing away. And for that, we're grateful.

Bibliography

INTERVIEWS

Anderson, Craig. October 3, 2013.
Appel, Marty. October 31, 2013.
Ardell, Jean Hastings. June 11, 2014.
Baldschun, Jack. November 7, 2013.
Bell, Gary. November 24, 2013.
Bergen, Steve. March 18, 2014.
Bouton, Bob. July 16, 2014.
Bouton, Jim. January 14–15, 2014; April 16, 2014; June 17, 2014; July 15, 2014; September 2, 2014.
Cecil, Dick. August 14, 2015.
Chass, Murray. April 7, 2014.
Cisco, Galen. October 3, 2013.
Davis, Ivor. September 22, 2015.
Dobson, Chuck. September 23, 2015.
Downing, Al. June 24, 2015.
Drysdale, Ginger. September 20, 2013.
Feinberg, Michael. July 13, 2015.
Feuer, Richard. March 20, 2014.
Fischer, Carl. July 23, 2015.
Gmelch, George. December 26, 2015.
Grant, James "Mudcat." December 13, 2015.
Harrelson, Ken. November 17, 2013.
Hickman, Jim. May 13, 2013.
Hinsley, Jerry. October 15, 2013.
Hochman, Stan. November 7, 2013.
Hook, Jay. October 3, 2013.
Howard, Arlene. June 22, 2015.
Jackson, Grant. July 14, 2015.
Jacobson, Steve. June 24, 2013; July 2, 2013; September 4, 2013.
Kane, Larry. September 30, 2015.
Kelly, Ray. May 24, 2015.
Linz, Phil. October 17, 2013; July 23, 2014.
Lipsyte, Robert. October 15, 2013; September 10, 2014.
Lois, George. July 28, 2015.
Marshall, Mike. November 17–18, 2013.
McCarver, Tim. June 20, 2015.
Meisner, Myron. July 1, 2015.
Merchant, Larry. June 28, 2013; September 1, 2013.
Miller, Norm. November 24, 2013.
Moss, Dick. April 12, 2014.
Newhan, Ross. June 27, 2014.
O'Malley, Peter. August 5, 2015.
Pepe, Phil. June 21, 2013; July 8, 2014; September 5, 2014.
Pepitone, Joe. September 8, 2015.
Peterson, Fritz. December 1, 2013.
Rader, Doug. May 27, 2014.
Schalman, Lynne. March 20, 2014.
Schreiber, Art. September 16, 2015.
Shelton, Ron. July 15, 2014.
Swoboda, Ron. October 14, 2013.
Tessler, Len. July 18, 2015.
Thomas, Frank. November 21, 2013.
Troester, Bonnie. July 17, 2015.
Trusty, John. July 6, 2015.
Vecsey, George. July 12, 2013.
Veeck, Mike. May 1, 2014.

Vincent, Fay. May 27, 2014.
White, Bill. July 22, 2015.
Wimbish, Ralph Jr. June 17, 2015.
Young, Andrew. August 11, 2015.

PUBLISHED SOURCES

Aaron, Henry, and Lonnie Wheeler. *I Had a Hammer*. New York: Harper Perennial, 2007.
Abrams, Roger I. "Arbitrator Seitz Sets the Players Free." *Baseball Research Journal*, SABR 38, no. 2 (Fall 2009).
Addie, Bob. "Assemblage Like World Series but Everyone Backed Some Team." *Washington Post*, August 29, 1963.
Alito, Samuel A., Jr. "Alito: The Origin of the Baseball Antitrust Exemption." *Journal of Supreme Court History*, 34, no. 2 (July 2009).
Allen, Dick. "After Jackie Robinson." *Time*, April 12, 2007.
Allen, Dick, and Tim Whitaker. *Crash: The Life and Times of Dick Allen*. New York: Ticknor & Fields, 1989.
Allen, Maury. "Our Mets are Rolling." *New York Post*, February 14, 1964.
American Law and Legal Information Website. "Curt Flood Trial and Appeals: 1970–72—The Playoffs." Law Library. http://law.jrank.org/pages/3195/Curt-Flood-Trial-Appeals-1970-72-Playoffs.html.
Anderson, Dave. "Sports of The Times; When Mantle Had to Battle for a Raise." *New York Times*, January 26, 1992.
Aronson, Harvey. "Long Island Looks to Future." *Newsday*, February 16, 1965.
Associated Press. "Allen Goes to Cards in 7-Player Deal." October 9, 1969.
———. "Allen Returns: $11,700 in Fine." July 21, 1969.
———. "Allen Walks Off Interview Show." June 14, 1969.
———. "Anthem Singing Is Criticized." October 8, 1968.
———. "Bob Gibson's Home Pelted." February 26, 1973.
———. "Cards Get Allen." October 8, 1969.
———. "Curt Flood Jumps Senators, Takes Off for Europe." April 8, 1971.
———. "Curt Flood Quits after Being Traded." October 9, 1969.
———. "Elston Howard Only Negro at Breakfast Given by Chamber." March 9, 1961.
———. "Ho Hum! Atlanta Greets Braves." April 12, 1966.
———. "Hotel Yanks Use Firm on Race Ban." February 3, 1961.
———. "Kuhn Displeased with Writings by Bouton." June 2, 1970.
———. "Kuhn Slaps Jim Bouton for Book." June 2, 1970.
———. "Phillies' Officials Claim They Hated to Trade Allen." October 9, 1969.
———. "Richie Allen Traded from Boobirds to Redbirds." October 9, 1969.
———. "Segregation Bit Flares in Camp." March 9, 1961.
———. "Segregation in Florida Camps of Majors Flares Up." March 9, 1961.
———. "Spring Camp Segregation: Baseball's Festering Sore." February 19, 1961.
———. "St. Petersburg 'Snub' Angers Cards' White." March 9, 1961.

———. "Writer Critical of Segregation." January 4, 1961.
Banks, Lacy J. "Richie Allen: 'I'm My Own Man.'" *Ebony*, July 1970.
Bart, Peter. "Koufax, Drysdale Are Philosophical." *New York Times*, March 27, 1966.
Baseball Reliquary. "The Shrine of the Eternals." http://baseballreliquary.org/awards/shrine-of-the-eternals/.
Basen, Ryan. "Fifty Years Ago, Last Outpost of Segregation in NFL Fell." *New York Times*, October 6, 2012.
Bass, Amy. *In the Game: Race, Identity, and Sports in the Twentieth Century*. New York: Palgrave Macmillan, 2005.
Baumann, Dan. "Reverence for Beatles?" *Arlington Heights Herald*, August 11, 1966.
Bavasi, Buzzie, and Jack Olsen. "The Great Holdout." *Sports Illustrated*, May 15, 1967.
———. "Money Makes the Player Go." *Sports Illustrated*, May 22, 1967.
———. "The Real Secret of Trading." *Sports Illustrated*, June 5, 1967.
———. "They May Have Been a Headache but They Never Were a Bore." *Sports Illustrated*, May 29, 1967.
Berkow, Ira. *Red: A Biography of Red Smith*. New York: Times Books, 1986.
Bernstein, Ralph. "Flood's Threat to Retire Causes Doubts on Trade." AP, October 9, 1969.
Berson, Lenora. *Case Study of a Riot: The Philadelphia Story*. New York: Institute of Human Relations Press, 1966.
Beschloss, Michael. "Jackie Robinson and Nixon: Life and Death of a Political Friendship." *New York Times*, June 6, 2014.
Bigart, Homer. "Lindsay's Rivals Score Him on War." *New York Times*, October 14, 1969.
Blum, Ronald. "Rose Affair Stirs Memories of McLain." AP, May 21, 1989.
Bouton, Jim. *Ball Four*. New York: World, 1970.
———. "Comeback, Part 2." *Look*, June 16, 1970.
———. "My Love/Hate Affair with Baseball, Part 1." *Look*, June 2, 1970.
Bouton, Jim, and Leonard Shecter. *I'm Glad You Didn't Take It Personally*. New York: William Morrow, 1971.
Boyd, Todd. *African Americans and Popular Culture*. Vol. 1. Westport CT: Praeger, 2008.
Breslin, Jimmy. "Worst Baseball Team Ever." *Sports Illustrated*, August 13, 1962.
Briley, Ron. *Class at Bat, Gender on Deck, and Race in the Hole: A Line-up of Essays on Twentieth Century Culture and America's Game*. Jefferson NC: McFarland, 2003.
Brooklyn Historical Society. Walter O'Malley Brooklyn Dodgers records, 1946–1957. Brooklyn, New York.
Brosnan, Jim. "I Broke Baseball's Rules." *Sport*, May 1961.
Bruns, Roger. *Martin Luther King, Jr.: A Biography*. Westport CT: Greenwood Press, 2006.
Bryant, Howard. "Atlanta Pro Sports and Integration." ESPN, January 12, 2011, http://espn.go.com/espn/commentary/news/story?id=6015125.

———. *The Last Hero: A Life of Henry Aaron*. New York: Random House, 2010.
———. *A Story of Race and Baseball in Boston*. New York: Routledge, August 30, 2002.

Bunch, Will. "'Gathering Storm': The Philly Riots of '64." *Philadelphia Daily News*, August 26, 2014.
———. "Link Between '64 Riot, Phillies' Collapse?" *Philadelphia Daily News*, August 28, 2014.

Burk, Robert F. *Marvin Miller, Baseball Revolutionary*. Champaign: University of Illinois Press, 2015.

Califano, Joseph A. Jr., "How the Government Prepared for the March on Washington." *Washington Post*, August 23, 2013.

Cannon, Jimmy. "Brosnan Chafes at Edict Forbidding Baseball Books." *New York Journal-American*, March 18, 1963.

Caro, Robert. *The Power Broker: Robert Moses and the Fall of New York*. New York: Vintage, 1975.

Carroll, Brian. *The Black Press and Black Baseball, 1915–1955: A Devil's Bargain*. New York: Routledge, 2015.

Carson, Clayborne. *The Autobiography of Martin Luther King Jr.* New York: Grand Central, 1998.

Charlton, Linda. "Day of Observance Here Declared by Lindsay." *New York Times*, October 3, 1969.
———. "War Moratorium Backers Believe Nixon Is Reacting." *New York Times*, October 12, 1969.

Chass, Murray. "Pappas First Class." AP, July 4, 1968.

Chester, Higgins. "Tigers Integrate Fla. Camp after Blast by Courier." *Pittsburgh Courier*, May 5, 1962.

Chicago Defender. "Phils Down Again, 14–8." September 28, 1964.

Chicago Tribune. "Cop Cleared in Negro's Killing." September 2, 1964.
———. "Eckert Facing End of Baseball Road." June 9, 1968.
———. "The Record: Democrats' 1968 Convention." September 9, 1968.

Clavin, Tom, and Danny Peary. *Gil Hodges: The Brooklyn Bums, the Miracle Mets, and the Extraordinary Life of a Baseball Legend*. New York: Penguin, 2012.

Clay, Cassius. "I'm a Little Special." *Sports Illustrated*, February 24, 1964.

Cleave, Maureen. "How Does a Beatle Live? John Lennon Lives Like This." *London Evening Standard*, March 4, 1966.

Cleveland Call and Post. "Negro Players Tired of Jim Crow Quarters." March 4, 1961.

Cohen, Stanley. *A Magic Summer: The Amazin' Story of the 1969 New York Mets*. New York: Skyhorse, 2013.

Cook, Alistair. "Moses's Promised Land." *London Guardian*. April 22, 1964.

Cook, Alton. "Koufax, Drysdale Sign . . . for Movie." *New York World-Telegram & Sun*, March 19, 1966.

Cope, Myron. "What, Then, Is Wrong with Richie Allen?" *Sport*, May 1966.

Cottrell, Robert C. *Two Pioneers: How Hank Greenberg and Jackie Robinson Transformed Baseball—and America*. Dulles VA: Potomac Books, 2012.

Curtis, Bryan. "No Chattering in the Press Box." Grantland Archives website. May 2, 2012, http://grantland.com/features/larry-merchant-leonard-shecter-chipmunks-sportswriting-clan/.

Daley, Arthur. "A Day for Mets." *New York Times*, October 21, 1969.

D'Antonio, Michael. *Forever Blue: The True Story of Walter O'Malley, Baseball's Most Controversial Owner, and the Dodgers of Brooklyn and Los Angeles*. New York: Riverhead Books, 2009.

Davis, Ivor. *The Beatles and Me on Tour*. Cockney Kid, 2014.

Davis, Jack E. "Baseball's Reluctant Challenge: Desegregating Major League Spring Training Sites, 1961–1964." *Journal of Sport History* 19, no. 2.

Deford, Frank. "Hot Pitchmen in the Selling Game." *Sports Illustrated*, November 17, 1969.

Dolson, Frank. *Jim Bunning: Baseball and Beyond*. Philadelphia: Temple University Press, 1998.

Donnelly, Joe. "Bouton Is Cheered by Houk's Pep Talk." *Newsday*, March 12, 1964.

Dreier, Peter. "The Real Story of Baseball's Integration That You Won't See in 42." *Atlantic*, April 11, 2013.

Dreifus, Claudia. "Voices: 7/20/69." *New York Times*, July 14, 2009.

Drysdale, Don, and Bob Verdi. *Once a Bum, Always a Dodger: My Life in Baseball From Brooklyn to Los Angeles*. New York: St. Martin's, 1990.

Durso, Joseph. "New York City Honors Its Amazing Mets with Parade." *New York Times*, October 21, 1969.

Ebony. "El Birdos Will Fly Again." June 1968.

———. "Found—An 'Abe Lincoln' of Baseball." March 1970.

———. "The Men behind Martin Luther King." June 1965.

———. "Needed—An Abe Lincoln of Baseball." April 1964.

———. "The Revolt of Negro Youth." May 1960.

Edmonds, Anthony O. *Muhammad Ali: A Biography*. Westport CT: Greenwood Press, 2006.

Edwards, Owen. "Courage at the Greensboro Lunch Counter." *Smithsonian Magazine*, February 2010.

Effrat, Louis. "Yanks Offer Reply." *New York Times*, February 3, 1961.

Einstein, Charles. *Willie's Time: Baseball's Golden Age*. Carbondale: Southern Illinois University Press, 1979.

Elias, Robert. *The Empire Strikes Out: How Baseball Sold U.S. Foreign Policy and Promoted the American Way Abroad*. New York: New Press, 2010.

Falls, Joe. "Golden 30 Stuns Even Denny." *Detroit Free Press*, September 15, 1968.

Ferkovich, Scott. "October 7 1968: Jose Feliciano Lights Tigers' Fire." Society for American Baseball Research website. http://sabr.org/gamesproj/game/october-7-1968-jose-feliciano-lights-tigers-fire.

Ferrick, Thomas, Jr., and Doreen Carvajal. "The 25-Year-Old Scars of a Riot, Violence of 1964 Devastated a Vital Neighborhood." *Philadelphia Inquirer*, August 27, 1989.

Fetter, Henry D. *Taking on the Yankees: Winning and Losing in the Business of Baseball, 1903–2003*. New York: W.W. Norton, 2003.

Finch, Frank. "Brosnan's Book Pulls No Punches." *Los Angeles Times*, September 1, 1960.

———. "Year's Layoff Could End Careers of K & D." *Los Angeles Times*, March 19, 1966.

Flood, Curt, and Richard Carter. *Curt Flood: The Way It Is*. New York: Trident, 1971.

Fountain, Charles. *Under the March Sun: The Story of Spring Training*. New York: Oxford University Press, 2009.

Frazier, George IV. "That Guy in New York Trying to Destroy the Reserve Clause." *Jock*, April 1970.

Frommer, Myrna Katz, and Harvey Frommer. *Manhattan at Mid-Century: An Oral History*. Lanham MD: Taylor Trade, 2013.

Furlong, Bill. "Brosnan's Book Bothers Baseball." *Chicago Daily News*, July 2, 1960.

Gibson, Bob, and Lonnie Wheeler. *Pitch by Pitch: My View of One Unforgettable Game*. New York: Flatiron Books, 2015.

Gibson, Bob, and Phil Pepe. *From Ghetto to Glory: The Story of Bob Gibson*. Englewood Cliffs NJ: Prentice Hall, 1968.

Gmelch, George. *Playing with Tigers*. Lincoln: University of Nebraska Press, 2016.

Goduti, Philip A., Jr. *Robert F. Kennedy and the Shaping of Civil Rights, 1960–1964*. Jefferson NC: McFarland, 2013.

Goldman, Robert M. *One Man Out: Curt Flood versus Baseball*. Lawrence: University Press of Kansas, 2008.

Golenbock, Peter. *Bums: An Oral History of the Brooklyn Dodgers*. New York: G. P. Putnam's Sons, 1984.

Gould, William B., IV. *Bargaining with Baseball: Labor Relations in an Age of Prosperous Turmoil*. Jefferson NC: McFarland, 2011.

Gross, Milton. "Baseball Needs More Color . . ." *Diner's Club Magazine*, July 1964.

Halberstam, David. "Baseball and the National Mythology." *Harper's*, September 1970.

———. *The Fifties*. New York: Villard Books, 1993.

———. *October 1964*. New York: Villard Books, 1994.

Haley, Alex. "Baseball in a Segregated Town." *Sport*, July 1961.

Hamill, Pete. "Two Minutes to Midnight: The Very Last Hurrah." *Village Voice*, June 13, 1968.

Hansen, Drew. "Mahalia Jackson, and King's Improvisation." *New York Times*, August 27, 2013.

Harrison, Claude E., Jr. "Richie Allen Is Ready for the Big Time?" *Philadelphia Tribune*, May 2, 1964.

Hartmann, Douglas. *Race, Culture, and the Revolt of the Black Athlete: The 1968 Olympic Protests and Their Aftermath*. Chicago: University of Chicago Press, 2003.

Helyar, John. *Lords of the Realm: The Real History of Baseball*. New York: Ballantine Books, 2011.

Hendrickson, Joe. "'We've Got Team for Whole World,' Shout Metnicks." *Pasadena Independent*, June 10, 1964.

Herbers, John. "Professional Sports Hail Stand on Full Integration." *Atlanta Daily World*, July 18, 1963.

Hobbs, Allison. "The Lorraine Motel and Martin Luther King." *New Yorker*, January 18, 2016.

Hoberman, John. *Darwin's Athletes: How Sport Has Damaged Black America and Preserved the Myth of Race*. New York: Houghton Mifflin, 1997.

Hochman, Stan. "Boo Birds of Unhappiness Find Nest in Allen's Glove." *Philadelphia Daily News*, September 4, 1964.

———. "Phils Find Relief in Bunning's Sunny Afternoon." *Philadelphia Daily News*, June 19, 1964.

Howard, Arlene, and Ralph Wimbish. *Elston and Me: The Story of the First Black Yankee*. Columbia: University of Missouri Press, 2001.

Howard-Cooper, Scott. "The Year of the Pitcher: 1968: Big Stars Were Drysdale, Gibson, McLain." *Los Angeles Times*, July 10, 1988.

Isaacs, Stan. "Brosnan Has Found New Literary Horizons." *Newsday*, May 8, 1963.

———. "Jim Bouton Is a Very Audacious Fellow." *Newsday*, June 2, 1970.

———. "Jim's Right to Write Becomes a Novel Affair." *Newsday*, April 2, 1964.

———. "The Yanks' Fans Are Not Coming." *Newsday*, June 8, 1965.

Izenberg, Jerry. "Richie Allen in St. Louis: Can the Love Affair Last?" *Sport*, July 1970.

Jackson, Marion E. "Sports of the World." *Atlanta Daily World*, April 7, 1962.

———. "Sports of the World." *Atlanta Daily World*, July 30, 1963.

Jacobson, Steve. "Bouton's Tranquilizer: He Read Scoreboard." *Newsday*, May 7, 1962.

———. *Carrying Jackie's Torch: The Players Who Integrated Baseball—and America*. Chicago Review Press, 2009.

———. "Dick Young: He Stood by His Beliefs." *Newsday*, September 4, 1987.

———. "Sandy Gets His Due, but Does Grant?" *Newsday*, June 19, 1965.

———. "Yankees Held Silence until Bulldog Snarled." *Newsday*, March 13, 1964.

Janson, Donald. "New Racial Topics." *New York Times*, July 18, 1963.

Jenkins, Mark Collins. *Muhammad Ali: Through the Eyes of the World*. New York: Skyhorse, 2007.

Johnson, Lyndon B. "Remarks at the Opening of the New York World's Fair." April 22, 1964. Online by Gerhard Peters and John T. Woolley. The American Presidency Project. Accessed June 22, 2016. http://www.presidency.ucsb.edu/ws/?pid=26179.

Kahn, Roger. *The Boys of Summer*. New York: Harper & Row, 1972.

Kappes, Serena. *Hank Aaron*. Minneapolis: Lerner, 2005.

Kashatus, William C. *September Swoon: Richie Allen, the '64 Phillies, and Racial Integration*. University Park: Pennsylvania State University Press, 2004.

Katz, Jeff. "Everybody's a Star: The Dodgers Go Hollywood." *The National Pastime*, SABR 41.

Keating, Larry. *Atlanta: Race, Class, and Urban Expansion*. Philadelphia: Temple University Press, 2001.

Kennedy, John F. *Public Papers of the Presidents of the United States, John F. Kennedy, 1962* (January 1 to December 31, 1962). Washington DC: United States Government Printing Office, 1963.

———. *Public Papers of the Presidents of the United States, John F. Kennedy, 1963* (January 1 to November 22, 1963). Washington DC: United States Government Printing Office, 1964.

Kerrane, Kevin. *Batting Cleanup, Bill Conlin*. Philadelphia: Temple University Press, 1997.

Kimball, George, and John Schulian. *At the Fights: American Writers on Boxing*. New York: Library of America, 2012.

King, Coretta Scott. *My Life with Martin Luther King*. New York: Henry Holt, 1993.

King, Joe. "Holdout Twins Turn a Plunder into a Blunder." *New York World-Telegram & Sun*, March 31, 1966.

King, Martin Luther, Jr. "Eulogy for the Young Victims of the Sixteenth Street Baptist Church Bombing." September 18, 1963. Lovearth Network website. http://drmartinlutherkingjr.com/birminghamchurchbombingeulogy.htm.

———. "I Have a Dream." August 28, 1963. American Rhetoric website. http://americanrhetoric.com/speeches/mlkihaveadream.htm.

———. "I've Been to the Mountaintop." April 3, 1968. ABC News website. http://abcnews.go.com/Politics/martin-luther-kings-final-speech-ive-mountaintop-full/story?id=18872817.

Kirk, John. *Martin Luther King Jr*. New York: Pearson/Longman, 2005.

Kiseda, George. "Phillies Shoot Holes in Pressure Theory." *Philadelphia Bulletin*. September 17, 1964.

Klein, Frederick C. "Miller Led Players Show Huge Economic Gains." *Sporting News*, March 23, 1974.

———. "Sportswriters Switch from 'Gee Whiz' Style to Analysis, Acerbity." *Wall Street Journal*, October 6, 1967.

Koppett, Leonard. *The New York Mets: The Whole Story*. New York: MacMillan, 1970.

———. "Shea Stadium Opens with Big Traffic Jam." *New York Times*, April 18, 1964.
———. "Yankees, Still Shooting for Moon, Down Senators, 3–2; White Tallies in 11th—Game Is Halted to Hail Landing." *New York Times*, July 21, 1969.
———. "Yanks: Healthy, Wealthy but Unwise." *New York Times*, January 18, 1964.
Korr, Charles P. *The End of Baseball As We Knew It: The Players Union, 1960–81*. Urbana: University of Illinois Press, 2002.
Koufax, Sandy. "My Battle with Arthritis." *Look*, July 12, 1966.
———. "My Salary Fights." *Look*, June 14, 1966.
———. "What Baseball Means to Me." *Look*, July 26, 1966.
Koufax, Sandy, and Ed Linn. *Koufax*. New York: Viking Adult, 1966.
Krell, David. *Our Bums: The Brooklyn Dodgers in History, Memory and Popular Culture*. Jefferson NC: McFarland, 2015.
Kuhn, Bowie. *Hardball: The Education of a Baseball Commissioner*. New York: Times Books, 1987.
Lacy, Sam. "Everybody Belongs in D.C. 'March.'" *Baltimore Afro-American*, August 24, 1963.
Laslett, John H. M. *Shameful Victory. The Los Angeles Dodgers, the Red Scare, and the Hidden History of Chavez Ravine*. Tucson: University of Arizona Press, 2015.
Leavy, Jane. *Sandy Koufax: A Lefty's Legacy*. New York: HarperCollins, 2002.
Lebovitz, Hal. "What Does Bowie Know?" *Plain Dealer*, June 28, 1970.
Leggett, William. "A Bird in Hand and a Burning Busch." *Sports Illustrated*, March 23, 1970.
———. "Never Pumpkins Again." *Sports Illustrated*, October 27, 1969.
———. "Not Just a Flood, but a Deluge. *Sports Illustrated*, August 19, 1968.
———. "Sportsman of the Year: Tom Seaver." *Sports Illustrated*, December 22, 1969.
———. "The Tigers See Too Much Red." *Sports Illustrated*, October 14, 1968.
———. "Trouble Sprouts for the Yankees." *Sports Illustrated*, March 2, 1964.
Leip, Dave. "1968 Presidential General Election Results." Dave Leip's Atlas of U.S. Presidential Elections website. Accessed 2012. uselectionatlas.org.
Lelyveld, Joseph. "Calm Returning to Philadelphia." *New York Times*, August 31, 1964.
Leonard, David. "What Happened to the Revolt of the Black Athlete?" *ColorLines*, June 10, 1998, http://colorlines.com/articles/what-happened-revolt-black-athlete.
Lewis, Allen. "Phils Attack Old Problem: Handling of Negro Players." *Sporting News*, November 20, 1971.
Lewis, John, and Michael D'Orso. *Walking with the Wind: A Memoir of the Movement*. New York: Simon and Schuster, 1998.
Lipsyte, Robert. "Waiting for Richie." *New York Times*, March 8, 1970.

———. "Yanks Woo Cabbies with 20,000 Tickets." *New York Times*, June 20, 1964.

Livingston, Charles J. "Finds Negro Athletes 'Chicken' on Rights." *Cleveland Call and Post*, May 4, 1963.

———. "Ralph Metcalf, Jesse Owens Row over Jackie Robinson." *Atlanta Daily World*, May 23, 1963.

Logan, Andy. "Mayoral Follies, the 1969 Edition." *New York Times*, January 25, 1998.

Los Angeles Times. "Braves Hand Philly 5th Loss in Row." September 26, 1964.

Lowenfish, Lee. *Branch Rickey: Baseball's Ferocious Gentleman*. Lincoln: University of Nebraska Press, 2007.

Madden, Bill. "In Leaving Vero Beach, Dodgers Cutting Last Tie to Glory Days of Brooklyn." *New York Daily News*, March 1, 2008.

———. *1954: The Year Willie Mays and the First Generation of Black Superstars Changed Major League Baseball Forever*. Boston: Da Capo, 2014.

Mann, Jack. "The $1,000,000 Holdout." *Sports Illustrated*, April 4, 1966.

Maraniss, David. *Clemente: The Passion and Grace of Baseball's Last Hero*. New York: Simon & Schuster, 2006.

Markusen, Bruce. *Roberto Clemente: The Great One*. New York: Sports Publishing, 1998.

———. "Thirty Years Ago . . . The First All-Black Lineup." BaseballGuru.com, http://baseballguru.com/markusen/analysismarkusen01.html.

Marmer, Mel, and Bill Nowlin. *The Year of the Blue Snow: The 1964 Philadelphia Phillies*. Phoenix: Society for American Baseball Research, 2013.

Marshall, Marilyn. "Movers and Shakers, They Helped Make the World Better for Blacks." *Ebony*, November 1985.

Martino, Alison. "The Tropicana Motel's Totally Rocking Heyday." *Los Angeles Magazine*, October 12, 2015.

Marzano, Rudy. *The Last Years of the Brooklyn Dodgers: A History, 1950–1957*. Jefferson NC: McFarland, 2008.

Massaquoi, Hans J. "The Breakthrough Stars." *Ebony*, August 1992.

Massey, Douglas S., and Nancy A. Denton. *American Apartheid: Segregation and the Making of the Underclass*. Cambridge MA: Harvard University Press, 1993.

Maule, Tex. "Cassius to Win a Thriller." *Sports Illustrated*, May 24, 1965.

Mayer, Robert. "Moonin' Over the Mets." *Newsday*, March 20, 1962.

McCue, Andy. *Mover and Shaker: Walter O'Malley, the Dodgers, and Baseball's Westward Expansion*. Lincoln: University of Nebraska Press, 2014.

McKenna, Brian. "Robert Cannon." Society for American Baseball Research website. http://sabr.com/bioproj/person/a7414ea2.

McLain, Denny, and Dave Diles. *Nobody's Perfect*. New York: Dial Press, 1975.

McLain, Denny, and Eli Zaret. *I Told You I Wasn't Perfect*. Chicago: Triumph Books, 2007.

Mee, Bob. *Ali and Liston: The Boy Who Would Be Kind and the Ugly Bear*. New York: Skyhorse, 2010.
Melanson, Philip H. *The Martin Luther King Assassination*. New York: Shapolsky, 1991.
Merchant, Larry. "Allen vs. Thomas: Round 10." *Philadelphia Daily News*, July 12, 1965.
———. "Fighting Phil Waived Goodbye." *Philadelphia Daily News*, July 6, 1965.
———. "Letters Bombard the Bomb Squad." *Philadelphia Daily News*, September 4, 1964.
———. "The Old Vic: New Face in Town." *Philadelphia Daily News*, September 11, 1964.
———. "Something Special." *Philadelphia Daily News*, July 13, 1964.
———. "Too Many Raves for Richie?" *Philadelphia Daily News*, May 4, 1964.
———. "Two Games and an Apology at Richie Allen Dell." *Philadelphia Daily News*, July 8, 1965.
Miller, Marvin. *A Whole Different Ball Game: The Inside Story of the Baseball Revolution*. Chicago: Ivan R. Dee, 2004.
Minter, Jim. "The Mayor Surrenders Atlanta." *Sports Illustrated*, July 12, 1965.
Moore, Kenny. "A Courageous Stand." *Sports Illustrated*, August 5, 1991.
Mulvoy, Mark. "Dizzy Dream for Jet-Set Denny." *Sports Illustrated*, July 29, 1968.
Murray, Arch. "Working Press." *New York Post*, February 4, 1961.
Murray, Jim. "Baseball Bad Boy and What's Wrong." *Los Angeles Times*, September 5, 1969.
———. "Flood Warning Goes Up." *Los Angeles Times*, January 25, 1970.
———. "Monument to Walter." *Washington Post*, April 10, 1962.
———. "O'Malley's Dilemma." *Washington Post*, July 10, 1963.
National Public Radio. "Final Words: Cronkite's Vietnam Commentary." July 18, 2009, http://npr.org/templates/story/story.php?storyId=106775685.
———. "Sports Reporting Hero Speaks of 'Silent Season.'" October 2, 2010, http://npr.org/templates/story/story.php?storyId=130287322.
Newhan, Ross. "Messersmith Defends Move." *Los Angeles Times*, April 17, 1976.
Newsday. "Island Population Rises 63,376 in Year." May 5, 1966.
———. "LI Population Gain Biggest in 4 Years." March 20, 1964.
———. "Mauch's 'Gene' Is Short for 'Genius'." September 5, 1964.
Newsweek. "Robert Kennedy Shot, Killed in Los Angeles." June 16, 1968.
New York Times. "Background of Northern Negro Riots." September 27, 1964.
———. "Baseball and U.S.O." November 19, 1967.
———. "Baseball Players Seek Federal Mediation in Negotiations with Owners." January 21, 1968.
———. "Boom Reshapes Atlanta Skyline; 100 Million Invested in 2 Years." July 8, 1962.
———. "Color Bar Lifted at Title Match." March 14, 1961.

———. "The New Breed and the Mets: Signs of the Times." August 24, 1964.
———. "Newspaper Strike Changed Many Habits but Left No Lasting Marks on Economy." December 8, 1963.
———. "Transcript of the Johnson Address on Voting Rights to Joint Session of Congress." March 16, 1965.
Nichols, Chris. "Rock 'n' Roll Coffee Shop Duke's Shutters." *Los Angeles Magazine*, May 12, 2012.
Nilsson, Jeff. "Religion Steps into the Boxing Ring: Ali in '64." *Saturday Evening Post*, January 21, 2012.
Normark, Don. *Chavez Ravine: 1949. A Los Angeles Story*. San Francisco: Chronicle Books, 1999.
Olbermann, Keith. "All Is Finally Forgiven." *Sports Illustrated*, August 3, 1998.
Olsen, Jack. "The Black Athlete: A Shameful Story. *Sports Illustrated*, July 1, 1968.
———. "Buzzie and Big D Go At It in L.A." *Sports Illustrated*, August 29, 1966.
Outlaw, Jesse. "Sir Walter's Palace." *Atlanta Constitution*, January 28, 1962.
Pauley, Garth E. *LBJ's American Promise: The 1965 Voting Rights Address*. College Station: Texas A&M University Press, 2007.
Pearson, Drew. "Believes Evictions Are behind the Negro Riots in Los Angeles." *Atlanta Constitution*, September 5, 1965.
Pepe, Phil. "Players Back K & D." *New York World-Telegram & Sun*, March 21, 1966.
———. "Them That Has Gits." *New York World-Telegram & Sun*, June 19, 1965.
Picou, Thomas. "Phils Out, Reds Lead." *Chicago Defender*, September 28, 1964.
Pittsburgh Courier. "Patterson Won't Fight in Miami If Jim Crow Holds." January 7, 1961.
Playboy. "Dick Gregory Interview." August 1964.
Poe, Randall. "The Writing of Sports." *Esquire*, October 1974.
Powers, Albert Theodore. *The Business of Baseball*. Jefferson NC: McFarland, 2003.
Purnell, Brian. *Fighting Jim Crow in the County of Kings: The Congress of Racial Equality in Brooklyn*. Lexington: University Press of Kentucky, 2013.
Pye, Brad, Jr. "A Note on Richie Allen." *Los Angeles Sentinel*, May 22, 1964.
Rampersad, Arnold. *Jackie Robinson: A Biography*. New York: Random House, 1997.
Randolph, Laura B. "Bill White: National League President." *Ebony*, August 1992.
Remnick, David. *King of the World: Muhammad Ali and the Rise of an American Hero*. New York: Random House, 1998.
Richman, Milton. "'Ball Four' Stirs Controversy; Players Critical." UPI, June 2, 1970.
———. "Dodgers Don't Resent Holdouts." UPI, March 3, 1966.
Rogin, Gilbert. "Still Hurt and Lost." *Sports Illustrated*, November 16, 1964.
Rosenbaum, Ron. "The House That Levitt Built." *Esquire*, December 1983.

Rosenthal, Harold. "Yanks Move to End Camp Jim Crow." *New York Herald Tribune*, February 2, 1961.
Ross, Charles K., and Guy Endore. *Outside the Lines: African Americans and the Integration of the National Football League*. New York: New York University Press, 1999.
Rothstein, Edward. "Four Men, a Counter and Soon, Revolution." *New York Times*, January 31, 2010.
Rowan, Carl. "How Kennedy's Concern for Negroes Led to His Death." *Ebony*, April 1967.
Rushin, Steve. "The Season of High Heat." *Sports Illustrated*, July 19, 1968.
Rutheiser, Charles. *Imagineering Atlanta: The Politics of Place in the City of Dreams*. Brooklyn: Verso, 1996.
Safire, William. "A Political Lesson from Jackie Robinson." *New York Times*, April 14, 1987.
Saylor, Jack. "Nobody Happier Than Diz." *Detroit Free Press*, September 15, 1968.
Schiavone, Michael. *Sports and Labor in the United States*. Albany: State University of New York Press, 2015.
Schmuhl, Robert. *Making Words Dance: Reflections on Red Smith, Journalism, and Writing*. Kansas City: Andrews McMeel, 2010.
Shantz, Randy. "Area Baseball Critics Approve of Phils Trade of Rich Allen." *Pottsdown Mercury*, October 9, 1969.
Shecter, Leonard. "Jim Bouton—Everything in Its Place." *Sport*, March 1964.
———. *The Jocks*. New York: Bobbs-Merrill, 1969.
———. "Richie Allen and the Use of Power." *Sport*, July 1967.
Sherman, Scott. "The Long Good-bye." *Vanity Fair*, November 30, 2012.
Sholley, Diana. "Retired LAPD Officer Recalls the Night He Arrested Robert Kennedy's Assassin." *Redlands Daily Facts*, June 2, 2012.
Siegel, Alan. "God vs. the World Series: Sandy Koufax's Yom Kippur Sacrifice." *Atlantic*, September 17, 2010.
Simons, William M. *The Cooperstown Symposium on Baseball and American Culture, 2005–2006*. Jefferson NC: McFarland, 2007.
Skornickel, George. "Characters with Character: Pittsburgh's All-Black Lineup." *Baseball Research Journal*, SABR 40, no. 2 (Fall 2011).
Smith, Brian. "The 50th Anniversary of the Phillies' 1964 Collapse Is Remembered." *Reading Eagle*, September 21, 2014.
Smith, Red. *To Absent Friends*. New York: Signet, 1986.
———. "To Buy and Sell Men Like Hogs." *New York Times*, June 18, 1976.
Smith, Thomas G. "Civil Rights on the Gridiron." ESPN, March 5, 2002, http://espn. go.com/page2/wash/s/2002/0305/1346021.html.
———. *Showdown: JFK and the Integration of the Washington Redskins*. Boston: Beacon Press, 2011.

Smith, Wendell. "Birdie Tebbets Should Quit Acting the Part of a 'Baby Chick.'" *Pittsburgh Courier*, February 18, 1961.

———. "Cardinal Exec Couldn't Contact Bill White for Hotel Breakfast." *Pittsburgh Courier*, March 18, 1961.

———. "Courier Drive against Baseball Camp Bias Gets Boost: Branch Rickey Backs Move." *Pittsburgh Courier*, February 4, 1961.

———. "Easy Seeing Why Willie Mays Is Still the Top Paid Player in World of Baseball." *Pittsburgh Courier*, January 25, 1964.

———. "Isn't It About Time for Negro Athletes to Be Heard from in Civil Rights Fight?" *Pittsburgh Courier*, March 14, 1964.

———. "Negro Ball Players Want Rights in South." *Chicago's American*, January 23, 1961.

———. "Negro Diamond Starts Tired of Second-Class Citizenship in South." *Pittsburgh Courier*, February 4, 1961.

———. "Negroes Find Themselves 'Caged.'" *Chicago's American*, February 4, 1961.

———. "No 'Uncle Toms' at Bat." *Pittsburgh Courier*, March 4, 1961.

———. "Raps Spring Camp Hotel Bias." *Pittsburgh Courier*, January 7, 1961.

———. "The Road to the Top Wasn't Easy for Elston Howard of the New York Yankees." *Pittsburgh Courier*, February 8, 1964.

———. "Taking a Stand and Paying the Price." *Chicago's American*, April 5, 1961.

———. "Time for Diamond Stars to Follow in Footsteps of Patterson's Fight against Bigotry." *Pittsburgh Courier*, January 28, 1961.

———. "What Allyn Has in Mind for Sox." *Chicago's American*, August 10, 1961.

———. "White Sox Spend $½ Million to End Bias." *Pittsburgh Courier*, November 26, 1961.

Snyder, Brad. *A Well-Paid Slave: Curt Flood's Fight for Free Agency in Professional Sports*. New York: Penguin Group, 2006.

Soderholm-Difatte, Bryan. "Beyond Bunning and Short Rest: An Analysis of Managerial Decisions That Led to the Phillies' Epic Collapse of 1964." *Baseball Research Journal*, SABR 30, no. 2 (Fall 2010).

Spoelstra, Watson. "Tiger Rally Gives McLain No. 30." *Detroit News*, September 15, 1968.

Sports Illustrated. "Through the Years with Ali." December 20, 1976.

"Stan Hochman on the Bout between Phillies Dick Allen and Frank Thomas." YouTube video. 1:51. Posted by "Philadelphia: The Great Experiment," April 6, 2012. https://www.youtube.com/watch?v=8g1Rs6PPhQQ.

Staples, Bill, and Rich Herschlag. *Before the Glory*. Deerfield Beach FL: HCI Books, 2007.

Staudohar, Paul D. *Diamond Mines: Baseball and Labor*. Syracuse: Syracuse University Press, 2000.

Stevens, Bill. "Hometown of Lacoochee Still in 'Mudcat' Grant's Heart." *Tampa Bay Times*, February 15, 2012.

Stone, Sumner. "300,000 March for Jobs, Freedom!" *Chicago Daily Defender*, August 29, 1963.

Stratton, W. K. *Floyd Patterson: The Fighting Life of Boxing's Invisible Champion*. New York: Houghton Mifflin Harcourt, 2012.

Sullivan, Neil J. *The Dodgers Move West*. New York: Oxford University Press, 1989.

Surdam, David G. *The Postwar Yankees*. Lincoln: University of Nebraska Press, 2008.

Swanson, Krister. *Baseball's Power Shift: How the Players Union, the Fans, and the Media Changed American Sports Culture*. Lincoln: University of Nebraska Press, 2016.

Talese, Gay. "Frank Sinatra Has a Cold." *Esquire*, April 1966.

———. *The Gay Talese Reader: Portraits and Encounters*. New York: Walker Books, 2003.

———. *The Kingdom and the Power: Behind the Scenes at the New York Times: The Institution That Influences the World*. New York: World, 1969.

———. "The Loser." *Esquire*, March 1964.

———. "The Silent Season of a Hero." *Esquire*, July 1966.

Taylor, Tony. "Jim Asks Phillies for Help." *Philadelphia Inquirer*, June 22, 1964.

Time. "Nation: M-Day's Message to Nixon." October 24, 1969.

———. "Nation: The Bombing Pause." April 5, 1968.

———. "South Viet Nam: Saigon under Siege." March 8, 1968.

———. "Time Looks Back: The Assassination of Martin Luther King, Jr." April 4, 2013.

Tirella, Joseph. "A Gun to the Heart of the City." *Slate*, April 22, 2014, http://www.slate.com/articles/news_and_politics/history/2014/04/core_s_1964_stall_in_the_planned_civil_rights_protest_that_kept_thousands.html.

Tischler, Barbara L. *Muhammad Ali: A Man of Many Voices*. New York: Routledge, 2015.

Travers, Steven. *The Last Icon: Tom Seaver and His Times*. Lanham MD: Taylor Trade, 2011.

Tuite, James. "War Casualties Demand Full-Staff Flag at Shea." *New York Times*, October 16, 1969.

Twombly, Wells. "Beware of Snoopy Colleagues." *San Francisco Examiner*, June 20, 1970.

United Press International. "'Ball Four' Way Outside, Cry Out Bouton's Foes." June 4, 1970.

———. "Bouton Receives Stern Reprimand." June 2, 1970.

———. "Bouton Spills Again." August 1, 1970.

———. "Clause Preserves Integrity, Kuhn Testifies in Flood Case." May 29, 1970.

———. "Jim Bouton to Quit Baseball." August 12, 1970.

———. "N.Y. Times, Newsweek Rip LBJ." March 11, 1968.

———. "Tom Seaver Says U.S. Should Leave Vietnam." October 11, 1969.

United States District Court, Southern District of New York. "Flood v. Kuhn (407 U.S. 258) Trial Transcript." In *Curt Flood Trial: May 19–June 10, 1970*. Book 1. http://scholarship.law.nd.edu/curt_flood_trial/1.

Vanderveld, Richard. "How Tenant O'Malley Became a Landlord." *Los Angeles Times*, April 8, 1962.

Vascellaro, Charlie. "Bucs Broke Ground with First All-Minority Lineup." MLB website, September 1, 1971, http://m.mlb.com/news/article/24052540/.

———. *Hank Aaron: A Biography*. Westport CT: Greenwood, 2005.

Vecsey, George. *Baseball: A History of America's Favorite Game*. New York: Random House, 2006.

———. "Dick Young, in His Time." *New York Times*, September 3, 1987.Veeck, Bill, and Ed Linn. *Veeck as in Wreck: The Autobiography of Bill Veeck*. Chicago: University of Chicago Press, 1962.

Voigt, David Q. "From Chadwick to the Chipmunks." *Journal of American Culture* 7, no. 3 (June 7, 2004).

Waldmeir, Pete. "Denny Wraps It Up in Style during and after the Game." *Detroit News*, September 15, 1968.

Welch, Matt. "Updated: On Jackie Robinson Day, Let's Remember When He Was Fired from the *New York Post* for Being Too Republican." *Reason*, April 15, 2015. http://reason.com/blog/2015/04/15/on-jackie-robinson-day-lets-remember-whe.

Wendel, Tim. *Summer of '68: The Season That Changed Baseball, and America, Forever*. Boston: Da Capo, 2013.

Wetzsteon, Ross. "Dick Young's America . . . The Reactionary Who Changed Sportswriting." *Sport*, August 1, 1985.

White, Bill, and Gordon Dillow. *Uppity: My Untold Story about the Games People Play*. New York: Hachette Book Group, 2011.

Whitman, Alden. "Robert Francis Kennedy: Attorney General, Senator and Heir of the New Frontier." *New York Times*, June 6, 1968.

Wiener, Jon. *Come Together: John Lennon in His Time*. Champaign: University of Illinois Press, 1991.

Wimbish, Ralph. "Mr. Robinson Let Me Watch the Yankees." *Tampa Bay Times*, April 15, 2007.

Wise, Aaron N., and Bruce S. Meyer. *International Sports Law and Business*. Vol. 3. Cambridge MA: Kluwer Law International, 1997.

Wolf, David. "Let's Everybody Boo Rich Allen!" *Life*, August 15, 1969.

———. "Tiger on the Keys and the Mound." *Life*, September 13, 1968.

Wolfe, Tom. "The Birth of 'The New Journalism'; Eyewitness Report by Tom Wolfe." *New York*, February 14, 1972.

———. "There Goes (Varoom! Varoom!) That Kandy Kolored Tangerine-Flake Streamline Baby." *Esquire*, November 1963.

Wright, Alfred. "Golden 30 For Show Biz Denny." *Sports Illustrated*, September 23, 1968.

Wulf, Steve. "Year of the Blue Snow." *Sports Illustrated*, September 25, 1989.

Young, Dick. "Brooklyn Dodgers Owner, Walter O'Malley Acquires L.A.'s Wrigley Field in 1957." *New York Daily News*, February 22, 1957.

———. "Soft Generals Never Last, Eckert Warned." *New York Daily News*, June 8, 1968.

Zimbalist, Andrew. *May the Best Team Win: Baseball Economics and Public Policy*. Washington DC: Brookings Institution Press, 2004.

Zirin, Dave. "An Interview with Marvin Miller." *CounterPunch*, January 10, 2004, http://www.counterpunch.org/2004/01/10/an-interview-with-marvin-miller.

Other works by John Florio and Ouisie Shapiro

One Punch from the Promised Land: Leon Spinks, Michael Spinks, and the Myth of the Heavyweight Title

Other works by John Florio

Sugar Pop Moon

Blind Moon Alley

Other works by Ouisie Shapiro

Autism and Me: Sibling Stories

Bullying and Me: Schoolyard Stories